Sol Bloom's Epoch "… Story of the Constitution"

The greatest remastering with major annotations of the greatest work ever on the Constitution—built for all Americans

A masterful work to read in order to refresh or gain knowledge of the greatest laws of our land, & how our government works. Understand your rights & your freedoms, so that nobody in government can take them from you!

Learn about why you love America so much by reading Sol Bloom's Epoch Story of the Constitution. Sol Bloom's book has been the best teaching tool about the Constitution in education for many years because it is written for ordinary people.

This book is the best starter book for anybody wanting to refresh some knowledge and gain a lot more about government and its most basic structure and laws. Listening to Sol Bloom's messages is like "hearing" the words of early colonialism and the fight for freedom from the founders themselves. This book will help all of us be better prepared to react to the over-reach of corrupt politicians at the highest levels of government. Bloom hated corruption, and you can learn why by reading this monumental historical work.

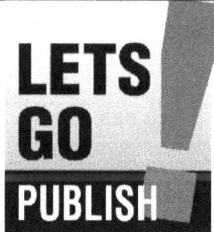

LETS GO PUBLISH

BRIAN W. KELLY

Published by: ....LETS GO PUBLISH!
Editor..Brian P. Kelly
Email: ....info@letsgopublish.com
Web site .... www.letsgopublish.com
Web site .... www.bookhawkers.com

Library of Congress Copyright Information Pending
Book Cover Design by Michele Thomas, Associate Editor—Brian P. Kelly

ISBN Information: The International Standard Book Number (ISBN) is a unique machine-readable identification number, which marks any book unmistakably. The ISBN is the clear standard in the book industry. 159 countries and territories are officially ISBN members. The Official ISBN For this book is   **978-0-9899957-6-4**

The price for this work is:								**$12.99 USD**	
10	9	8	7	6	5	4	3	2	1

Release Date: August 2014, August 2016

LETS GO PUBLISH!

Acknowledgments

In every book that I write or edit, I publicly acknowledged all of the help that I have received from many sources. Some of these wonderful people are still one earth and others have made their way to heaven.

I would like to thank many people for helping me in this effort.

I have listed their names and the story I usually tell on the Lets Go Publish! Web site-- www.letsgopublish.com. Look for the main menu. Please take a run out there and you will find the up to date text about all of those who are acknowledged for their help in bringing my books to you.

God bless them all

My plan is to update the acknowledgments on the LGP web site at least once every six months so that I can correct the names that are recorded wrongly, and add names that I have forgotten or who deserve credit for their new work.

Thank you all for all your help in keeping Lets Go Publish and our sales division BookHawkers.com (www.bookhawkers.com) on the top of the heap for so long.

As always, I must thank Nancy Lavan, our sponsor at Offset Paperback, our printer. She continually encourages us in our writing and publishing efforts. Arlene O'Malley, our customer service person from Offset took over for stalwart Chris Grieves and makes working with the printing process an easy task. Jozer Mickey (Joe McDonald) thinks both are the best! A special thanks goes to Michele Thomas, who still does these wonderful covers as a freelance cover designer. She takes ideas and makes wonderful images from them, such as this wonderful cover. She is a great talent. Dennis Grimes spent hours getting the book scans right. Thank you very much Bucko!

To sum up my acknowledgments, as I do in every book that I have written, I am compelled to offer that I am truly convinced that "the only thing one can do alone in life is fail." Thanks to my family, good friends, and a wonderful helping team, I am not alone.

Thank you all

Brian W. Kelly

Brian W. Kelly

Preface / Foreword Annotation

This popular vintage historical book was first published in 1937, when honoring America was commonplace. It was written for the 150th anniversary of the creation of the U.S. Constitution.

"It is a book for the people," wrote Sol Bloom, Chairman of the Sesquicentennial Commission. "

The original book and this remastering tell the origins of our country and what the steps were that led to the formation of the Constitution.

After telling how and why the national government came to be, the book then goes on to tell what the Constitution stands for; its principles; and the means by which it operates.

This preface / foreword by your author, Brian W. Kelly, considered by many to be a prolific patriotic book writer, sets the book in its proper historical context and explains why it is a classic in constitutional studies.

The original hard cover edition of this book, which I possess, was prepared in 1937 for the 150th anniversary of the U.S. Constitution. Its full-color pasteboard cover featured the painting of Liberty looking over the delegates to the Constitutional Convention by Howard Chandler Christy (1973-1952) is breathtaking. I would love to have the original.

My 1937 copy (which I bought used on eBay) is plain vanilla. However, there was a special print run made for Boy Scouts attending the First National Jamboree. I include a message to the Boy Scouts at the end of this note as well as a nice picture. The note in Bloom's special edition book included a short message by Chief Scout Executive James E. West (1876-1948) and a B&W reproduction of another Christy painting, "Boy Scout, 1937" facing the title page.

The text of the book was prepared under the supervision of Representative Sol Bloom (1870-1949) of New York, who was the able Director General of the United States Constitution Sesquicentennial Commission. Historians David M. Matteson, Ira E. Bennett, John C. Fitzpatrick, and Charles A. Cusick also "prepared various portions."

In 1937, this book gathered a great deal of useful reference information in one place—the full text of the Constitution as well as the Amendments through number 21. This re-mastering contains the full 27 Amendments to the Constitution, including those ratified after the printing of Bloom's book in 1937. Also included in Bloom's 1937 book is the Declaration of Independence, and Washington's Farewell Address; portraits of the signers and Chief Justices; text notes; details of the ratification of the Constitution and its amendments. Most notably, there is an "Alphabetical Analysis" that functions as a concordance and index. Finally, there is a set of detailed Q&A's on the Constitution that can test one's knowledge very effectively.

A very interesting notion for twenty-first century readers is the work's 1937 views of the Constitution and American history. This is found within "The Story of the Constitution" (pp. 7-53) and within "National Development Under the Constitution, with Maps" (pp. 146-156).

A reader who commented on Bloom's book in a separate archive noted that "There have been so many developments in the understanding of American history and in Constitutional law that reading this volume is like watching an old B&W movie in the age of HD and Blu-Ray." Quite so!

Indeed we are citizens of a truly exceptional country as Sol Bloom well knew and loved to write about. America is the exception to the rule of nations, having been founded on principles of liberty and freedom and ruled by the people. The Founders knew that even the great Constitution they wrote might not be enough to keep knaves and scoundrels from subverting their work. But they sure hoped it would serve us well, and they labored many hours and days so it would last through time.

Today, 230 + years after the Constitution, all is not perfect in America, but the principles of the Constitution are so sound and so powerful that even knave politicians, in high ranking positions, have yet to bring us under, though admittedly they seem to be trying very hard to do so. The big concern of course for many Americans today is that if we don't smarten up, things can get lots worse. I suspect that is part of your reasoning for choosing this great book to read.

Nobody can deny that Sol Bloom's Epoch masterpiece titled "The Story of the Constitution" is a unique and excellent expose on America's founding documents. In later versions, it was even cast as a United States government text. At the time, the government was teaching patriotism as well as the facts of the founding. This perspective seems to be missing from the education our children receive today.

Bloom tells the story of the origins, purpose, and nature of our nation's most important document in a very nice, engaging way.

Even when Bloom gave rights to the US Government to use his book, it was not a fully government text. You see, the book focuses exclusively on those aspects of the U.S. government defined and affected by the Constitution.

In Bloom's time, the education and government leaders suggested that to get the full picture of the founding, some additional reading was required and they suggested *The Land of Fair Play* as a companion to The Story of the Constitution. Bureaucrats in the 1930's and later felt the other book filled in many of what they saw as gaps in the Bloom book. I find the Bloom Book to be a great starter book for a great adventure into the history of the founding, and its play forward.

As a side note, Christian Liberty Press' bestselling *Land of Fair Play* was updated in 2008. It features clear lessons on the duties of citizenship as well as the workings of the government. Let's Go Publish is considering publishing this master work in much the same way the company remastered the Federalist Papers and this book by Sol Bloom. T

In the *Land of Fair Play*, the theory, machinery and services of national government are explored, as well as the relation between national, state and local governments, elections, and the importance of the Constitution. Yet the primary emphasis remains on providing young adults with the knowledge and skills for them to exercise appropriate and responsible citizenship as a Christian. In this respect, this is a wonderful read for all Americans, especially the young.

In the second edition of Bloom's *The Story of the Constitution* the booked morphed into a teacher / student version in a work effort shared with author Lars Johnson. Bloom put together what many saw as an eighth grade text. Because facts are facts, the book could also be used for older students and adults, though the "experts" slotted this book with Johnson as a text for younger students. Would it not be wonderful if our children today were versed in Bloom's understanding of the U.S. Constitution?

This book is illustrated with black and white drawings that help bring it to life. In 1937, color was not as easy to come by, but the pictures add a great dimension to the work, and make it easy to read, and desirable as a great read.

As many as fifteen chapters of this book discuss the conditions that led to the fight for American independence, the drafting of the Constitution, and the ratification process. Each article of the Constitution is covered in detail. Bloom also adds the Bill of Rights and Constitutional amendments which had been ratified before the 1937 time frame, when the book was written.

In this version of Bloom's Epoch Book, your author and re-mastering agent, Brian W. Kelly has added the missing amendments. Kids and adults can get an intimate sense of the value, complexity and novelty of the government that our Founding Fathers set up by reading this book. It is that well done.

Of course we laud the book that you are about to read, done before the cooperative effort with Lars Johnson and others. This is a defining work, worthy of text-book or companion-book status in America's finest universities, and in introductory courses on the Federal Government.

You will find the Bloom text to be very readable, though there is a lot of it and sometimes, when chapter and verse are quoted, such as the full Constitution, it can seem dry and stilted. Despite these sections of the book, overall it is invigorating and exciting to see how bright and how brave our Founders were. And, Sol Bloom had a major gift in the use of his pen to communicate great thoughts.

In the US today, some would suggest that our ailments are large and growing. Neither Sol Bloom, nor his contemporaries suffered as we do today from intrusive government, and so he could not write specifically about our travails.

For sure, in our day, taxes are way too high, elected officials are out of touch, government is too big, spending is out of control; the new healthcare program is a train wreck, much of the federal government is incompetent, the people have no voice in government, too many people are too lazy to hold government accountable, too many are on the take, and worse than that, the list of ailments is growing, not shortening.

Your intention no doubt in learning about the structure of America and its most fundamental laws in choosing to read this book is to help you understand why all this is happening. Thank you for picking this great book. You will enjoy it.

That is why Sol Bloom wrote about it and it is why I am bringing his work forth, written for today's America. I am betting that sooner or later, all Americans will better understand our great country and our great form of government by reading this great work by Mr. Bloom.

As noted, this book has been used many times as a starter book on America. That is because it is a book for anybody wanting to refresh their knowledge or learn about the government of the United States of America. It helps the reader be better prepared to react to anything the government throws your way.

If you have been paying attention to what is going on in America today, you know we are in trouble. We have a busted economy, high unemployment, no jobs, and our basic rights to freedoms such as speech, religion, the press, and our right-to-bear-arms are being impinged upon. The Founders saw it as a civic duty for Americans to pay attention to our government so that we can avoid being chumps and being snookered by crooked politicians. Sol Bloom finds areas in the Constitution to help us all.

There are more issues than just those noted above, and we better fix them quickly while we still have a Constitution upon which to lean.

We are on the same side in this battle for the Constitution and for the survival of America. Together we can all help. We first must understand what is going on by checking out Mr. Bloom's words, and we then must understand our rights as delivered in the Declaration of Independence; The Constitution; and the Bill of Rights.

My concern is that when we all wake up from our deep fog, there may be no Bill of Rights or Constitution left for our progeny. We will have blown it for sure if that is permitted to happen.

In this book, Sol Bloom stays away from suggesting we no longer trust our government. Your author Brian Kelly however, unabashedly recommends that we stop completely trusting government since the founders suggested a watchful eye for the press and for citizens. Besides, unfortunately, today government is clearly not working for the people's best interests. It would be great to see Bloom's opinion of Brian Kelly's conservative work. Kelly's message for this reading adventure is to pay attention by understanding Bloom's book.

The sooner we can understand the threats coming from progressive communists in our country, the sooner we all can move on to solving the problem for our values, our country, and our freedom.

The smarter we are, the more chance we have for success. Understanding America's founding and the founding documents, especially the Constitution and The Bill of Rights, is a sure way to become an American forever. I know you love America as I do. Sol Bloom wrote his book because in 1937, there was no doubt that the majority of Americans loved America.

Your author continually monitors what is happening to our government and he has written extensively on the major problems our country faces. Brian Kelly loves Sol Bloom's treatment of constitutional issues. Yet, he is also one of America's most outspoken and eloquent conservative spokesmen.

Mr. Kelly is the author of many other patriotic books including America 4 Dummmies, The Constitution 4 Dummmies, The Bill of Rights 4 Dummmies, No Amnesty! No Way!, Saving America!, Taxation Without Representation!, Kill the EPA!, Jobs! Jobs! Jobs! And many others. Kelly also analyzed and remastered the Federalist Papers, originally written by the Framers, and he has written many other patriotic books in his own pen. All books are available at www.bookhawkers.com.

Like many Americans, Brian Kelly, your author and remastering agent, is fed up with stifling socialist progressive Marxists in many of the top seats in Washington. They place the needs of everybody else in front of the needs of Americans. Like many Americans, Kelly is shocked at how brazen the government is today in ignoring our Constitution and our Bill of Rights! This must be stopped.

Like Sol Bloom long before him, Brian W. Kelly has read the founding documents, the underlying intelligence reports, and he has researched and written about such topics for years. Brian has written fifty-four books and hundreds of patriotic articles. He is deeply concerned about how intolerable the results of poor government policy can be within our neighborhoods and our lives. His comprehensible and sane recommendations in this book on top of Sol Bloom's insights, are explained in detail within the covers of many books including this soon-to-be classic edition.

Sol Bloom's Epoch: The Story of the Constitution is a title to get your attention for sure. I hope we got your attention. In addition to a review of the founding history, Sol Bloom has delivered major civics lesson in this book to bring you up to date on the national scene.

You are going to love this book since it has been written by an American hero and remastered by an American for Americans. Perhaps if Sol Bloom were here today, lovers of America would be calling on him to run for President.

Few books are a must-read but ***Sol Bloom's Epoch: The Story of the Constitution*** will quickly appear at the top of America's most read list.

Sincerely,

Brian P. Kelly, Editor
Brian W. Kelly, Author/Remasterer

Sol Bloom Supported the Boy Scouts

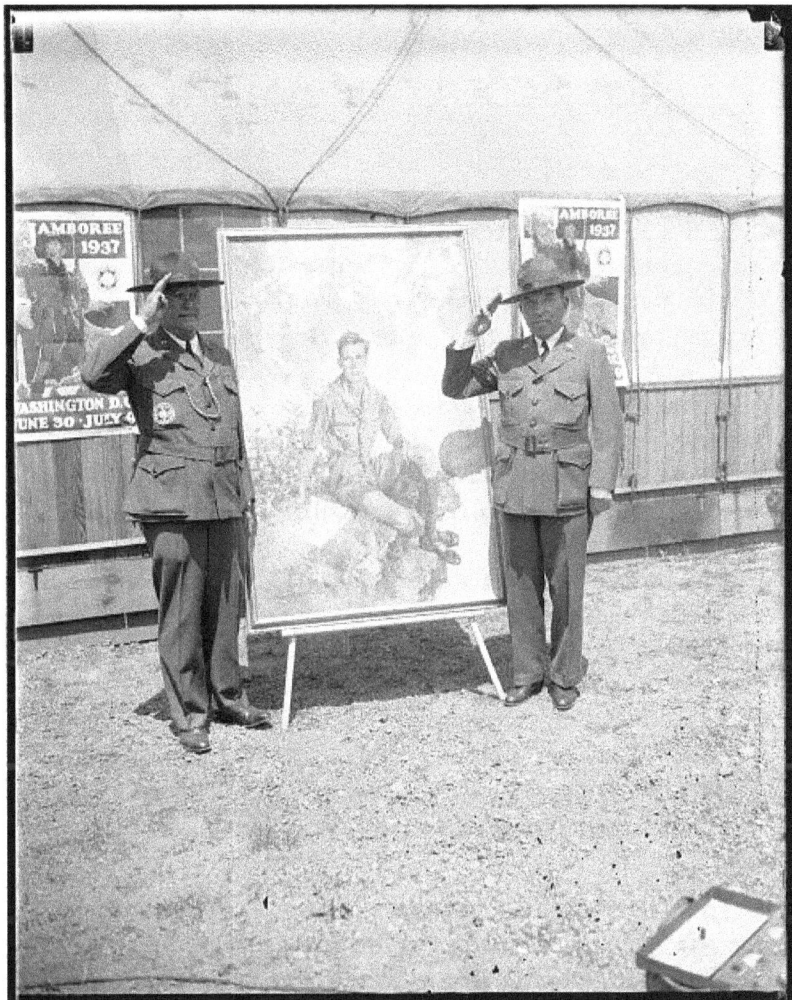

Title: Official Boy Scout poster. Dr. James E. West, Chief Scout Executive of the Boy Scouts (left) and Rep. Sol Bloom of New York with the official poster. This poster was painted and donated to the Boy Scout Jamboree by Howard Chandler Christy. It, the poster, will be distributed all over the world for the coming Boy Scout Jamboree which will be held in Washington from June 30th to July 9th with 30,000 Boy Scouts in attendance. Rep. Bloom has been one of the most active leaders in promoting this Boy Scout Jamboree, 5/21/1937

Creator(s): Harris & Ewing, photographer

A MESSAGE

TO THE

BOY SCOUTS OF AMERICA

It is a matter of great satisfaction to me that it has been made possible for Scouts attending our National Jamboree in Washington, D. C., commencing June 30, 1937, to participate in a pilgrimage to the Shrine of the Declaration of Independence and the Constitution of the United States. This pilgrimage will result, I am confident, in a greatly stimulated interest on the part of all in Scouting and indeed all others, in these two great documents in our country's history. I have again and again urged a more profound understanding of the fundamental principles on which our country is organized, based upon a study of the Constitution. It is one of the first essentials of good citizenship. A democracy is dependent upon a voluntary process of thinking, feeling, and acting, individually, for the good of the community, the State, and the Nation. Such a democracy can only be sustained by an understanding of its fundamental principles, and a habit of thinking about others and caring about others, such as we in Scouting try to develop through our program, our Scout ideals, and our daily Good Turn.

To all those Scouts and friends of Scouts who participate in the pilgrimage to the Shrine of our Constitution, I extend my greetings; on your behalf I express appreciation to those who made possible this enrichment of your experience.

James E. West

Chief Scout Executive and
Editor of BOYS' LIFE.

The Remastering of Saul Bloom's Epoch
Introduction to annotation technique

You will soon learn that this is a remastering of a *great book written originally by a great man and a great patriot,* Sol Bloom. Thank you for taking the time to learn about Sol Bloom's Constitution.

This book has been remastered structurally so that it is better than the Bloom original. In this endeavor I had the benefit of modern tools from scanners to spell checkers to automatic pagination, and of course the very powerful Table facility.

You can imagine how many old words that were used in 1937 that are not used today or words that are spelled differently today than back then. I left them be so I could recreate the flavor of the 1937 part of the work. However, when the problem was merely a typo, I changed it because nobody can catch all book errors. Sol Bloom, who I respect more and more as I learn about him, surely was not looking for errors to be included in his presentation to the people.

When I write my books from scratch today, I use a header on the left with the book title and page # and on the right, I use the chapter title and page #. Sometimes the page # in this book is on the left, sometimes the right and sometimes the bottom. I chose to let this stand as in the original and did not use automatic page numbering or headers / footers. The book looks more original though it is more readable.

Unfortunately, I could not stay true to physical page numbering. Once I hit a certain spot in the book, I had to change. Bloom has a section entitled, *Alphabetic Analysis of the Constitution. In here he also analyzes the* Bill of Rights and the Amendments to the 21st. From my observations as a book author and editor, this is a unique notion and it is very helpful for those studying the Constitution. The reader can look for a few easier answers rather than reading through the entire text of the Constitution each time a question arises.

In an effort to conserve space, Congressman Bloom used what appears to be a 6 or 7 point type font (very small) and minimal spacing and so these pages are difficult to read in the original. For each of these pages, in this remastered edition, we use two pages at 10.5 points. However, so the reader can follow the book using Bloom's guides and page references , we keep the same page # for both pages. For the second page, we label it with the page # and the designation *part 2.*

And so—though I have remained true to the writer's intentions and the writer's wording, most of the book is retyped or otherwise remastered in a more easily readable font and format. Thus, as noted, this book has more pages than shown in Sol Bloom's page numbering scheme. However, the original table of contents works perfectly with the original page numbers.

In the original book, which is a treasure to possess, and which I have referenced many times in producing this work, Mr. Bloom squeezed everything he could into every page. Bloom also added excitement to his formatting by changing the font at times and he sometimes used the small caps notion instead of small letters. He also sprayed italics and all-caps and dark / light highlighting to help him make sections stand out. Both he and his editors did a fine job. For the 1930's, an even for today, this is a fine work.

Last thought… most authors begin sections / chapters on odd pages and on the even pages, they place the book title, with page # to the left, and on odd pages, they put the Chapter or Verse Title with page # to the right. Since we use two pages for each original page, during this section, we use the page numbering of the "header" on the odd page. The even page (Part 2 of the page) shows the page number on the bottom with the part 2 designation.

Public Biography of Sol Bloom:
Sol Bloom

**Member of the US House of Representatives
From New York's 20th district**

Sol Bloom was a member of the US House of Representatives From New York's 20th district. He was born in Pekin, Tazewell County, Ill., March 9, 1870, and moved with his parents to San Francisco, Calif., in 1873.

Bloom engaged in the newspaper, theatrical, and music-publishing businesses and he was the superintendent of construction of the Midway Plaisance at the World's Columbian Exposition at Chicago in 1893.

He moved to New York City in 1903 and engaged in the real estate and construction business; was a captain in the New York Naval Reserve in 1917; and was elected as a Democrat to the Sixty-eighth Congress by special election, to fill the vacancy caused by the death of United States Representative-elect Samuel Marx. Bloom was reelected to the thirteen succeeding Congresses.

Among many other accomplishments in the Congress over the years, he was chairman of the Committee on Foreign Affairs, Special Committee on Chamber Improvements, and he was a director of the United States George Washington Bicentennial Commission. He wrote The Land of Fair Play while serving as the director general of the United States Constitution Sesquicentennial Commission. Sol Bloom died on March 7, 1949, in Washington, D.C.

About the Author / Remasterer

Brian W. Kelly retired as an Assistant Professor in the Business Information Technology (BIT) program at Marywood University, where he also served as the IBM i and midrange systems technical advisor to the IT faculty. Kelly has designed, developed, and taught many college and professional courses. He is also a contributing technical editor to a number of IT industry magazines, including "The Four Hundred" and "Four Hundred Guru" published by IT Jungle. On the Patriotic side, you can often find a Kelly article at www.conservativeactionalerts.com Look up Brian Kelly or go to http://www.conservativeactionalerts.com/author/Brian-Kelly/

Kelly is a former IBM Senior Systems Engineer and he has been a candidate for US Congress and the US Senate from Pennsylvania. He has an active information technology consultancy. He is the author of 53 books and numerous articles. Kelly is a frequent speaker at COMMON, IBM conferences, and other technical conferences. Ask him to speak at your next TEA Party rally! You might be surprised!

Over the past eleven years, Brian Kelly has become one of America's most outspoken and eloquent conservative protagonists. Besides America 4 Dummmies, Kelly is also the author of No Amnesty! No Way!, Taxation Without Representation, and many other patriotic books. Books available at Amazon and www.bookhawkers.com

Endorsed by the Independence Hall Tea Party in 2010, Kelly ran for Congress against a 13-term Democrat and, took no campaign contributions, spent enough to buy signs and T-shirts, and as a virtual unknown, he captured 17% of the vote— www.briankellyforcongress.com.

1787

UNITED STATES
SESQUICENTENNI

Acknowledges its grateful appreci

in the Sesquicentennial Celebration

UNITED STATES SENATE COMMISSIONERS		PRESIDENTIAL
HENRY F. ASHURST	ARIZONA	C. O'CONNOR COOLIDGE
JOSEPH T. ROBINSON	ARKANSAS	CARYL J. TITUS
FREDERICK HAGEDTS	IDAHO	WILLIAM FITTS
WILLIAM E. BORAH	IDAHO	MAURICE E. HARRISON
CHARLES L. MCNARY	OREGON	HARRY A. DUTOIS

1937
CONSTITUTION
AL COMMISSION
ion of the patriotic participation of
the Formation of the Constitution.

CONSTITUTION

SESQUICENTENNIAL

E PLURIBUS UNUM

We The People

EX LIBRIS

1787   1937

THE STORY OF THE CONSTITUTION

SOL BLOOM

UNITED STATES CONSTITUTION
SESQUICENTENNIAL COMMISSION

HOUSE OFFICE BUILDING
WASHINGTON, D. C.

UNITED STATES CONSTITUTION
SESQUICENTENNIAL COMMISSION
Established by a Joint Resolution of the Congress of the United States, Approved August 23, 1935

THE PRESIDENT OF THE UNITED STATES
Chairman
THE VICE PRESIDENT OF THE UNITED STATES
THE SPEAKER OF THE HOUSE OF REPRESENTATIVES

UNITED STATES SENATE *COMMISSIONERS*	HOUSE OF REPRESENTATIVES *COMMISSIONERS*
HENRY F. ASHURST, Vice Chairman Arizona	SOL BLOOM New York
JOSEPH T. ROBINSON ARKANSAS	CHARLES F. MCLAUGHLIN NEBRASKA
FREDERICK VAN NUYS Indiana	FRANK J.G. DORSEY Pennsylvania
WILLIAM E. BORAH IDAHO	JOHN TABER NEW YORK
CHARLES L. MCNARY Oregon	GEORGE P. DARROW Pennsylvania

Presidential Commissioners

C. O'CONOR GOOLRICK Virginia	WILLIAM HIRTH Missouri
DANIEL J. TOBIN Indiana	MAURICE E. HARRISON California

HARRY AUGUSTUS GARFIELD
Massachusetts

DIRECTOR GENERAL
SOL. BLOOM
New York

[2]

Introduction

The [original] front of this book shows the official poster of the United States Constitution Sesquicentennial Commission, painted by Howard Chandler Christy; and like that poster and the work which the Commission expects to do, this book is dedicated to "We the People"-to the 128,000,000 [over 300,000,000 today] who desire to know something about the story of the Constitution, and to have it told to them in such a way that they can understand what it is all about. It tries to reach the millions who are not judges or lawyers or professors or historians or otherwise trained in a knowledge of the Constitution, which governs the daily lives of all of us. It is a book for the people. Accordingly, it tells briefly the origins of our country, and what the steps were that led up to the formation of the Constitution. Having told how and why the National Government came about, the book tells what the Constitution stands for, its principles and the means by which it operates.

That the people may study the document itself, the text of the Constitution and of all the amendments is given, and given as nearly as possible exactly as in the originals from the en grossed parchment of the Constitution as signed by George Washington to the Twenty-first Amendment as proclaimed by Franklin D. Roosevelt. It is the Constitution from our first President to our present President.

For those who wish to know what the Constitution and amendments say upon a particular subject, there is an alphabetical analysis made after the successful plan devised by William Hickey some ninety years ago. For those who are interested in the changes which the Nation has undergone while under the rule of the Constitution, there are a series of historical maps and a short sketch of national development to be read in connection with the maps. Pictures are given of the men who signed the Constitution and thumbnail sketches of their careers. Also there are various tables of dates of ratification by the States of the original Constitution, of later admission of States, and of territories and dependencies; as well as an explanation of when the various amendments went into force. A series of Questions and Answers gives information on many details of the making and operation of our Government. Among the many valuable state papers of the Nation two are most intimately connected with the Constitution.

[3]

These are the Declaration of Independence, which opened the way for it, and Washington's Farewell Address on keeping in the path. It is fitting, therefore, to include these in a book which is itself a fingerpost. The Supreme Court of the United States has been called a "continuous constitutional convention," which statement, even if considered an exaggeration, correctly marks the importance of the court in our constitutional history, and the interest which centers in the eleven men who have been the Chief Justices. Portraits and sketches of these judges are included in this volume. An index binds the contents together; and to stamp the character of the whole, a reproduction and short history of the Great Seal close the work.

This book was planned and edited by the Director General, and prepared under the more immediate supervision of the Historian, David M. Matteson, who is mainly responsible for the accuracy of the texts and statements. Other workers upon the book, who prepared various portions of it, are Mr. Ira E. Bennett, Dr. John C. Fitzpatrick, and Mr. Charles A. Cusick. Accuracy as to all facts and dates has been a constant aim in the publication, and especially of literal exactness in the reprint of the original documents. It is believed that the care which has been taken in these matters justifies a claim of unusual correctness.

Upon application, permission will be granted for the reprint or use of any portion of this book, provided that no change be made, and that full credit be given to the Commission.

SOL. BLOOM,
Director General.

SPECIAL NOTICE This book contains on page 164, under the heading, "Questions and Answers," the record that the engrossing of the Constitution was the work of Jacob Shallus, Assistant Clerk of the Pennsylvania State Assembly. This is the first time the question as to the penman who actually engrossed the text of the Constitution after it had been agreed upon prior to the signing, has ever been answered in any publication. The many historical data contained in this book, of which this is a striking example, give it an unusual value.

[Let's Go Publish! Hereby Gives the Commission Full Credit.]

CONTENTS

The People

The Thirteen Colonies

The Continental Congress

The Revolutionary War

The Declaration of Independence
of the United States

The State Governments

The Articles of Confederation

Independence

The Constitution of the United States

The United States Government

. . .

THE STORY OF
THE CONSTITUTION
PART I.

Origin of the United States

CHAPTER I. Discovery—Title to the Soil

King Henry VII of England turned a cold shoulder upon Christopher Columbus when he asked for financial aid in undertaking a highly speculative voyage in search of India by sailing westward from Europe. But Henry, a keen and enterprising monarch, quickly realized the importance of Columbus's discovery, and in 1496 commissioned John Cabot to go out and discover countries then unknown to Christian people and take possession of them in the name of the English king.

Cabot made two voyages, and by 1498 had sailed along what is now the coast of the United States and claimed it for England. By tacit agreement the European sovereigns rested their respective claims upon priority of discovery. The natives were regarded as heathens possessing no rights of sovereignty. Quarrels arose between the European powers over boundary questions, but the British claims based upon right of discovery were made good by sword and by treaty, so that ultimately the title to all lands embraced in the thirteen original States was vested in the British crown.

The first permanent English settlement on this continent was made under the charter granted by King James I to Sir Thomas Gates and others in 1606. Three years later a new and more enlarged charter was given to the "Treasurer and Company of Adventurers of the City of London for the First Colony in Virginia." The colony was given in absolute property all the lands extending along the sea-coast 400 miles northward from near the 34th degree of north latitude and running back from the coast "from sea to sea." In 1620 another charter was granted to the Duke of Lenox and others, denominated the Council for New England, conveying to them in absolute property all the lands between the 40th and 48th degrees of north latitude.

[7]

Under these patents the settlement of Virginia and New England was accomplished. Subsequent charters brought about the settlement of New Jersey, New York, Pennsylvania, Maryland, the Carolinas, and Georgia. Wars followed by treaties resulted in the acquisition by England of the remaining territory now comprised in the thirteen original States, together with the western country east of the Mississippi.

By the treaty which ended the War of the Revolution the boundaries of the United States were agreed upon, and all the powers of government and right to soil passed to the United States.

CHAPTER II. Colonial Government

British subjects outnumbered all other immigrants to the colonies under British dominion. They brought with them the traditions of British' rights, liberties, and immunities, British laws and customs, and the English language.

Centuries of struggle had won for Englishmen many guaranties of rights, liberties, and immunities. English common law was fairly established when the colonies were begun. Some rights and immunities which had been enjoyed from time immemorial were reduced to writing in Magna Charta, which was wrung from King John by the barons of England at Runnymede in 1215. Other individual rights were formally guaranteed in writing, notably the Bill of Rights under William and Mary. The system of constitutional government safeguarded by a parliament elected by the people was well established when the first colonial charter was granted.

The liberties and rights of Britons were concessions from kings who ruled as by divine right and were originally seized of all authority. This theory underlies the monarchical system to this day.

The colonies, beginning with Virginia and New England, were settled under charters granted by the king of England. These grants made large reservations of royal privilege and relatively small concessions to the emigrants. Broadly speaking, the colonists did not at first enjoy civil and political liberties as they were known in England. Protests against denial of privileges enjoyed by British freemen were made in Virginia as early as 1612. Gradually the colonies were given larger powers of government, always provided that colonial laws should be in conformity to the laws of England and that allegiance to the crown should be acknowledged.

The colonial period of the people who became Americans was longer than the period extending from the establishment of the Constitution to the year 1937. The colonists had abundant experience during 169 years in various forms of government under British authority. In some respects eventually there was substantial home rule and enjoyment of individual liberties equal to those enjoyed in England. But in matters of trade the British government persisted in sacrificing the rights of the colonies to the advantage of Britain. This situation developed endless friction, complaint, and evasion of the British regulations.

CHAPTER III. Causes of the Revolution

From the early days of the colonies, the people claimed for themselves and their posterity exemption from all taxation that was not imposed by their own representatives. Since it was impossible for them to be represented in the British parliament, they denied the right of that body to tax them. Attempts by Parliament to impose taxes as a means of regulating commerce were opposed, with increasing tension on both sides, but the climax was not reached until after the French and Indian war of 1754-63. During this war the colonists were drawn nearer the British sovereign as their legitimate protector, but bitter experiences and common impositions also served to draw them closer toward a colonial union which was, however, mainly for more effective protest.

This war, which was part of the Seven Years' War in Europe, left Great Britain with many new colonial possessions all over the world, with a great burden of debt, and with a driving incentive for developing the imperial system. It was felt in Britain that the American colonies should help pay the cost of removing the French menace and for continued British protection. The imperialistic spirit awakened a desire for more strict control over all British possessions. This control was to be exercised through Parliament. A specific declaration to this effect was made in 1766, in the statute of 6 Geo. 3, ch. 12, in which Parliament declared that "the colonies and plantations in America have been, are, and of right ought to be, subordinate unto, and dependent upon, the Imperial Crown and Parliament of Great Britain," and that the king, with the advice and consent of Parliament, "had, hath, and of right ought to have, full power and authority to make laws and statutes of sufficient force and validity to bind the colonies and people of America in all cases whatsoever."

Violent opposition to this assertion of the power to tax the colonies arose both in England and America. Lord Chatham, in December, 1765, declared that while British authority over the colonies was supreme in matters of government and legislation, taxation is no part of the governing or legislative power; taxes are the voluntary grant of the people alone."

Efforts were made on both sides to avoid a collision. Parliament modified its declaration by providing that no duty or tax would be imposed on the colonies except for the regulation of commerce; and that the net revenue from the duty or tax would be devoted to the use of the colony in which it was levied. Many plans were suggested for reorganization of the governments in the colonies, with a view to reconciling the differences that disturbed good relations with Great Britain.

As early as 1754 a plan of union was suggested to the Albany Congress of the colonies by Benjamin Franklin, but, foreshadowing the irrepressible conflict that was to come, the colonies rejected the plan because it gave too much control to the British government, and that government rejected it because it gave too much liberty to the colonies.

Aside from the resistance to "taxation without representation," numerous grievances were nursed by the Americans against Great Britain—grievances arising from differences that had grown up in the economic and social life of the colonies, for which no allowance was made by the British government. The colonies were moving toward separation from Britain. The more the colonists studied the subject, the more doubt they entertained as to the right of Parliament to assert supreme authority over them.

The first united action of protest in the preliminaries of the War for Independence was the Stamp Act Congress of 1765. Held at New York and attended by delegates from nine of the thirteen colonies, mostly appointed by the assemblies. Voting by colonies, each having one vote, it framed petitions to the king and to Parliament and adopted an important Declaration of Rights, the first platform of American

principles. The next step was a common policy of boycotting English goods, known as nonimportation agreements, followed by the appointment of intercolonial committees of correspondence to keep the leaders of the different regions in mutual touch and consultation. When affairs with the home government reached a crisis with the destruction of imported tea and the acts to coerce Massachusetts into obedience to British measures, the colonies took the step which led directly to the present Union. This was the meeting of the First Continental Congress on September 5, 1774, in Carpenters' Hall at Philadelphia.

CHAPTER IV The Continental Congress

This important body was attended by delegates from all the colonies save Georgia, the representation of the people being indirect. It continued to be so throughout the Continental Congress and Articles of Confederation, except that Connecticut and Rhode Island delegates were popularly elected. Another highly important fact was that this meeting, following the practice of the Stamp Act Congress, adopted the rule of one vote for each colony without respect to size, population, or wealth. This decision for equality was undoubtedly inevitable. It had great effect upon the subsequent legislative events down' to 1789, for the system was continued under the Second Continental Congress and by the Articles of Confederation. It was a rule that often impeded congressional action and hindered the development of a competent general government; the efforts to continue it almost disrupted the Constitutional Convention.

While there were some conservative members in the First Continental Congress, the radicals were in control; the roll of the Congress included the prominent men of all the colonies. The petitions and declaration were similar to those of the Stamp Act Congress. More important was the regulation of the enforcement of the nonimportation and nonconsumption agreemcnt-the boycott. The carrying out of this remained with the people of the colonies, the coercive power remained there; but the direction was at least given by a united action. Before the Congress adjourned on October 26, 1774, it provided for another Congress if the crisis continued.

The Second Continental Congress met at Philadelphia on May 10, 1775, and continued until finally superseded in 1789 by the government organized under the new Constitution. It passed without break from the extra-legal conditions of its earlier existence to those of a constitutional body under the Articles of Confederation after March 1, 1781. It and its agents were during the years 1775-88 the only organ of union; in it were all the national powers not then withheld by the States-legislative, executive, and judicial—that existed to keep the States together as one nation, and to it belonged all the responsibility. But neither before nor after the Articles of Confederation went into operation did it possess the power to enforce its measures. The only instrument for this was the States; as Washington said, Congress could "merely recommend and leave it to the States afterwards to do as they please, which is in many cases to do nothing at all." This was an almost fatal weakness but it was not an unnatural condition. Originally, the colonies probably had no further idea of union than such common action as would force respect for the rights of the individual colonies under British suzerainty. Circumstances alter cases, and experience teaches.

Independence was not an element of the antebellum struggle. Circumstances literally forced it upon the attention of the leaders and then it was reluctantly incorporated into their policy. They were proud of being Englishmen so long as they were permitted to be such with full recognition of what they claimed as their rights. The Declaration was made inevitable by armed conflict. Independence of thirteen little nations engaged in a common war would have been an absurdity; but localism was still too powerful to permit a union stronger than the minimum necessary to give it status in the family of nations, especially after the need of united military effort had ceased. It was only when it was realized that a nation without a backbone could not remain a nation even in name, that events compelled the "more perfect union"; and the ratification struggle showed how difficult it was even then to get public opinion to support measures deemed necessary for this by the farsighted men who drafted the Constitution. The evolution did not end there, or the strife between localism, or State rights, and national power.

CHAPTER V. Articles of Confederation

When the Second Continental Congress met, hostilities had begun and the Minute Men of New England were besieging the British forces in Boston. The delegates were much the same as in the earlier Congress, and they realized the need of assuming the war power necessary to carry on the conflict. It was an entirely extra-legal action, acquiesced in because the control of the colonies was in the hands of those who sympathized with the measures, even though they often became reluctant to assume the burden essential to carrying them out.

Independence, national standing, confederation, and State rights were conjoined speedily. The resolution of the Virginia Convention, May 15, 1776, instructing the colony's delegates to propose independence, also gave assent to "whatever measures may be thought proper and necessary by the Congress for forming foreign alliances, and a Confederation of the Colonies, ...Provided, That the power of forming Government for, and the regulation of the internal concerns of each Colony, be left to the respective Colonial Legislatures." Also the resolves which Richard Henry Lee introduced under the above directions, and which were adopted by Congress on July 2, 1776, included: "That a plan of confederation be prepared and transmitted to the respective Colonies for their consideration and approbation."

In 1774 a plan of union had been proposed by a conservative, but this was ignored as it was distinctly pro-British. Franklin offered an outline in 1775 which also was neglected. Finally the Articles of Confederation were agreed to and submitted to the states in 1777. The victory of the small States in establishing their right to an equal vote was not considered by some of them as sufficient, however. New Jersey, Delaware, and Maryland demanded that the States that had large claims to western lands renounce them in favor of the Confederation. Maryland was the last State to ratify the Articles, holding out until March 1, 1781, when she became satisfied that the western claims would become the expected treasure of the whole nation.

This delay caused almost the whole of the American Revolution to be fought under a gentlemen's agreement, and one that was by no means favorable to efficient operation, either civil or military. The correspondence of Washington, the commander-in-chief, during the war is one long plaint of things that were lacking-soldiers, supplies, funds, and cooperation. Undoubtedly, the Continental Congress was not an ideal instrument for the work that it had to do; it deteriorated in personnel, much time was wasted on unimportant matters and in bickering; but in spite of this the evidence is strong that Congress was better than its results. Time and again it passed measures admirable for military efficiency and success, only to see them fall by the wayside because of the obduracy of the State governments that alone had the power to make the acts operable.

No war was ever won through enthusiasm alone, and as this died down and the realization of the burden increased, the reluctance of the States to face necessary conditions increased both the burden and the duration of the contest. In the end the war was won because of the character of the commander-in-chief and because of French aid. Without these it undoubtedly would have failed, and the failure would have been due to the attitude of the State governments, to their unwillingness to forget the selfish claims of the parts in the needs of the whole.

CHAPTER VI. Confederation Fails—The Critical Period

Conditions were not improved under the Articles of Confederation. This direct predecessor of the Constitution brought no transformation of the government; it merely placed on a legal foundation a structure that needed rebuilding throughout. The main, and fatal, character of the government under the Articles is indicated by Article II, "each state retains its sovereignty, freedom, and independence, and every Power, Jurisdiction and right, which is not by this confederation expressly delegated to the United States." It was a "league of friendship" only, of which the Congress was the unique organ and in which " each state shall have one vote." The vote of nine States in Congress was necessary to important action by that body. The Articles "shall be inviolably observed by every state, and the union shall be perpetual;" and the consent of the legislature of each State was necessary to any amendment of the fundamental law.

The Articles contained many wise details which were later perpetuated in the Constitution; but the compact gave Congress no control and no power to raise money. It could only make requisitions on the States (as it had done during the war) on an ascertained basis, and then hope and pray that the States would respond favorably. They never did. Congress was given control over foreign affairs but was given no means of making the states obey even the treaty requirements, or provide for the payment of the foreign debt. It was a government of responsibility without power; to foreign nations it was the United States, to the states, it was merely what they chose to allow it to be. Its dealing with the people was through States and not otherwise.

During the war most of the States had adopted constitutions. These provided for governments in separate departments—executive, legislative, and judicial—with bills of rights to protect the citizens especially from such evils as had caused the revolt against British control. They were based on the practices of colonial times and the current theories of government; and they gave control through the elective franchise over the lower house of legislature in all cases, as had been the rule of the colonies. There was usually an upper house, but the character of its election varied. The governor was chosen by the legislature. In only five cases, the four New England States and New York, were both the entire legislature and the executive popularly elected. The Articles of Confederation were, however, a thing apart from this movement, a concession to necessity rather than an inherent element of American polity.

There is small wonder that the Confederation was not a success. Congress recognized at once the financial need; but several efforts to get the States to amend the Articles, by adding the right to levy import duties, failed through lack of unanimous authorization. The binding force of war conditions having ended, there was the collapse of moral fiber that seems always to follow a great clash of arms. Interest in the Union steadily waned. It became increasingly difficult to secure a quorum of attendance in Congress, and when there was a sufficiency of States represented important measures were blocked by the need of nine State votes, especially as a State frequently lost her vote because of differences among her delegates. Localism became more and more rampant; interstate difficulties and discriminating commercial legislation arose; and within the States depression with its following of radicalism and class and ignorant sectional demands, bred anarchy. It is, however, easy to put too much emphasis on the evils of this critical period and upon the economic distress. It was a time of experimentation, of learning a hard lesson that would be remembered. The Continental Congress and Articles of Confederation not only remained a symbol of union; they also prepared the way for a better national government and left on hand agencies of government in good working order and various substantial acts of legislation, such as the ordinance for the government of the Northwest Territory, and that for the public-land survey.

PART II.
Formation of the Constitution

CHAPTER VII. Genesis of the Convention

Thoughtful men, both in and out of public life, were fully aware of the distressful state of affairs and its only too evident consequences; and there were many exchanges of ideas on the possible remedies. Pamphlets were also issued on the subject, such as those of Noah and Pelatiah Webster. Washington was then in retirement on his Mount Vernon estate, but in touch with affairs through visitors and an extensive correspondence. He wrote Lafayette in 1783: "We stand, now, an Independent People, and have yet to learn political tactics experience, which is purchased at the price of difficulties and distress, will alone convince us that the honor, power, and true interest of this country must be measured by a Continental scale, and that every departure therefrom weakens the Union, and may ultimately break the band which holds us together."

Since the attempts for stronger central government through the regular agency were failing to produce results, efforts for a better understanding and cooperation were sought in outside ways. Virginia led in the measures which had direct results, and the economic interests of the late commander-in-chief were involved in the matter. He was concerned with the improvement of the navigation of the Potomac River and was instrumental in getting a joint Virginia-Maryland commission, in 1785, to sign a compact for the regulation of the river that was their mutual boundary. Consideration led to the suggestion to include Pennsylvania and Delaware in the adjustment of commercial matters which they had in common with the other two States. On January 21, 1786, the legislature of Virginia enlarging upon this idea and ignoring entirely the requirements of the Articles of Confederation, suggested a general convention of commissioners from the States to view the trade of the Union, and "consider how far a uniform system in their commercial relations may be necessary to their common interests and their permanent harmony."

This convention met at Annapolis in September, 1786, but was attended by only five States, New York, New Jersey, Pennsylvania, Delaware, and Virginia, though other States had appointed delegates. Because of the limited attendance, nothing was done except to make a report, drafted by Alexander Hamilton, to the legislatures of the five States and also to Congress. This called attention to the fact that the delegates of New Jersey had been authorized to consider not only commercial regulations but "other important matters" necessary to the common interest and permanent harmony of the several States; and suggested the calling of another convention with enlarged powers, since the "power of regulating trade is of such comprehensive extent, and will enter so far into the general System of the foederal government, that to give it efficacy, and to obviate questions and doubts concerning its precise nature and limits, may require a corresponding adjustment of other parts of the Foederal System." It is interesting to note how farseeing Hamilton was in this statement of the importance of the commercial power of the Union.

Congress took this report into consideration and on February 21, 1787, eleven States being represented, resolved that such a convention appeared "to be the most probable means of establishing in these states a firm national government," and that it considered it "expedient" that such a convention be held in May, 1787, at Philadelphia, "for the sole and express purpose of revising the Articles of Confederation and reporting to Congress and the several legislatures such alterations and provisions therein as shall when agreed to in Congress and confirmed by the states render the federal constitution adequate to the exigencies of Government & the preservation of the Union." This resolve brought the acts of the proposed convention within the legal requirements 'of amendment of the Articles, since whatever was proposed by the convention must be agreed to by Congress and then confirmed, presumably, by all the State legislatures.

CHAPTER VIII. THE DEPUTIES

The legislatures of all the States, except Rhode Island, appointed deputies to the Constitutional Convention. Six of them did this before Congress passed the above resolve. Seventy-four men were appointed deputies; of these nineteen declined or did not attend. Of the fifty-five who attended, fourteen left before the convention closed and three more refused to sign the final draft; thirty-eight signing, with the added signature of an absent deputy. Rhode Island, where localistic radicals were in control, ignored the whole proceedings.

Who were the fifty-five men who, in varying degrees, were the framers of our National Constitution? The knowledge concerning some of them is indefinite, but the following facts are substantially correct. All of them except eight were natives of the colonies. Franklin, the oldest, was 81; Dayton the youngest, was 26; fourteen were 50 or over; twenty-one were less than 40. Twenty-five were college men. Eighteen had been officers in the Continental army, of whom ten were in the Society of the Cincinnati. One had been a British army officer before the Revolution. Thirty-four of them were lawyers, or men who had at least studied the law, some of them trained at the Middle Temple in London; of these six had been or were to be State attorney generals, five chief justices of the State Supreme Courts, four chancellors, three national judges, and five justices of the Supreme 'Court of the United States, of whom one was to be chief justice and another after a term as associate justice was to be rejected for the higher office by the Senate. Eight of the deputies were merchants or financiers. Six of them were planters, while others were planters in addition to legal or other activities. There were three physicians and two former ministers of the gospel, several college professors and one present and one future college president. The Fourth Estate was represented by Benjamin Franklin.

These men were almost without exception acquainted with public affairs: forty-six had been members of one or both of the houses of the colonial or State legislatures; ten attended State constitutional conventions; sixteen had been or were to be governors.

In national affairs forty-two were delegates to the Continental Congress, eight were signers of the Declaration of Independence, six signers of the draft of the Articles of Confederation, seven had attended the Annapolis Convention, and three had been executive officers under the Congress. Fourteen were to be congressmen and nineteen national senators, one territorial governor, four members of the President's Cabinet. One had been a minister abroad and six more were to be later. Two future Presidents of the United States took a prominent part in the proceedings of the Convention and one future Vice-President. Two others were to be candidates for the highest office in the land and these and one other, candidates for the Vice-Presidency. The positions which these men had occupied or were later to fill are indicative of the regard in which they were held by their fellow citizens, and of their character and worth.

The most important man in the convention was George Washington; indeed, his acceptance of the deputyship, made reluctantly and after long consideration, was the initial triumph of the movement, and a foreshadowing of success, so great was his prestige. Madison and Randolph, his fellow deputies from Virginia, were very active in the work of the convention; and Wythe and Mason, older men, added the weight of their knowledge and experience as prominent participants in earlier affairs. Madison's great knowledge of political science, the fact that to him more than to any other deputy public life was a profession, and his grasp of the essential problems before the convention and the means by which they could be solved, enabled him to become the principal architect of the Constitution.

Franklin was the seer of the convention. His great age and infirmities forbade very active participation, and he was probably responsible for little of the detailed results, but his very presence gave the gathering importance and dignity and his advice must have been eagerly sought and carefully considered. He and Washington were the two great harmonizers. Washington presided over the formal sessions, taking little part in the debate, but in committee of the whole, and in the private conferences which were such an important underpinning of the formal structure as it arose, he was in constant consultation with his colleagues. Also, as the must be a leading man in the early operation of the new government, and this of necessity influenced its shape.

It is not possible here to do more than mention the other most prominent men of the convention. In the reflection of his later fame much influence has been attributed to Alexander Hamilton. This, however, was not the case. His ideas of central power were too extreme; he was hindered by the reactionary character of his two colleagues, and he was also absent during half of the convention. His great services came later. In the ratification contest and the successful operation of the new government his work was masterful.

Gouverneur Morris brilliant and cogent debater and firm believer in a national system, was responsible for the final very apt wording of the Constitution. James Wilson, leader in law and political theory, ably seconded Madison's efforts, especially in details. Roger Sherman, from small but progressive Connecticut, was a signer of the documents of the First Congress, the Declaration, the Articles of Confederation, and the Constitution; and Oliver Ellsworth was his lawyer colleague.

Gerry and King of Massachusetts were Harvard graduates, the one fluctuating in his attitude and the other a calm thinker and careful speaker, an advocate of an efficient system with due consideration of the rights of the States. William Paterson of New Jersey, John Dickinson of Delaware, and Luther Martin of Maryland, were prominent as small State leaders, bent upon the preservation of the equality of the States. Martin was from the beginning an opponent of anything other than amendment of the Articles of Confederation and continued implacable. John Rutledge, Charles Pinckney, Charles Cotesworth Pinckney, and Pierce Butler of South Carolina, saw the need of a completely new system, but were also eager to preserve the advantage of the slave system then dominating the economic conditions of the lower south. Charles Pinckney, one of the youngest men in the convention, was especially eloquent in his advocacy of a workable "American System" for the nation whose future growth he clearly envisioned.

CHAPTER IX. Organization

The convention was called for the second Monday in May, 1787, which was the 14th, and Washington arrived at Philadelphia, prompt as always, on the day before, when, as he said in his diary, "the bells were chimed." There was, however, not the necessary quorum until the 25th, when seven States were represented. Before the end of the month ten States were present and voting. Maryland participated on June 2, but New Hampshire, the twelfth State, was not on hand until July 23, and New York was not voting after July 10.

The meeting was held in Independence Hall, where the Congress had sat and where the Declaration of Independence was adopted and signed. Little time was wasted in organization. Washington was the unanimous choice for President. The voting was by the prevailing system of one State, one vote; and complete secrecy was ordered in accordance with the rule, often violated, of the Continental Congress.

The credentials of most of the deputies merely voiced the purpose of the assembly as given by the resolution of the Continental Congress to provide effectual means to remedy the defects; but the Delaware members were forbidden to amend the right of each State to one vote. On the other hand, South Carolina wished the central authority to be "entirely adequate to the actual situation and future good government." Delaware's warnings were preliminary notes of discord that later reached full development in the main theme.

Thus began the meetings of one of the greatest sessions of wise men in the history of the world. But these meetings were so secret that the President would not give any hint concerning them even in the intimacy of his private diary. There was a formal journal kept, but, except for its list of motions and votes, it is the least important of the records which have come down to us. Far surpassing it and all other sources combined were the notes on the debates kept by Madison, notes that were not made public as a whole until 1840. Thus he doubled the debt the nation owes him for his work in the formation of the national government, and later he added still further to the obligation by his energetic participation in the ratification contest. Various other members made notes that occasionally add to the knowledge derived from Madison, or throw light upon the position of members. None of these, however, covers the whole proceedings, the Yates notes being the most extensive next to Madison's.

There were meetings on eighty-seven days of the one hundred sixteen between May 25 and September 17, inclusive, of 1787. Of these meetings we have more or less knowledge, but of the work under the surface, of the special committee meetings and of the private discussions, we have scarcely anything, and most of this through the unreliable form of later recollection. Yet it was here, in the give and take of informal gatherings, that much of the real work was done and understandings were reached.

CHAPTER X. The Virginia Plan

On May 29, 1787, the convention having been organized, Randolph "opened the main business" by introducing the "Virginia Plan." This plan, drafted by Madison, had been submitted by him in outline to Washington on April 16, and was later worked up in preliminary meetings of the Virginia delegation of seven members. It provided for apportioned representation, a legislature of two houses, the lower house elected by the people, the upper one elected by the lower. The legislature was to have all the legislative powers of the Continental Congress, and also "to legislate in all cases to which the separate States are incompetent, or in which the harmony of the United States may be interrupted by the exercise of individual Legislation; to negative all laws passed by the several States, contravening in the opinion of the National Legislature the articles of Union; and to call forth the force of the Union against any member
of the Union failing to fulfill its duty under the articles thereof."

There was to be a national executive and a national judiciary, with a council of revision formed out of them which should have a conditional veto on national legislation and also on the national legislature's negative of State acts. The central power was to guarantee a republican form of government and its territory to each State. Provisions for the admission of new States were included, and provisions for amendment without the assent of the National Legislature." Also State officers should be "bound by oath to support the articles of Union."

This was the germ of the Constitution of the United States. For its form it went back to practices of colonial and State governments; for its powers to the lessons of wartime and later experiences. It gave the central government coercive power over the State governments, while it guaranteed their continued existence. Since it made no provision for operation through the State governments, it contained the idea of direct action on the people, and the great "law of the land" principle was foreshadowed. This was far more than a mere amendment of the Articles of Confederation and entirely contrary to the instructions given the delegates from Delaware. It was a large-State proposal.

Charles Pinckney also introduced a plan, the text of which has not come down to us, but probable extracts and an outline exist. Its general character was similar to the Virginia plan and its influence upon the final draft seems to have been considerable.

The next thirteen meetings were in committee of the whole upon the Virginia plan. To enforce the idea of this plan three resolutions, urged by Gouverneur Morris, were introduced declaring that a federal (that is, confederate) union of individual sovereigns was not sufficient; that a "national Government ought to be established consisting of a supreme Legislative, Executive, & Judiciary."

The report which the committee of the whole made to the convention on June 13 was a development of the Virginia plan, with changes that gave the election of the upper house of the
national legislature to the State legislatures; made the executive consist of a single individual, and gave him alone the provisional veto; and added a resolution for the ratification of the new
Constitution by State conventions.

CHAPTER XI. The Paterson Plan

Meanwhile the deputies who feared a strong central government and were concerned with the preservation of the power of the States had been devising an alternative plan, which was introduced by Paterson of New Jersey on June 15, 1787. This merely added to the powers of Congress the right to levy an impost and to regulate foreign and interstate commerce. It authorized a plural executive and a federal judiciary. It made the acts of Congress and the treaties with foreign powers "the supreme law of the respective States so far forth as those Acts or Treaties shall relate to the said States or their Citizens," and bound the judiciary of the States to proper observance. It also gave the national executive the right to call forth the power of the States to compel obedience by the States to such acts or treaties.

This plan left the character of Congress unchanged, with an equal State vote and choice of delegates by the State legislatures; it adopted the separation of national powers; and specified the supremacy of the Union within its sphere. There were thus concessions to the recognized need for a more efficient government, but they did not go far. They merely patched up the old Articles.

CHAPTER XII. The Compromise

The battle between the large and small States was joined. Out of the conflict, which threatened to disrupt the convention, emerged on July 16, 1787, the adoption of the Great Compromise, urged by the Connecticut deputies. This gave representation based on population in the lower house, with the exclusive power to originate money bills in that house; but in the upper house an equal State vote. The special financial power of the lower house was also a provision in some of the State constitutions; but it was later practically nullified by giving the Senate the right of unrestricted amendment. During the discussion of this, the cleavage between the northern and southern States developed, due to the latter's demand, when population was substituted for wealth as the basis of representation, for representation of its slave population. A part of the compromise was, therefore, that three-fifths of the slaves should be counted as inhabitants. A similar proposal as a basis of requisitions upon the States had been before the Continental Congress; and as a phase of this agreement the direct taxes, which under the new government would take the place of the old requisitions, were given the same basis of levy upon the States. This compromise, together with the election of the Senate by the State legislatures, did much to quiet the apprehension of the small-State party; but it was not a victory for those who wished to preserve the principles of the Articles of Confederation, and when later each senator was given a separate vote the idea of State representation in the upper house was weakened.

This compromise made it evident that sectional questions as well as those involving State rights were to be met—evidences that were prophetic of future trouble.

Much of the history of the nation throughout its first six decades was to turn, not upon State rights as they involved the differences between small and large States, but upon State sovereignty in combination with sectional divergences. The southern deputies, from a region entirely agricultural, were fearful that unrestrained control by the central government over foreign commerce might result in navigation acts unfavorable to their section. Out of this another compromise developed which left the commercial power unrestricted but forbade an export tax, or interference with the foreign slave trade until 1808.

CHAPTER XIII. Law of the Land

The next important question was that of national control over State laws and actions; its need was generally recognized, but a direct veto and military enforcement of obedience were objectionable. The plan introduced by Paterson on June 15, 1787, suggested the remedy, which was adopted unanimously on July 17. This made the laws and treaties of the national government the supreme law, to which the State judiciaries were bound in their decisions. Later the Constitution itself was added to the laws and treaties and the "supreme law of the States" was made the "supreme Law of the Land," which change might be considered as emphasizing the origin of the Constitution as the work of the whole-of the people-and not of the States.

This great "Law of the Land" clause has been called the linchpin of the Constitution, since it effectively binds the parts into the whole. It has always been the chief basis upon which the courts have passed on the constitutionality of legislation, whether State or national. It embodies the principle of direct action by the national government upon the inhabitants, for the enactments of the Congress are laws directly binding upon the people themselves.

CHAPTER XIV. Method of Ratification and Amendment

The Virginia plan had called for ratification of the Constitution by State conventions especially chosen by the people. Only two of the existing State constitutions had been framed by conventions chosen exclusively for this task; and only in these two had the Constitution been submitted to the people for approval or rejection. Elsewhere legislatures, all but three of them freshly chosen, however, framed the constitutions and put them in force. The amendments proposed to the Articles of Confederation were also voted upon by the legislatures.

The more direct appeal under the new Constitution to the freemen themselves, through the action of conventions especially chosen for the purpose, was in harmony with the main principles of a document which began with "We the People," and which cut loose so completely from the existing confederate principles. Attention may be called here to the fact that in this as in other respects the Constitution led toward that greater democratic spirit that operated more and more within the State governments themselves; an element that had no small influence in cementing the Union.

More was to follow the convention's adoption on July 23, 1787, of this method of ratification, for on August 31 it was voted that ratification by nine States would be sufficient for establishing the Constitution over the States so ratifying, and that the approbation of the Continental Congress was not required. Both of these decisions were clearly revolutionary. The Articles of Confederation required unanimous ratification of amendment, and the resolution calling the convention stated that the alterations and provisions made by the convention should be submitted to Congress as well as to the States; in other words, that the convention should act, not as an independent body, but as a committee or agent of Congress. The method by which the new Constitution might be amended also did away with the need of unanimity; but left to the Congress under the new Constitution to decide, in proposing amendments, whether the ratification should be by legislatures or conventions of the people.

CHAPTER XV. FINISHING THE WORK

The rest of the work of the convention was largely detail —important detail, but little that involved great principles. Like the basic ideas, the results were arrived at for the most part through compromise. A definite statement of the national powers had to be made, since the residuary ones were left to the States; the national judiciary and its jurisdiction stated; and the election and powers of the President decided upon.

The demand for a single executive won; but the idea of a council, inherited from colonial times, when such a body was both the upper house of legislature and the governor's adviser, persisted, and finally the Senate was given power to ratify treaties and also approve appointments. But the Cabinet has no legal existence as a body. The method of choosing the President had to be worked out without aid from precedents, except the provision in the Maryland constitution of an electoral college for senatorial elections; and the original intention has been twisted entirely out of shape by the development of political parties.

Committees of detail and of style performed their tasks, and finally on September 17, 1787, the draft was ready for the signatures of the deputies. Of the fifty-five who had attended the convention, only forty-one remained, and three of these re-fused to sign. To the thirty-eight signatures was added, at his request, that of one absent deputy, and it is probable that a large majority of those absent would have signed if present. With Hamilton signing for New York, though he had refrained from voting on its final passage since alone he could not represent the State, the draft was sent forth by the "Unanimous Consent of the States present." This form was itself a com-promise which induced various members to sign who would not otherwise have done so. These were willing to certify by their signatures that the draft had received the votes of all of the States, but not that it had their personal approval. Most truly has the Constitution been called a "bundle of compromises . . . a mosaic of second choices accepted in the interest of union."

CHAPTER XVI. RATIFICATION

The draft was submitted to the consideration of the "United States in Congress assembled," with the expression of opinion that Congress pass it on to the State legislatures, to be submitted by them to the mercies of State conventions. Doubtless, had Congress refused to do this, the States could and probably would have taken independent action. The Pennsylvania deputies presented the draft to their legislature on September 18, 1787, before it was known to Congress, and other copies were sent by delegates to their States or to friends. The Congress accepted its modest role. On September 28, eleven States being present, without a word of favorable comment upon the contents of the document, it was unanimously transmitted to the State legislatures. The unanimity, like that of the convention itself, was rather fictitious, and possibly only because comment was withheld.

During the convention there had been newspaper speculation and statements as to its progress, based for the most part merely on rumor; but .with the publication of the signed Constitution the expression of public opinion came at once to full flood. The extensive and virulent use of newsletters and pamphlets was greater than on any previous occasion; and wherever people gathered, whether for town meetings, church, or gossip at the country stores on the crossroads, the topic was evidently a universal one. It raged for months, and it is to be noticed that ratification became more difficult as the discussion progressed.

The honor of first ratification went to Delaware. Her convention was a mere formality, and approval was unanimously given on December 7, 1787. Five days later Pennsylvania, under the influence of Wilson's vigorous arguments, added her name, though the Anti-federalists raised the cry of trickery. The convention of New Jersey resolved on ratification without dissent on December 18, 1787. Georgia gave her adherence on January 2, 1788, and Connecticut was just a week later. One large State, two small States, and two that occupied rather a middle position on this question had now given their approval. The convention of Massachusetts came next and here, where but recently the Shays Rebellion, the worst of the radical outbreaks, had threatened the stability of the State itself, there was a real battle.

The issue fought out in the ratification contest had many phases: the old question of State rights and sovereignty; the danger to the liberties of the people from a strong central government; sectional antagonism; class prejudices; desire to escape obligations and enjoy the unearned increment of cheap money; backwoods life where ignorance of the real needs prevailed; and fear of anything new or novel.

There were strong leaders on both sides. Samuel Adams was in doubt. Hancock inclined to wait and see which way the popular wind would blow, and Gerry voiced his reasons for refusing to sign the Constitution.

Governor George Clinton of New York strongly opposed ratification. Patrick Henry, Richard Henry Lee. George Mason, who had refused to sign the Constitution, and James Monroe headed the opposition in Virginia. The leaders of the convention rallied to its support—King and Strong in Massachusetts, and Hamilton, assisted by Jay and Benson, in New York. Madison was a tower of strength in Virginia, ably seconded by Randolph, even though he also had refused to sign, and by the young John Marshall, ignorant of what his own career would mean in constitutional history, but already firm in the principles which were to give him immortal fame and his government a dynamic entity. Above all, the fact that Washington and Franklin had signed the draft was of immeasurable importance. Both sides realized this: the Federalists pointed with pride; the Antifederalists declared that these great men had been deceived and that the claim of their support of the plan was misleading.

Washington took no direct active share in the ratification contest, but he made no secret of his support. His correspondence teemed with the subject and his almost daily intercourse with visitors at Mount Vernon seconded his written admonitions. Above all, he disapproved of the idea of a second convention, which was one of the favorite proposals of the Antifederalists. He had too much knowledge of the difficulties met in the first gathering to believe that a second one could do any better, especially as there was no agreement among those opposed as to the proper remedy. There was nothing, in his opinion, constructive in the arguments against the Constitution; they were all "addressed to the passions of the people and obviously calculated to alarm their fears."

The most influential publication of the contest was the series of newsletters written by Hamilton, Madison, and Jay under the signature of "Publius" and called "The Federalist." So fair and so cogent was this work that it continues to this day as a great exposition of the Constitution, a survival which Washington prophesied.

It was in the Massachusetts contest that the proponents, facing a crisis, devised a remedy that made ratification possible. This was the proposal of amendments by the State conventions, not as a condition of ratification, though this was generally demanded by the opposing leaders, but as a recommendation, of the proper consideration of which they were "convinced." A chief feature of all these amendments was a bill of rights that the new central government might not become an instrument of tyranny. which the newly emancipated colonists considered the British government to have been.

Ratification in Massachusetts, the second large State, was thus secured on February 6, 1788, by the close vote of 187 to 168. All the States but one of those which followed Massachusetts in 1788 suggested amendments. In New Hampshire the convention met and adjourned, which alarmed Washington and other Federalists; but this was really a wise act, because a majority of the delegates of this rural State had been instructed to oppose adherence. Maryland, in spite of Luther Martin and Samuel Chase, who later were to become strong Federalists, ratified on April 28, 1788, by a vote of 63 to 11, and South Carolina on May 23 by a vote of 149 to 73.

The reassembled New Hampshire convention on June 21, 1788, by a vote of 57 to 47, gave the ninth ratification necessary for putting the Constitution into effect.

Practically, however, the approval of Virginia and New York was necessary; the former because of its importance and the latter because of its geographical position. In both of these conventions the struggle was desperate. Finally ratification was obtained in Virginia on June 26, 1788, by a vote of 89 to 79. In New York a large majority of the delegates were hostile, but the efforts of Hamilton, Jay, R. R. Livingston, and Duane converted a sufficient number, in spite of Lansing, who had been a member of the Federal Convention, Governor Clinton, and Melancton Smith. Ratification won by a vote of 30 to 27 on July 26, 1788.

North Carolina and Rhode Island remained outside. In the former State a convention adjourned on August 4, 1788, after resolving by a vote of 184 to 83 or 84 that a long list of submitted amendments should be laid before Congress, or a second convention called, previous to ratification. Rhode Island did not even call a convention. When, however, the new government was in operation without these States and they were in danger of being treated as foreign countries, they changed their mind. North Carolina ratified on November 21, 1789, and Rhode Island on May 29, 1790, but even then by the narrow vote of 34 to 32.

On September 13, 1788, the Continental Congress prepared for its own demise by directing that the electors of the President should be chosen on the first Wednesday in January, 1789; that the electors [Electoral College] should vote on the first Wednesday in February; and that the new government should begin operations at New York on the first Wednesday in March. Electors were accordingly chosen in ten States; the New York legislature failing to pass the necessary measure on method of appointment, that State lost its vote. A month later the electors chose George Washington President and John Adams Vice-President. But the newly elected Congress failed to have a quorum on the first Wednesday in March, which was the 4th; and it was not until April 6, 1789, that enough members were assembled legally to organize and declare the electoral vote. Washington, duly notified, arrived at New York on April 23 and was inaugurated President April 30, 1789. Thus the government of the United States of America began actual operations under the Constitution, except that the Supreme Court did not organize
until February 2, 1790.

PART III.
THE CONSTITUTION IN OPERATION

CHAPTER XVII. The People and the Constitution

The league embodied in the Articles of Confederation was made by the States. The Constitution was made by the People.

The first three words of the Constitution—"We the People"—declare by what authority the United States of America is ruled.

Having won their liberty and independence by force of arms, and having experienced distress and danger because of an imperfect union, the people finally succeeded in forming the more perfect Union which is ordained and established by the Constitution.

The Constitution is a direct emanation from the people. It not only prescribes the kind of government which shall hold the States and the people together, but it limits and defines the powers of the government itself. Neither the United States Government nor the

States can modify, enlarge, or restrict their own powers. They depend for their existence upon the people, who reserve the right as set forth in the Declaration of Independence, to alter or abolish their government.

Until the people decide otherwise, the United States is, in the noble phrase of Chief Justice Chase, "an indissoluble Union of indestructible States." It is made indissoluble by the Constitution, which also provides for the indestructibility of the States by guaranteeing to each State a republican form of government and equal suffrage in the Senate.

The people have ordained in the Constitution that the national government shall depend for its existence upon the perpetuity of the States. There is, however, no guarantee of unchangeable State areas; but all elections are by States, including election of senators and representatives in Congress and presidential electors [Electoral Collage]. When the House of Representatives is called upon to elect a President of the United States each State has one vote. Failure of the States to perform their functions would annihilate the national government.

The people who ordained the Constitution were passionately attached to their State and local governments. They knew that they were masters of their States, but they feared that a national government would become a tyranny like the British tyranny they had just thrown off. The States and the people enjoy immense powers that are denied to the United States. It is this dual system of government that distinguishes the United States from other countries.

England has no written constitution. Its constitution or fundamental law is whatever Parliament says it is. Therefore the judges of England enforce the laws of Parliament without any question as to their constitutionality. But under a written constitution creating a government with limited powers a nation must have some means of determining if laws are in accord with the basic principles set forth by the constitution.

The liberties enjoyed by Englishmen were wrested from the Crown. The American colonists claimed these liberties as their inheritance, and won. by force of arms, the final right to them and to further ones which had been fostered by the conditions of the colonial governments. The government of the United States is not a concession to the people from some one higher up. It is the creation and the creature of the people themselves, as absolute sovereigns.

CHAPTER XVIII. A Limited Government

The objects sought by the American people in their aspirations for the preservation of their liberties are well stated in the Preamble to the Constitution. But while the scope of these objectives recognizes the unlimited power of the people, the Constitution itself imposes severe limitations upon the government. In general, the national government is granted only such powers as are absolutely necessary for the discharge of purely national functions, such as could not be discharged by the States acting either separately or through interstate compacts.

New conditions and an uncertain future faced the people when they ratified the Constitution, and it was framed to meet the situation that confronted them. This was well set forth by Justice Story in Martin v. Hunter, 1 Wheat. 326:

"The Constitution unavoidably deals in general language. It did not suit the purposes of the people, in framing this great charter of our liberties, to provide for minute specifications of its powers or to declare the means by which those powers should be carried into execution. It was foreseen that this would be a perilous and difficult, if not an impracticable, task. The instrument was not intended to provide merely for the exigencies of a few years, but was to endure through a long lapse of ages, the events of which were locked up in the inscrutable purposes of Providence."

The determination of the people to hold a check-rein upon the government they were creating is shown in the many prohibitions contained in the Constitution. Great reserve powers, many of them unexplored, are retained to the States and to the people. This is well stated by the court in Livingston v. Van Ingen, 9 Johns. (N. Y.) 507:

"When the people create a single, entire government, they grant at once all the rights of sovereignty. The powers granted are indefinite and incapable of enumeration. Everything is granted that is not expressly reserved in the constitutional charter, or necessarily retained as inherent in the people. But when a federal government is erected with only a portion of the sovereign power, the rule of construction is directly the reverse, and every power is reserved to the members that is not, either in express terms or by necessary implication, taken away from them, and vested exclusively in the federal head. This rule has not only been acknowledged by the most intelligent friends of the Constitution, but is plainly declared by the instrument itself."

No power to enact any statute is derived from the Preamble.

Although the powers of the national government are limited in number, they are not limited in degree. Wherever the people have granted a power to the government it is a complete power, and that which is implied is as much a part of the Constitution as that which is expressed.

Experience in colonial governments and under the Confederation had taught the people that safety lay in preventing concentration of powers in any one authority. By separating the legislative, executive, and judicial powers, and making each of them a check upon the others, it was felt that all powers necessary could be entrusted to the government without danger of tyranny. But as a further precaution the people reserved to the States and to themselves all powers that were not entrusted to the national government; and in other clauses of the Bill of Rights they set barriers against encroachment upon individual liberty by any branch of this government.

By retaining large powers in the States the people erected a further barrier against encroachment upon their liberties by the central government they were creating. This division or balance of powers between the national government and the States has been the cause of endless debate and controversy.

CHAPTER XIX. CONGRESS

The limitation upon the law-making power of the United States government is clearly shown by the words "herein granted" in the following sentence, from Article 1, Section 1:

All legislative Powers herein granted shall be vested in a Congress of the United States, which shall consist of a Senate and House of Representatives."

Neither branch of Congress acting separately can enact a law. Congress cannot delegate its power to make laws to an executive department or to an administrative officer, nor can any department or officer repeal, extend, or modify an act of Congress.

But Congress may vest in executive officers the power to make necessary rules and regulations to enforce a law.

Senators and representatives are paid out of the United States Treasury, but it has been held that they are not officers of the United States. They are not subject to impeachment. Either House by a two-thirds vote may expel a member, but otherwise they are not removable. With some exceptions, they are exempt from arrest during attendance upon Congress; and they cannot be questioned elsewhere for their actions or words in Congress. No Senator or Representative may be appointed to any national office during his term if the office has been created or the salary thereof increased during that time. No national officer may be a member of Congress.

The general process of making laws is set forth in the Constitution. Every bill must have the approval of the President of the United States; and if he should disapprove, it cannot become a law unless repassed by a two-thirds vote of each house of Congress.

Proposals to amend the Constitution may be submitted to the States by a two-thirds vote of both houses of Congress, and such a resolution need not be submitted to the President for his approval.

The chief power conferred upon the government is that of taxation. When Congress acts within its constitutional authority, its power to tax is unlimited; but Congress cannot under the pretext of taxation exercise powers which are denied to it.

Next to the power to tax, the power to regulate interstate and foreign commerce is the most important function of Congress as affecting the everyday affairs of the people. Commerce is traffic, intercourse, navigation, trade, and shipping; and the power to regulate includes power to foster, protect, control, restrain, and prohibit, with appropriate regard for the welfare of the public. But here, as elsewhere, this power does not carry with it the right to destroy the guaranties which are placed in the Constitution and amendments.

The exclusive power to coin money and regulate its value is conferred upon Congress. All power over coinage is denied to the States, so that there shall be a national coinage and a uniform value of money throughout the United States. Although the States are prohibited from making "anything but gold and silver coins a tender in the payment of debts," there is no prohibition against the issuance of paper money by the United States.

The Supreme Court has held that Congress may determine this question, according to the necessities of the Nation.

Only seven words are contained in the Constitution in regard to the mails. Congress is given power "to establish Post Offices and Post roads." But this is a complete and exclusive power, and it has been held to include the power to define and punish crimes against the mails.

Under its power to confer upon authors and inventors "the exclusive Right to their respective Writings and Discoveries" Congress has powerfully stimulated the inventive faculties of the American people.

The exclusive power to declare war is vested in Congress. The Constitution does not define the limits of this power. This subject was earnestly discussed by the framers of the Constitution. They very wisely concluded that since it is impossible to foresee the dangers of war or the measures that may be necessary to maintain our independence the government should not be denied the power to make war and peace in any way it deems wise. The power to declare war and make treaties enables the United States to do anything necessary to preserve the Nation. But even extreme war measures must be directed toward saving the Constitution. The government cannot, under the exercise of the war power, extinguish a State or abolish the Constitution. The Constitution takes precautions against a possible military dictatorship by providing that no appropriation of money to raise and support armies shall be for a longer term than two years. Congress is not at liberty to grant permanent funds to the President for the support of an army.

Several prohibitions are imposed upon Congress in the body of the Constitution. The privilege of the writ of habeas corpus may not be suspended unless the public safety shall require it; no bill of attainder may be enacted; no ex post facto law may be passed; no export tax or duty may be imposed; no preference may be given to the ports of one State over those of another; no money may be drawn from the Treasury except by appropriations made by law; and no title of nobility may be granted.

To prevent encroachments on national powers, certain prohibitions are imposed by the Constitution upon the States.

No State may enter into any treaty or alliance, grant letters of marque, coin money, emit paper money or make it a legal tender, pass any bill of attainder, ex post facto law, or law impairing the obligation of contracts, or grant any title to nobility. No State may keep troops or ships of war or enter into any agreement with any other State, or with a foreign power, without the consent of Congress.

CHAPTER XX. The President

The executive power is "vested in a President"; he is the sole responsible constitutional officer. There is a Vice President, but as an executive officer he is merely the heir apparent, ready to take over the presidential functions when occasion requires. In the meantime he presides over the Senate without a vote except in cases of a tie. Unofficially he may at times act as a liaison between the President and Congress; but ordinarily his place in the scheme of government is but little considered, so slightly that this reacts at times upon the proper consideration to be given to the nominations for an office of such great potentiality.

The President must be a native born citizen, the only office in the country of which this was a qualification in the original Constitution, though a similar qualification was implied for the Vice President. In the Twelfth Amendment these requirements for the lesser office are distinctly stated.

The office of President of the United States is one of the most important and powerful in the world; yet to its duties and powers the Constitution gives only some 320 words, not including those upon the veto power. These duties and powers are to have command of the military and naval forces, grant reprieves and pardons, make treaties, appoint and commission officers, give information to Congress, receive foreign ministers, and "take care that the Laws be faithfully executed." In addition he has the power of provisional veto.

It is evident that while the President is head of the executive department, his duties and powers are not confined to the execution of the laws; though this is perhaps his most important duty. Various of his functions, not actually executive, were also combined in the office of colonial governor or later state governor and which were primarily those of the deputy of a king possessed with general powers. The power of veto is distinctly legislative, as is also the treaty-making power and the right to advise Congress. The pardon power is judicial.

The Senate shares in both the appointing and treaty power, possessing in this respect, the character of a council.

The President himself does not execute the laws. He is responsible for seeing that they are executed, the actual tasks being performed by a host of officials under him, who are answerable to him. The Constitution directs that he shall appoint diplomatic and consular officers, judges of the Supreme Court, and "all other Officers of the United States," except that Congress may direct the appointment of "inferior Officers" by courts of law or heads of departments. So far as his power is derived from the Constitution, he is beyond the reach of any other department of the government. In directing national policy, the President possesses almost unlimited discretionary powers which are not subject to question by the legislative or judicial departments. All official acts performed by the heads of departments are presumed to be the acts of the President.

The President is exempt from mandamus or injunction, and is not subject to the writ of habeas corpus. Theoretically, he may be subpoenaed, but in practice he is exempt.

As commander-in-chief of the army and navy the President may make rules and regulations for the government of these forces. Such regulations have the force of law. Without waiting for the action of Congress, the President may use the military forces to put down insurrection or meet invasion. During war he possesses enormous powers. He may invade enemy territory and set up a military government therein. He may establish provisional courts in occupied territory and set up a temporary tariff system. He may recognize and revoke recognition of foreign governments. He may declare a blockade of foreign ports and employ secret agents to enter the enemy's lines for the purpose of gaining information. In a time of invasion or civil war the President may declare martial law.

The President's power to pardon is not subject to regulation by Congress. Congress cannot limit the effect of his pardon nor exclude any class of offenders from the exercise of a pardon.

Under the treaty-making power the President, with the advice and consent of the Senate, may make contracts with foreign nations of the most far-reaching character, and these treaties are the supreme law of the land.

During war, treaties with the enemy are usually suspended or terminated automatically, and peace is usually made by treaty. Additions to the territory of the United States have been made by treaty, notably the Louisiana Purchase, the acquisition of California and other territory from Mexico, the purchase of Alaska, and the acquisition of the Philippine Islands and Puerto Rico from Spain.

CHAPTER XXI. THE JUDICIARY

One of the most striking and novel features of the Constitution is the establishment of the judicial branch as an independent and coequal department of the government. The lack of a judicial system was one of the vital defects of the United States before the establishment of the Constitution. At the time, in no other government did the judiciary exercise the powers now exercised by the courts of the United States; since ratification of our Constitution, various nations have adopted similar provisions. Justice Story says:

"Where there is no judicial department to interpret, pronounce, and execute the law, to decide controversies, and to enforce rights, the government must either perish by its own imbecility, or the other departments of government must usurp powers, for the purpose of commanding obedience, to the destruction of liberty. The will of those who govern will become, under such circumstances, absolute and despotic; and it is wholly immaterial, whether power is vested in a single tyrant or in an assembly of tyrants."

The Constitution provides for "one supreme Court, and such inferior Courts as the Congress may from time to time ordain and establish." The judicial power of the United States is vested in these courts.

Neither the number nor the qualifications of justices of the Supreme Court, or of other courts, are provided for in the Constitution. All judges are appointed by the President, with the advice and consent of the Senate, and hold their offices during good behavior.

Careful provision was made not to have the national courts conflict with State courts in jurisdiction, and the functions and powers of State courts were left intact except in matters outside their province. The national judicial power extends to cases arising under the Constitution, the laws of the United States, and treaties; in addition, other cases which do not properly come under the jurisdiction of State courts are under the jurisdiction of the national courts, such as those of maritime jurisdiction, controversies between States, and cases affecting ambassadors, ministers, and consuls. Cases arising under State laws, of course, may be appealed to the Supreme Court when constitutional rights are involved.

This new branch of government revealed its importance from the very first, and with the growth of the nation, the framework of national courts has become of profound significance. Only a relatively small part of the work done by the national courts, including the Supreme Court, involves decisions on the constitutionality of legislation. The vast majority of cases are those of interpretation and application of laws whose constitutionality is unquestioned.

The Supreme Court hears very few cases that have not been heard before in inferior courts, as the Constitution gives it original jurisdiction only in cases affecting ambassadors, ministers, and consuls, and those in which a State itself is a party. As such cases are relatively few, the Supreme Court devotes most of its time to its appellate jurisdiction, which extends to all the other cases named in the Constitution.

It was for the purpose of enabling the Constitution and laws in pursuance of it to be enforced in specific cases, in this way securing the rights of life, liberty, and property, that the people committed the judicial power, not to a part of the legislature or executive power, but to a separate, distinct and independent body of men. The independence of the judicial branch is secured by providing that judges cannot be removed except by impeachment, and their salaries cannot be diminished during their continuance in office.

Congress cannot impose upon the courts any but judicial duties. Quasi-judicial functions may be conferred by Congress upon administrative officers.

CHAPTER XXII. Pertaining to the States

Article IV of the Constitution provides that full faith and credit shall be given by each State to the public acts, records, and judicial proceedings of every other State. This clause is intended to preserve the rights and immunities of citizens and to promote uniformity and harmony in the administration of justice under State laws.

It is also provided that the privileges and immunities of citizens shall be common throughout the States. Fugitives from justice are required to be returned to the State having jurisdiction of the crime.

Provision is made for the admission by Congress of new States into the Union. A State when admitted has equal sovereignty with the older ones. It must pledge to the other States that it will support the Constitution; and it cannot, by a compact with the United States, enlarge or diminish its constitutional rights or liabilities.

Congress is given power to dispose of property belonging to the United States. The full extent of this power has never been developed; but the Supreme Court has held that it includes the right to acquire means of conveying to market surplus electric power developed as an incident to regulation of navigation. The government of territories is within the power of Congress under the same paragraph, as well as the reclamation of public lands.

A republican form of government is guaranteed by the United States to every State, and they must be protected against invasion. In case of domestic violence the legislature or governor may call upon the United States for protection. The courts have ruled that the authority to decide whether the exigency requires action by the United States rests in the President.

CHAPTER XXIII. Method of Amendment

Much time and labor was devoted by the framers to working out a method whereby the Constitution might be changed to meet the needs of the people, while at the same time guarding against hasty and ill-considered experiments suggested by mere speculation or theory.

Two modes are provided for bringing about alterations in the Constitution. One may be begun at the instance of the government, through a resolution of Congress proposing amendments; the other may be begun at the instance of the States, through the instrumentality of a convention. A resolution by Congress proposing a constitutional amendment requires a two-thirds vote; and no general convention can be called unless two-thirds of the States concur in the demand. In either case, three-fourths of the States must concur, either through their legislatures or conventions called for the purpose, before any amendment can become a part of the Constitution. The States cannot substitute a popular vote for the constitutional method of acting upon proposed amendments.

The provisions whereby the Constitution provides for its own amendment by the people is one of the most novel and ingenious developments ever recorded in the history of the art of government. It enables the people, without turbulence or bloodshed, to alter their government as they see fit. Changes of government in other countries have usually been attended by wild disorders. Inability to improve the Articles of Confederation was one of the reasons for the virtual collapse of the Union before the Constitution was adopted.

Attempts have been made by States to rescind their ratification of amendments to the Constitution, but without effect. It is believed that when a State legislature has voted to ratify an amendment it has exhausted its constitutional authority in the premises.

Thousands of resolutions have been offered in Congress for amendments to the Constitution. But the unwisdom of rushing through an amendment by surprise or in response to a sudden wave of public impulse has been provided against by securing deliberation in proposing and ratifying amendments. Only after full discussion by all the people can the Constitution be changed. Yet the knowledge that they have it in their power to make any change they desire is a factor in insuring the devotion of the people to the Constitution they have ordained and established.

CHAPTER XXIV. Supremacy of the Constitution and Laws

After recognizing the validity of the public debt, the sixth article of the Constitution declares that the Constitution and the laws of the United States made in pursuance thereof, and all treaties made under the authority of the United States, shall be the supreme law of the land; and that the judges in every State shall be bound thereby, anything in the constitution or laws of any State to the contrary notwithstanding.

This majestic declaration makes of the United States a Nation, with an effective national government. The law of a State, though enacted in the exercise of powers not controverted, must yield to an act of Congress or a treaty. "It must always be borne in mind," says the Supreme Court,

"that the Constitution, laws and treaties of the United States are as much a part of the law of every State as its own local laws and constitution. This is a fundamental principle in our system of complex national polity."

No act of Congress is of any validity unless it rests upon the authority conferred by the Constitution. But a constitutional law of Congress supersedes a State law, even if the latter be enacted within the State's powers, if the two statutes are in conflict.

A treaty is regarded as equivalent to an act of Congress if it operates of itself without the aid of any legislative provision. Where a treaty and an act of Congress are in conflict the latest in date must prevail. A treaty may supersede a prior act of Congress, and an act of Congress may supersede a prior treaty.

"The guardianship of the Constitution," says Dicey, "is in America confined not only to the Supreme Court, but to every judge throughout the land. The power, moreover, of the courts which maintains the articles of the Constitution as the law of the land, and thereby keeps each authority within its proper sphere, is exerted with an ease and regularity which has astounded and perplexed Continental critics. The explanation is that while the judges of the United States control the action of the Constitution, they nevertheless perform purely judicial functions, since they never decide anything but the cases before them."

In order to compel observance of the Constitution as the supreme law it is further provided that all national legislators, judges and officers, and all State legislators and officers shall be bound by oath or affirmation to "support this Constitution"; but no religious test is required as a qualification to office.

It is indispensably necessary that members and officers of State governments should be under obligation to support the Constitution; for these authorities are agents in keeping the United States government in operation. The election of the President, senators, and representatives in Congress is dependent upon the faithful action of the States. State judges are called upon to pass judgment upon the Constitution, laws, and treaties of the United States.

Governors exert important powers in filling vacancies in the Senate and in issuing writs of election to fill vacancies in the House of Representatives, as well as in regard to the militia.

CHAPTER XXV. Amendments to the Constitution

Only twenty-one amendments have been attached to the Constitution [as of 1937]. Of these the first ten constitute the Bill of Rights. The conventions of several States consented to ratify the Constitution only after they became satisfied that the Bill of Rights would be made a part of it.

In an eloquent address to the United States Senate on March 18, 1936, dealing specifically with the fourth and fifth amendments, Senator Ashurst of Arizona gave a vivid picture of the genesis of the Bill of Rights. Referring to the ancient right expressed in the phrase, "Every man's house is his castle," Mr. Ashurst said:

"A gentleman calling upon me once asked, 'Did you ever read Lord Coke's famous maxim in Semayne's case?' to wit, 'The house of every one is to him as his castle and fortress, as well for his defense against injury and violence as for his repose.' I said, 'I am familiar with Coke, but that was law 1,000 years before my Lord Coke adorned the bench. ' "

Senator Ashurst added:

"The makers of our Federal Constitution and the framers of the first 10 amendments were never tired of quoting the immortal words of the elder Pitt, used in his speech on The Excise:

"'The poorest man may in his cottage bid defiance to all the force of the Crown. It may be frail; its roof may shake; the wind may blow through it; the storms may enter; the rain may enter-but the King of England cannot enter. All his forces dare not cross the threshold of the ruined tenement.'

"When the ratification of the Federal Constitution was pending before the Virginia convention, called to pass upon that momentous question, Virginia was a pivotal State—a diamond pivot—on which mighty events turned. Patrick Henry, whom Lord Byron said was 'the forest-born Demosthenes who shook the Phillip of the seas,' was a delegate to the Virginia convention; and although the proposed Federal Constitution had come forth with the sanction of the revered name of

General Washington and therefore justly carried with it the vast prestige which the name of Washington could not fail to
attach to any proposition, Patrick Henry did not approve the Constitution and, to use his own expression, he was 'most awfully alarmed,' as he considered the document to be threatening to the liberties of his country—amongst other reasons because it lacked a bill of rights—and Mr. Henry challenged the view of Mr. James Madison, he of the superb intellect; Mr. Henry challenged the Wythes, the Pendletons, and the Innesses, and that splendid galaxy of scholars and statesmen who enriched the annals not only of Virginia but all America; and he demanded to know why a Bill of Rights, guaranteeing the privileges and immunities of the citizen, had been omitted from the Federal Constitution. The Virginia State convention, after a prolonged debate, was able to ratify the Federal Constitution by a majority of only 10 votes, so ably did Patrick Henry argue against it because it did not contain the Bill of Rights which English liberty had affirmed for centuries.

James Madison pledged his word that at the earliest opportunity he would use his energy toward placing into the Federal Constitution the requisite amendments guaranteeing the citizens' rights, privileges, and immunities, and as soon as the Virginia convention had finished the work of ratification it adopted resolutions expressing its desire for the Bill of Rights, demanded by Patrick Henry. These resolutions were forwarded to the governors of the various States, and as far as men could be bound in faith and honor, as far as men could be bound in statesmanship and in politics, the amendments guaranteeing the citizen's individual rights and his liberties were by common consent agreed to, and it was generally understood that these amendments would be proposed to the States by the First Congress. The first bill to be considered by the First Congress under the Constitution was quite naturally a bill to raise revenue to pay the expenses of the Government; but on July 21, 1789, James Madison, who was a Member of the House, arose and asked the House 'to indulge him in further consideration of amendments to the Constitution,' and he pointed out that the faith and honor of Congress were pledged; that the faith and honor of public men everywhere were pledged to amendments securing to the citizens such guaranties as were comprehended within the first 10 amendments.

"The Bill of Rights amendments were then proposed to the States, including of course the fourth and fifth, and were ratified within 2 years and 3 months. Thereafter, as far as Americans are concerned, and as far as the Constitution itself is concerned, they were and are a part and parcel of the original Constitution, as much so as if they were signed on the 17th of September, 1787, when the main instrument itself was signed."

The ten amendments constituting the Bill of Rights are restrictions upon national power. The rights and immunities enumerated were already in existence. The people had all their rights and liberties before they made the Constitution. The Constitution was established, among other purposes, to make the people's liberties secure against oppression by the government which they were setting up.

I.

The First Amendment, relating to religion, free speech, right of assembly and petition, debars Congress from establishing a religion or prohibiting free exercise of religion, or abridging the freedom of speech or of the press, or the right of the people peaceably to assemble and to petition the Government for a redress of grievances.

Efforts to check the evil practices of lobbying have been checked when they sought to abridge the right of petition; but freedom of speech and of the press does not permit the publication of libels, blasphemous or other indecent articles, or other publications injurious to morals or private reputation. A publisher is subject to punishment for contempt if his articles tend to obstruct the administration of justice. The right of free speech does not give immunity for every possible use of language. (See [original] page 81.)

II.

The Second Amendment does not confer upon the people the right to bear arms. It merely forbids Congress from infringing upon that right. [It helps to know that this is Sol Bloom's personal opinion and it is not in the Constitution]. But a law forbidding the carrying of concealed weapons does not violate this amendment (Again this is Sol Bloom's opinion]. (See "The Constitution in Operation 47")

III.
The Third Amendment protects the people against military intrusion in their homes. (See page 81 [of original text.])

IV.
The Fourth Amendment guarantees the security of the people in their persons, houses, papers, and effects against unreasonable searches and seizures. Almost up to the hour of the evolution the American people had suffered from such injuries at the hands of the British government; and they were determined that their own government should not have power to invade their privacy by "writs of assistance," as general search-warrants were called. John Adams, speaking of James Otis' heroic protest against that practice, declared,

"The child Independence was born on that occasion." (See [original] page 81.)

V.
The Fifth Amendment protects the citizen against double jeopardy, self-incrimination, deprivation of life, liberty, or property without due process of law, and loss of property taken for public use. Far-reaching decisions by the courts have protected the citizen under these clauses. (See [original] page 81.)

VI.
The Sixth Amendment secures the right of trial by jury, and other rights while under criminal trial. The prohibitions are laid upon Congress, and not upon the States. (See [original] page 82.)

VII.
The Seventh Amendment guarantees the rights of citizens in civil trials. (See [original] page 82.)

VIII.
The Eighth Amendment prohibits excessive bail and fines, and cruel and unusual punishment. The Supreme Court will interfere with the action of State courts if they impose fines which amount to a deprivation of property without due process of law, but will do this under the Fourteenth Amendment. (See [original] page 82.)

IX.

The Ninth Amendment provides that the enumeration of certain rights shall not be construed to deny or disparage other rights retained by the people. "This amendment," said the Supreme Court (Livingston v. Moore, 7 Pet. 551) "indicates that the Federal Constitution is but a delegation of powers, which powers, together with the implied powers, constitute all that the Federal Government has or may presume to exercise." The people retain many rights which are not enumerated, and the Government has no power to interfere with these rights. (See page 82.)

X.

The Tenth Amendment is vitally important in preserving the powers of the States and the people against encroachment by Congress. It retains to the States or the people all powers not delegated to the United States nor prohibited to the States by the Constitution. In observance of this amendment the Supreme Court has halted attempts to invade the powers of the States, notably in the matter of commerce (there have been numerous examples of this in recent years). The power of the States to regulate matters of internal police applies not only to the health. morals, and safety of the public, but also to whatever promotes the public peace, comfort, and convenience. State laws enacted under this power may be harsh and oppressive without violating the Constitution, but the restrictions of the Fourteenth Amendment apply. (See page 82.)

XI.

The Eleventh Amendment exempts a State from suit by a citizen of another State or a foreigner. It does not deprive the Supreme Court of jurisdiction over suits between States. Nor does it prevent suits against individuals holding official positions under a State, to prevent their committing wrong or trespass under sanction of an unconstitutional statute. (See page 82.)

XII.

The Twelfth Amendment was declared in effect September 25, 1804, after a deadlock in the election of a President of the United States. Under the original electoral provision the elector voted "for two Persons," without designating either for President or Vice President. Jefferson and Burr received an equal number of votes in the election of 1800, and 35 ballots were taken in the House of Representatives before the choice fell to Jefferson. The amendment requires electors to vote separately for President and Vice President. (See page 83.)

XIII.

The Thirteenth Amendment abolishes slavery. It differs from the first ten amendments in that it restricts the power of the States as well as that of the national government. It removes legal doubt as to the validity of the Emancipation Proclamation.

The drafting of men for military service does not violate this amendment, since a soldier is not a slave; and the contract of a seaman does not violate the spirit of the amendment.

An act of Congress declaring that no distinction should be made between race or color in denying admission to accommodations and privileges in inns, public conveyances and theaters was held unconstitutional, because denial of these privileges does not subject any person to any form of servitude or fasten upon him any badge of slavery. (See page 8}.)

XIV.

The Fourteenth Amendment puts beyond doubt that all persons, white or black, whether former slaves or not, born or naturalized, and owing no allegiance to any foreign power, are citizens of the United States and of the State in which they reside. The States are prohibited from abridging the immunities of citizens, and from depriving any person of life liberty, or property, without due process of law, or denying to any person equal protection of the laws. A State law fixing the employment of mine workers at eight hours per day does not contravene the amendment. Statutes regulating the manufacture and sale of goods are within the amendment.

The amendment does not add to constitutional privileges and immunities. The right of suffrage is not one of these. (See page 84.)

XV.

The Fifteenth Amendment provides that the right of citizens to vote shall not be denied or abridged on account of race, color, or previous condition of servitude. It does not confer upon any one the right to vote. The power to determine qualifications of voters is left to the States; but they may not confine the voting right to white persons. (See page 85.)

XVI.

The Sixteenth Amendment gives Congress power to tax incomes, from whatever source derived, without apportionment among the several States. This is not an extension of the taxing power, but it removes all occasion for an apportionment among the States of taxes laid upon incomes. The salaries of United States judges are not subject to tax, since the Constitution provides that they shall not be diminished. (See page 83.)

XVII.

The Seventeenth Amendment changes the mode of election of United States Senators. Contests in State legislatures over election of senators had caused great dissatisfaction, and it was believed that election by the people would be an improvement. (See page 85.)

XVIII.

The Eighteenth Amendment provided for prohibition of the manufacture, sale, transportation, importation, and exportation of intoxicating liquors for beverage purposes. Congress and the States were given concurrent power to enforce the amendment. The amendment became effective January 16, 1920. It proved to be unsatisfactory, for many reasons. Confusion arose because of the division of police powers. Enforcement by the national government was impossible. It was urged that this amendment was in conflict with the fifth, by taking property without due process of law. It conflicted with the provision which makes the acts of Congress the supreme law of the land. Personal liberty, it was claimed, was abridged. On this point the Supreme Court said (Corneli v. Moore, 267 Fed. 456) :

"It may be a matter of regret that age-old provisions making for the liberty of action of the citizen have been encroached upon, and to a degree whittled away; but this is not a matter wherein the courts may relieve. It is a political question and not a judicial one."

After 13 years of trial, with increasing confusion, dissatisfaction, and expense, the Eighteenth Amendment was repealed by the Twenty-first Amendment, which became effective December 5, 1933. (See page 85.)

XIX.

The Nineteenth Amendment provides that the right of United States citizens to vote shall not be denied or abridged by the United States or any State on account of sex. It was declared adopted August 26, 1920. The first proposal to amend the Constitution to provide for woman suffrage was offered by Senator Sargent, of California, in 1878, at the request of Miss Susan B. Anthony.

Fifteen States had granted complete suffrage to women before the amendment was adopted, and in all but nine of the rest they had partial suffrage. A woman was elected to the House of Representatives from Montana in 1916. Women first voted on a national scale in the presidential election of 1920, and apparently their total vote was about 6,000,000. It is believed that at least 12,000,000 women voted in 1932. (See page 86.)

XX.

The Twentieth Amendment was adopted primarily for the purpose of abolishing "lame duck" sessions of Congress. It changes the dates when the terms of the President, senators and representatives shall begin and end. The presidential term now begins on January 20 every fourth year, and the terms of senators and representatives begin on January 3, the length
of term remaining six and two years, respectively. Consequently a new Congress convenes in the January following the presidential election of the preceding November.

Since only 17 days elapse between the convening of Congress on January 3 and the inauguration of the President on January 20, it is possible that embarrassment may arise in case of delay in counting and declaring the electoral vote, or in electing a President by the House in the event of failure of the electors to elect. The amendment provides that if the President-elect shall have died before inauguration day the Vice President-elect shall be President; and that if a President shall not have been chosen or shall have failed to qualify by inauguration day, the Vice President-elect shall act as President until a President shall have qualified. Congress is authorized to provide for filling a vacancy occurring through failure of both a President-elect and Vice President-elect to qualify, and the person selected shall act until a President or Vice President shall have qualified.

Congress has provided that it shall meet in joint session on January 6 following a presidential election, to count the electoral vote and declare the result. This allows only three days for organization of the House of Representatives by the election of a Speaker. Serious difficulties might arise if the House should fail to organize in time to count the vote, or to elect a President if that duty should fall upon it. Failure of the House to elect a President might be attended by failure of the Senate to elect a Vice President. It is quite conceivable, also, that passions might be aroused if failure to elect a President by a House con-trolled by one political party should be followed by election of a Vice President by a Senate controlled by another party. It is also conceivable that the two houses of Congress might deadlock upon the selection of a person to fill a vacancy in the Presidency. (See page 86.)

XXI.

The Twenty-first Amendment repeals the Eighteenth Amendment and prohibits the transportation or importation into any State of intoxicating liquors in violation of its laws. (See page 87.)

CONCLUSION.

The symmetry of arrangement and beautiful co-ordination of motion in the several governments constituting the American system may be compared with the solar system.

As the Sun is the center of attraction and controlling power that binds and moves the planets in one system, so the People are the center and controlling power that binds and moves their governments in one system.

The Law which the solar system obeys is not written, but its operation is partly disclosed and partly understood. The Law which the American political system obeys is partly written, for all men to read. It is the Constitution of the United States.

The limits of the powers of the Sun and the People are not known. They have never been tested to the limit. The composition of the Sun is hidden in Nature. The composition of the People is hidden in human nature.

Reason assumes that the Sun has powers beyond those known to us. Reason reinforced by knowledge asserts that the People have reserved powers which never have been expressed in written law.

The United States and the States may be compared to planets revolving around their Sun, the People.

In order to comprehend the peculiar nature of the American system it must be borne in mind that the States existed before the United States was created. It was to bind them together, to swing them into their coordinated orbits that the Union was perfected.

Some of the powers possessed by the People are exerted in the States. Others are kept in reserve.

The powers necessary to bind the States together in one solar Union are set forth in the Constitution. All other powers are kept in reserve.

The States perform certain functions which the United States cannot perform. The United States performs functions which the States separately cannot perform. The People retain a sphere of personal liberties into which neither the States nor the United States can enter.

The law which controls the solar system is divine, and therefore perfect. The law which controls the American political system is human, and therefore imperfect. But under a trial of 150 years it has been found to approach more nearly the symmetry of the law that rules the universe than any other emanation of the human mind and will.

Several unique features of the Constitution distinguish it from any previous inventions in the art of government. Among these are:

The Constitution binds individuals as well as States. Under it all individuals have equal duties and rights.

The legislative, executive, and judicial powers are lodged in separate bodies of public servants whose powers and duties compel them to check and balance one another. No uncontrolled power is lodged in any one.

The written Constitution is made paramount to any legislative, executive, or judicial authority.

A court is created with power to hold all authorities within their allotted spheres, and this court itself is bound to remain within its allotted sphere.

The Constitution contains within itself a method whereby it may be amended by the People.

These principles, never practiced before, are the bone and sinew of a fabric suitable to a nation whose government obeys those whom it rules, and whose people rule the government which they obey.

PORTRAITS AND SKETCHES OF THE SIGNERS
OF THE CONSTITUTION

INTRODUCTION

These portraits and brief facts pertain, it should be borne in mind, to the thirty-eight deputies who signed the Constitution, and an absent deputy, Dickinson of Delaware, who requested his colleague, George Read of Delaware, to sign for him; the other sixteen men who attended and had more or less to do with framing the document are not given here. There is no known portrait of FitzSimons or Broom. Others, though included, are not entirely authenticated. These are the portraits of Brearley, Livingston, Wilson, and Blair. The statements concerning the careers of the men are intended to emphasize the public services and to show, by dates, length of participation in activities of the Union. Each one is called, in connection with the Constitutional Convention, by the title given him in his credentials.

WASHINGTON, GEORGE, 1732-1799

VIRGINIA

Planter, soldier, statesman; colonial officer in French and Indian War; Virginia Legislature; Continental Congress, 1774-75; Commander-in-Chief of Continental Army; "Deputy" to Constitutional Convention, President of it; President of the United States, 1789-97; Commander-in-Chief of United States Provisional Army.

WASHINGTON, by Stuart, in Boston Museum of Fine Arts, property of Boston Athenaeum.

[54]

LANGDON, JOHN, 1741-1819
NEW HAMPSHIRE

Merchant; militia service during Revolution; Continental Congress, 1775-76; New Hampshire Legislature, Speaker; Continental Navy Agent; President of New Hampshire; "Deputy" to Constitutional Convention; Governor; United States Senator, 1789-1801.

GILMAN, NICHOLAS, 1755-1814
NEW HAMPSHIRE

Statesman; officer in Continental Army; Continental Congress, 1787-88; "Deputy" to Constitutional Convention; Congressman, 1789-97; New Hampshire Senate; United States Senator, 1805-14.

GORHAM, NATHANIEL, 1738-1796
MASSACHUSETTS

Merchant, land owner; Massachusetts Legislature, Speaker; Massachusetts Board of War and Constitutional Convention; Continental Congress, 1782-83, 1786-87; judge; "Delegate" to Constitutional Convention, chairman of committee of the whole; Massachusetts Council.

KING, RUFUS, 1755-1827
MASSACHUSETTS

Lawyer; Massachusetts Legislature; Continental Congress, 1784-87; "Delegate" to Constitutional Convention; United States Senator from New York, 1789-96, 1813-25; Minister to Great Britain; Federalist candidate for Vice President and President.

LANGDON, by Savage. GILMAN, from Bowen's "Centennial of the Inauguration of Washington." GORHAM, by Sharples, courtesy Frick Art Reference Library. KING, by Trumbull, courtesy of Gallery of Fine Arts, Yale University.

JOHNSON, WILLIAM SAMUEL,
1727-1819

CONNECTICUT

Lawyer; Stamp Act Congress; Connecticut
Agent in England; Connecticut Council;
judge; Continental Congress, 1784-87; "Delegate" to Constitutional Convention; United
States Senator, 1789-91; President of Columbia College.

SHERMAN, ROGER, 1721-1793

CONNECTICUT

Shoemaker, lawyer; Connecticut Legislature
and Council of Safety; Continental Congress,
1774-81, 1784, signer of Declaration of Independence and Articles of Confederation;
"Delegate" to Constitutional Convention;
mayor of New Haven; Congressman, 1789-91;
United States Senator, 1791-93.

HAMILTON, ALEXANDER, 1757-1804

NEW YORK

Lawyer; aide to Washington and line colonel
in Continental Army; Continental Congress,
1782-83, 1788; New York Legislature; Annapolis Convention; "Delegate" to Constitutional Convention; part author of *Federalist*;
Secretary of the Treasury, 1789-95; inspector
general in United States Provisional Army.

LIVINGSTON, WILLIAM, 1723-1790

NEW JERSEY

Lawyer; New York Legislature; local New
Jersey Committee of Correspondence; Continental Congress, 1774-76; commander of New
Jersey Revolutionary militia; Governor of
New Jersey; "Commissioner" to Constitutional
Convention.

JOHNSON, by Stuart, from collection of Mrs. Jonathan Bulkley, courtesy Frick Art Reference Library.
SHERMAN, by Rosenthal, in Independence Hall. HAMILTON, by Trumbull, courtesy Essex Institute.
LIVINGSTON, by Rosenthal.

[56]

BREARLEY, DAVID, 1745-1790
NEW JERSEY

Lawyer; officer in Continental Army; New Jersey Constitutional Convention; Chief Justice of New Jersey; "Commissioner" to Constitutional Convention; United States District Judge.

PATERSON, WILLIAM, 1745-1806
NEW JERSEY

Lawyer; New Jersey Provincial Congress, Constitutional Convention, Attorney General, and Council; "Commissioner" to Constitutional Convention; United States Senator, 1789-90; Governor; Chancellor; Associate Justice of Supreme Court, 1793-1806.

DAYTON, JONATHAN, 1760-1824
NEW JERSEY

Land owner; officer in Continental Army; New Jersey Legislature, Speaker; "Commissioner" to Constitutional Convention; Continental Congress, 1788; New Jersey Council; Congressman, 1791-99, Speaker; United States Senator, 1799-1805.

FRANKLIN, BENJAMIN, 1706-1790
PENNSYLVANIA

Printer, statesman, scientist, philosopher; Pennsylvania Legislature; Deputy Postmaster General of Colonies; Albany Congress; Colonial Agent in England; Continental Congress, 1775-76, signer of Declaration of Independence; Commissioner and Minister to France; President of Pennsylvania; "Deputy" to Constitutional Convention.

MIFFLIN, THOMAS, 1744-1800
PENNSYLVANIA

Merchant, politician; Pennsylvania Legislature, Speaker; Continental Congress, 1774-75, 1782-84, President of it, 1783-84; aide to Washington, major general and quartermaster general in Continental Army; Continental Board of War; "Deputy" to Constitutional Convention; President of Pennsylvania and Governor; Pennsylvania Constitutional Convention.

MORRIS, ROBERT, 1734-1806
PENNSYLVANIA

Merchant, financier; Continental Congress, 1775-78, signer of Declaration of Independence and Articles of Confederation; Pennsylvania Legislature and Council of Safety; Superintendent of Finance, 1781-84; established Bank of North America; "Deputy" to Constitutional Convention; United States Senator, 1789-95.

(No known portrait)

CLYMER, GEORGE, 1739-1813
PENNSYLVANIA

Merchant; Pennsylvania Council of Safety; Continental Congress, 1776-77, 1780-82, signer of Declaration of Independence; Pennsylvania Legislature; "Deputy" to Constitutional Convention; Congressman, 1789-91.

FITZSIMONS, THOMAS, 1741-1811
PENNSYLVANIA

Merchant; militia officer in Revolution; Pennsylvania Council of Safety and Navy Board; Continental Congress, 1782-83; Pennsylvania Legislature and Board of Censors; Bank of North America; "Deputy" to Constitutional Convention; Congressman, 1789-95.

MIFFLIN, by Peale, in Independence Hall. MORRIS, by Stuart, courtesy Lt. Col. Robert Morris. CLYMER, by Rosenthal.

INGERSOLL, JARED, 1749-1822
PENNSYLVANIA

Lawyer; Continental Congress, 1780; Pennsylvania Attorney General, "Deputy" to Constitutional Convention; United States District Attorney; municipal officer in Philadelphia; judge of Pennsylvania District Court; Federalist candidate for Vice President.

WILSON, JAMES, 1742-1798
PENNSYLVANIA

Lawyer; Pennsylvania Provincial Convention; Continental Congress, 1775-77, 1783, 1785, 1786, signer of Declaration of Independence; Continental Board of War; Advocate General for France in America; "Deputy" to Constitutional Convention; Associate Justice of Supreme Court of the United States, 1789-98.

MORRIS, GOUVERNEUR, 1752-1816
PENNSYLVANIA

Lawyer; New York Provincial Congress and Constitutional Convention; Continental Congress from New York, 1778-79, signer of Articles of Confederation; Assistant Superintendent of Finance; "Deputy" to Constitutional Convention; special mission to England; Minister to France; United States Senator from New York, 1800-03.

READ, GEORGE, 1733-1798
DELAWARE

Lawyer; Delaware Attorney General and Legislature; Continental Congress, 1774-77, signer of Declaration of Independence; Delaware Constitutional Convention and Council; Continental Court of Appeals; Annapolis Convention; "Deputy" to Constitutional Convention; United States Senator, 1789-93; Chief Justice of Delaware.

INGERSOLL, by Peale, courtesy of Frick Art Reference Library. WILSON, by Seyffert. MORRIS, by Sharpless, courtesy of John S. Turnbull. READ, by Sully, courtesy of Mrs. Harmon P. Read.

[59]

(No known portrait)

BEDFORD, GUNNING, JR., 1747-1812
DELAWARE

Lawyer; Delaware Legislature and Council; Continental Congress, 1783-85; Delaware Attorney General; Annapolis Convention; "Deputy" to Constitutional Convention; United States District Judge.

BROOM, JACOB, 1752-1810
DELAWARE

Surveyor, business man, manufacturer; "Deputy" to Constitutional Convention; borough officer in Wilmington; Delaware Legislature; postmaster at Wilmington; bank director.

BASSETT, RICHARD, 1745-1815
DELAWARE

Lawyer; militia service in Revolution; Delaware Council of Safety, Legislature, and Constitutional Convention; Annapolis Convention; "Deputy" to Constitutional Convention; United States Senator, 1789-93; judge of Delaware Court of Common Pleas; Governor; United States Circuit Judge, but office soon abolished.

DICKINSON, JOHN, 1732-1808
DELAWARE

Lawyer; Delaware and Pennsylvania Legislatures, Speaker in Delaware; Stamp Act Congress; Continental Congress, 1774-76, 1779, signer of Articles of Confederation; President of Delaware; President of Pennsylvania; Annapolis Convention; "Deputy" from Delaware to Constitutional Convention. (Though not present at the signing, his signature was added, at his request, by George Read of Delaware.)

BEDFORD, by Peale, in Independence Hall. BASSETT, by Rosenthal. DICKINSON, by Rosenthal.

McHENRY, JAMES, 1753-1816
MARYLAND

Physician; surgeon in Continental Army, military secretary to Washington, aide to Lafayette; Maryland Legislature; Continental Congress, 1783-85; "Deputy" to Constitutional Convention; Secretary of War, 1796-1800.

JENIFER, DANIEL OF ST. THOMAS, 1723-1790
MARYLAND

Planter; Agent and Receiver General for Lord Proprietary of Maryland; Maryland Legislature, Council, Council of Safety, and President of Senate; Continental Congress, 1779-81; Maryland-Virginia Conference of 1785; "Deputy" to Constitutional Convention.

CARROLL, DANIEL, 1730-1796
MARYLAND

Planter; Continental Congress, 1781-83, signer of Articles of Confederation; "Deputy" to Constitutional Convention; Congressman, 1789-91; Commissioner for District of Columbia.

BLAIR, JOHN, 1732-1800
VIRGINIA

Lawyer; Virginia Legislature, Provincial Convention, and Council; judge of General Court and Chancery of Virginia; "Deputy" to Constitutional Convention; Associate Justice of the Supreme Court of the United States, 1789-96.

McHENRY, by Rosenthal. DANIEL OF ST. THOMAS JENIFER, by Rosenthal. CARROLL, by Wollaston, courtesy of Maryland Historical Society. BLAIR, by Rosenthal.

[61]

MADISON, JAMES, 1751-1836
VIRGINIA

Lawyer, statesman; Virginia Convention, Legislature, and Council; Continental Congress, 1780-83, 1787-88; Virginia-Maryland Conference of 1785; Annapolis Convention; "Deputy" to Constitutional Convention; part author of *Federalist*; Congressman, 1789-97; Secretary of State, 1801-09; President of the United States, 1809-17; Virginia Constitutional Convention; Rector of University of Virginia.

BLOUNT, WILLIAM, 1749-1800
NORTH CAROLINA

Land owner; paymaster in Continental Army; North Carolina Legislature, Speaker; Continental Congress, 1782-83, 1786-87; "Deputy" to Constitutional Convention; Governor of Territory South of the Ohio River and Superintendent of Indian Affairs; Tennessee Constitutional Convention; United States Senator from Tennessee, 1796-97; Tennessee Senate.

SPAIGHT, RICHARD DOBBS, 1758-1802
NORTH CAROLINA

Planter; North Carolina Legislature; Continental Congress, 1783-85; "Deputy" to Constitutional Convention; Governor of North Carolina; Congressman, 1798-1801; North Carolina Senate.

WILLIAMSON, HUGH, 1735-1819
NORTH CAROLINA

Merchant, physician; surgeon general of North Carolina militia; North Carolina Legislature; Continental Congress, 1782-85, 1787-88; "Deputy" to Constitutional Convention; Congressman, 1789-93.

MADISON, copy of Stuart, courtesy of Frick Art Reference Library. BLOUNT, by Rosenthal. SPAIGHT, by Rosenthal. WILLIAMSON, by Rosenthal.

RUTLEDGE, JOHN, 1739-1800
SOUTH CAROLINA

Lawyer; South Carolina Legislature; Stamp Act Congress; Continental Congress, 1774-75, 1782-83; South Carolina Council of Safety, Constitutional Convention, President, and Governor; judge of Chancery Court; "Deputy" to Constitutional Convention; Associate Justice of Supreme Court of United States, 1789-91; Chief Justice of South Carolina.

PINCKNEY, CHARLES COTESWORTH, 1746-1825
SOUTH CAROLINA

Lawyer, soldier; South Carolina Provincial Congress, Council of Safety, Legislature, and President of Senate; colonel in Continental Army; "Deputy" to Constitutional Convention; declined Cabinet positions; Minister to France; major general in United States Provisional Army; candidate for President.

PINCKNEY, CHARLES, 1757-1824
SOUTH CAROLINA

Lawyer; militia service in Revolution; South Carolina Legislature; Continental Congress, 1784-87; "Deputy" to Constitutional Convention; South Carolina Council, Governor, and Constitutional Convention; United States Senator, 1799-1801; Minister to Spain; Congressman, 1819-21.

BUTLER, PIERCE, 1744-1822
SOUTH CAROLINA

Planter; officer in British Army before the Revolution; South Carolina Legislature; Continental Congress, 1787; "Deputy" to Constitutional Convention; United States Senator, 1789-96, 1803-04.

FEW, WILLIAM, 1748-1828

GEORGIA

Lawyer; Georgia Constitutional Convention, Legislature, and Council; militia service in Revolution; judge of Georgia County and Circuit Courts; Continental Congress, 1780-82, 1786-88; "Deputy" to Constitutional Convention; United States Senator, 1789-93; New York Legislature and Prison Inspector; bank director; New York City Alderman.

BALDWIN, ABRAHAM, 1754-1807

GEORGIA

Clergyman, lawyer; tutor at Yale; chaplain in Continental Army; Georgia Legislature; author of charter and President of University of Georgia; Continental Congress, 1785, 1788; "Deputy" to Constitutional Convention; Congressman, 1789-99; United States Senator, 1799-1807.

FEW, by Rosenthal. BALDWIN, by Rosenthal.

NOTE ON TEXT OF THE CONSTITUTION

Secretary William Jackson took the engrossed Constitution to New York and delivered it to the Continental Congress. Congress, receiving it on September 20, 1787, placed it with its other papers. After the new government went into operation these records, which evidently included both the Declaration of Independence and the Constitution, were turned over to President Washington, and, in accordance with the act of September 15, 1789, to the custody of the Department of State.

When the capture of Washington by the British was imminent in 1814, the Secretary of State, James Monroe, was able to remove all the papers of his office to a place of safety, so that both of the great documents escaped destruction in the burning of the public buildings by the enemy.

The original Declaration was exhibited for many years, until light and air threatened its destruction; but the Constitution was not. On September 29, 1921, both documents were transferred to the Library of Congress. A special shrine was prepared for them in which they have been on view since February 28, 1924, but under conditions that prevent deterioration.

During the early years of the National Government the printed copies of the Constitution seem to have made no attempt to be literally exact. In 1820, however, an edition was prepared in the Department of State which was "copied from and compared with the roll." In 1846 William Hickey published his manual on the Constitution, in which he gave a very exact reprint, generally followed ever since.

The reprint of the Constitution given on the following pages is from a photograph of the original. It endeavors to be accurate in every particular capitals, spelling, punctuation, and paragraphing being exactly as in the engrossed parchment. Two things must, however, be borne in mind. The engrosser seems to have intended to write all nouns with a capital, but forgot his rule in some cases, and in other cases for his capital he has used an enlarged small letter. His enlargements vary in degree and it is not always possible to decide what his intention was. The parchment has wrinkled here and there and become rubbed, especially on the margins, causing occasional blurs that make punctuation particularly doubtful.

The signatures here follow the order in the original. Washington as president signed first, and the deputies followed in State groups in geographical order, beginning their signing immediately below the name of the president.

Attention is called to the fact that in the note after Article VII, respecting the interlineations, the references are to the pages and lines of the original and not to this reprint. That note is not complete; there is a final interlineation to which it does not refer.

The text of the Constitution follows; and, in turn, the resolves which the Convention passed for getting the Constitution ratified and put in operation, the letter sent to the Continental Congress with the draft of the Constitution, and the resolves of Congress submitting the draft to the States and later, after eleven States had ratified, for starting the new government. The text of the Amendments follows these. This last text is taken from the original rolls in the Department of State, the early Amendments being subject to the

We the People of the United States, in Order to form a more perfect Union, establish Justice, insure domestic Tranquility, provide for the common defence, promote the general Welfare, and secure the Blessings of Liberty to ourselves and our Posterity, do ordain and establish this Constitution for the United States of America.

Article. 1.

Section. 1. All legislative Powers herein granted shall be vested in a Congress of the United States, which shall consist of a Senate and House of Representatives.

Section. 2. The House of Representatives shall be composed of Members chosen every second Year by the People of the several States, and the Electors in each State shall have the Qualifications requisite for Electors of the most numerous Branch of the State Legislature.

No Person shall be a Representative who shall not have attained to the Age of twenty five Years, and been seven Years a Citizen of the United States, and who shall not, when elected, be an Inhabitant of that State in which he shall be chosen.

Representatives and direct Taxes shall be apportioned among the several States which may be included within this Union, according to their respective Numbers, which shall be determined by adding to the whole Number of free Persons, including those bound to Service for a Term of Years, and excluding Indians not taxed, three fifths of all other Persons. The actual Enumeration shall be made within three Years after the first Meeting of the Congress of the United States, and within every subsequent Term of ten Years, in such Manner as the shall by Law direct. The Number of Representatives shall not exceed one for every thirty Thousand, but each State shall have at Least one Representative; and until such enumeration shall be made, the State of New Hampshire shall be entitled to chuse three, Massachusetts eight, Rhode-Island and Providence Plantations one, Connecticut five, New-York six, New Jersey four, Pennsylvania eight, Delaware one, Maryland six, Virginia ten, North Carolina five, South Carolina five, and Georgia three.

When vacancies happen in the Representation from any State, the Executive Authority thereof shall issue Writs of Election to fill such Vacancies.

The House of Representatives shall chuse their Speaker and
[66]

Officers; and shall have the sole Power of Impeachment..

Section. 3. The Senate of the United States shall be composed of two Senators from each State, chosen by the Legislature thereof, for six Years; and each Senator shall have one Vote.

Immediately after they shall be assembled in Consequence of the first Election, they shall be divided as equally as may be into three Classes. The Seats of the Senators of the first glass shall be vacated at the Expiration of the second Year, of the second Class at the expiration' of the fourth Year, and of the third Class at the Expiration of the sixth Year, so that one third may be chosen every second Year; and if Vacancies happen By Resignation, or otherwise, during the Recess of the Legislature of any State, the Executive thereof may make temporary appointments until the next Meeting of the Legislature, which shall then fill such Vacancies.

No Person shall be a Senator who shall not have attained to the age of thirty Years, and been nine Years 3a Citizen of the United States, and who shall not, when elected, be an Inhabitant of that State for which he shall be chosen.

The Vice President of' the United States shall be President of the Senate but shall have no Vote, unless they be equally divided.

The Senate shall chuse their other Officers, and also a President pro tempore, in the Absence of the Vice President, or when he shall exercise the Office of President of the United States.

The Senate shall have the sole Power to try all Impeachments. When sitting for that Purpose, they shall be on Oath or 'Affirmation. When the President of the United States is tried, the Chief Justice shall preside: And no Person shall be convicted Without concurrence of two thirds of the Members present.

Judgment in Cases of impeachment shall not extend further than to removal from Office and disqualification to hold and enjoy any Office of honor, Trust or Profit under the United States: but the Party convicted shall nevertheless be liable and subject to Indictment, Trial, Judgment and Punishment, according to Law.

Section. 4. The Times, Places and Manner of holding Elections for Senators and Representatives, shall be prescribed in each State by the legislature thereof; but the Congress may at any time by Law make or alter 'such Regulations, except as to the Places of chusing Senators. The Congress shall assemble at least once in every Year, and such Meeting shall be on the first Monday in December (Jan.3) , unless they shall by Law appoint a different Day.

Section. 5. Each House shall be the Judge of the Elections, Returns and Qualifications of its own Members, and a Majority of each shall constitute a Quorum to do Business; but a smaller Number may adjourn from day to day, and may be authorized to compel the Attendance of absent Members, in such Manner, and under such Penalties as each House may provide.

Each House may determine the Rules of its Proceedings, punish its Members for disorderly behaviour, and, with the Concurrence of two thirds, expel a Member.

Each House shall keep a journal of its Proceedings, and from time to time publish the same, excepting such Parts as may in their Judgment require Secrecy; and the Yeas and Nays of the Members of either House on any question shall, at the Desire of one fifth of those Present, be entered on the Journal.

Neither House, during the Session of Congress, shall, without the Consent of the other, adjourn for more than three days, not to any other Place than that in which the two Houses shall be sitting.

Section. 6. The Senators and Representatives shall receive a Compensation for their Services, to be ascertained by Law, and paid out of the Treasury of the United States. They shall in all Cases, except Treason, Felony and Breach of the Peace, be privileged from Arrest during their Attendance at the Session of their respective Houses, and in going to and returning from the same; and for any Speech or Debate in either House, they shall not be questioned in any other Place.

No Senator or Representative shall, during the Time for which he was elected, be appointed to any civil Office under the Authority of the United States, which shall have been created, or the Emoluments whereof shall have been increased during such time; and no Person holding any Office under the United States, shall be a Member of either House during his Continuance in Office.

Section. 7. All Bills for raising Reyenue shall originate in the House of Representatives; but the Senate may propose or concur with Amendments as on other Bills.

Every Bill which shall have passed the House of Representatives and the Senate, shall, before it become a Law, be presented to the President of the United States; If he approve he shall sign it, but if not he shall return it, with his Objections to that House in which it shall have originated, who shall enter the Objections at large on their Journal, and proceed to reconsider it.

[68]

If after such Reconsideration two thirds of that House shall agree to pass it as a Bill, it shall be sent, together with the Objections, to the other House, by which it shall likewise be reconsidered, and if approved by two thirds of that House, it shill become a Law. But in all such Cases the Votes of both Houses shall be determined by yeas and Nays, and the Names of the Persons voting for and against the Bill shall be entered on the Journal of each House respectively. If any Bill shall not be returned by the President within ten Days (Sundays excepted) after it shall have been presented to him, the Same shall be a Law, in like Manner as if he had signed it, unless the Congress by their Adjournment prevent its Return, in which Case it shall not be a Law.

Every Order, Resolution, or Vote to which the Concurrence of the Senate and House of Representatives may be necessary (except on a question of Adjournment) shall be presented to the President of the United States; and before the Same shall take effect, shall be approved by him, or being disapproved by him, shall be repassed by two thirds of the Senate and House of Representatives, according to the Rules and Limitations prescribed in the Case of a Bill.

Section. 8. The Congress shall have Power To lay and collect Taxes, Duties, Imposts and Excises, to pay the Debts and provide for the common Defence and general Welfare of the United States; but all Duties, Imposts and Excises shall be uniform throughout the United States;

— To borrow money on the credit of the United States;
— To regulate Commerce with foreign Nations, and among the several States, and with the Indian Tribes;
— To establish an uniform Rule of Naturalization, and uniform Laws on the subject of Bankruptcies throughout the United States;
— To coin Money, regulate the Value thereof, and of foreign Coin, and his the Standard of Weights and Measures;
— To provide for the Punishment of counterfeiting the Securities and current Coin of the United States;
— To establish Post Offices and post Roads;
— To promote the Progress of Science and useful Arts, by securing for limited Times to Authors and Inventors the exclusive Right to their respective Writings and Discoveries;
— To constitute Tribunals inferior to the supreme Court;
— To define and punish Piracies and Felonies committed on the high Seas, and Offences against the Law of Nations;

- To raise and support Armies, but no Appropriation of Money to that Use shall be for a longer Term than two Years;
- To provide and maintain a Navy;
- To make Rules for the Government and Regulation of the land and naval Forces;
- To provide for calling forth the Militia to execute the Laws of the Union, suppress Insurrections and repel Invasions;
- To provide for organizing, arming, and disciplining, the Militia, and for governing such Part of them as may be employed in the Service of the United States, reserving to the States respectively, the Appointment of the Officers, and the Authority of training the Militia according to the discipline prescribed by Congress;
- To exercise exclusive Legislation in all Cases whatsoever, over such District (not exceeding ten Miles square) as may, by Cession of particular States, and the Acceptance of Congress, become the Seat of the Government of the United States, and to exercise like Authority over all Places purchased by the Consent of the Legislature of the State in which the Same shall be, for the Erection of Forts, Magazines, Arsenals, dock Yards, and other needful Buildings;—And
- To make all Laws which shall be necessary and proper for carrying into Execution the foregoing Powers, and all other Powers vested by this Constitution in the Government of the United States, or in any Department or Officer thereof.

Section. 9. The Migration or Importation of such Persons as any of the States now existing shall think proper to admit, shall not be prohibited by the Congress prior to the Year one thousand eight hundred and eight, but a Tax or duty may be imposed on such Importation, not exceeding ten dollars for each Person.

The Privilege of the Writ of Habeas Corpus shall not be suspended, unless when in Cases of Rebellion or Invasion the public Safety may require it.

- No Bill of Attainder or ex post facto Law shall be passed.
- No Capitation, or other direct, Tax shall be laid, unless in Proportion to the Census or Enumeration herein before directed to be taken.
- No Tax or Duty shall be laid on Articles exported from any State.
- No Preference shall be given by any Regulation of Commerce or Revenue to the Ports of one State over those of another: nor shall Vessels bound to, or from, one State, be obliged to enter, clear, or pay Duties in another.

— No Money shall be drawn from the Treasury, but in Consequence of Appropriations made by Law; and a regular Statement and Account of the Receipts and Expenditures of all public Money shall be published from time to time.
— No Title of Nobility shall be granted by the United States: And no Person holding any Office of Profit or Trust under them, shall, without the Consent of the Congress, accept of any present, Emolument, Office, or Title, of any kind whatever, from any King, Prince, or foreign State.

Section. 10. No State shall enter into any Treaty, Alliance, or Confederation; grant Letters of Marque and Reprisal; coin Money; emit Bills of Credit; make any Thing but gold and silver Coin a Tender in Payment of Debts; pass any Bill of Attainder, ex post facto Law, or Law impairing the Obligation of Contracts, or grant any Title of Nobility.

No State shall, without the Consent of the Congress, lay any Imposts or Duties on Imports or Exports, except what may be absolutely necessary for executing it's inspection Laws: and the net Produce of all Duties and Imposts, laid by any State on Imports or Exports, shall be for the Use of the Treasury of the United States; and all such Laws shall be subject to the Revision and Controul of the Congress.

No State shall, without the Consent of the Congress, lay any Duty of Tonnage, keep Troops, or Ships of War in time of Peace, enter into any Agreement or Compact with another State, or with a foreign Power, or engage in War, unless actually invaded, or in such imminent Danger as will not admit of delay.

Article. II.

Section. 1. The executive Power shall be vested in a President of the United States of America. He shall hold his Office during the Term of four Years, and, together with the Vice President, chosen for the same Term, be elected, as follows

Each State shall appoint, in such Manner as the Legislature thereof may direct, a Number of Electors, equal to the whole Number of Senators and Representatives to which the State may be entitled in the Congress: but no Senator or Representative, or Person holding an Office of Trust or Profit under the United States, shall be appointed an Elector.

The Electors shall meet in their respective States, and vote by Ballot for two Persons, of whom one at least shall not be an Inhabitant of the same State with themselves.

And they shall make a List of all the Persons voted for, and of the Number of Votes for each; which List they shall sign and certify, and transmit sealed to the Seat of the Government of the United States, directed to the President of the Senate. The President of the Senate shall, in the Presence of the Senate and House of Representatives, open all the Certificates, and the Votes shall then be counted. The Person having the greatest Number of Votes shall be the President, if such Number be a Majority of the whole Number of Electors appointed; and if there be more than one who have such Majority, and have an equal Number of Votes, then the House of Representatives shall immediately chuse by Ballot one of them for President; and if no Person have a Majority, then from the five highest on the List the said House shall in like Manner chuse the President. But in chusing the President, the Votes shall be taken by States, the Representation from each State having one Vote; A quorum for this Purpose shall consist of a Member or Members from two thirds of the States, and a Majority of all the States shall be necessary to a Choice. In every Case, after the Choice of the President, the Person having the greatest Number of Votes of the Electors shall be the Vice President. But if there should remain two or more who have equal Votes, the Senate shall chuse from them by Ballot the Vice President.

The Congress may determine the Time of chusing the Electors, and the Day on which they shall give their Votes; which Day shall be the same throughout the United States.

No Person except a natural born Citizen, or a Citizen of the United States, at the time of the Adoption of this Constitution, shall be eligible to the Office of President; neither shall any Person be eligible to that Office who shall not have attained to the Age of thirty five Years, and been fourteen Years a Resident within the United States.

In Case of the Removal of the President from Office, or of his Death, Resignation, or Inability to discharge the Powers and Duties of the said Office, the Same shall devolve on the Vice President, and the Congress may by Law provide for the Case of Removal, Death, Resignation or Inability, both of the President and Vice President, declaring what Officer shall then act as President, and such Officer shall act accordingly, until the Disability be removed, or a President shall be elected.

The President shall, at stated Times, receive for his Services, a compensation, which shall neither be increased nor diminished during the Period for which he shall have been elected, and he shall not receive within that Period any other Emolument from the United States, or any of them.

Before he enter on the Execution of his Office, he shall take the following Oath or Affirmation:—"I do solemnly swear (or affirm) that I will faithfully execute the Office of President of the United States, and will to the best of my Ability, preserve, protect and defend the Constitution of the United States."

Section. 2. The President shall be Commander in Chief of the Army and Navy of the United States, and of the Militia of the several States, when called into the actual Service of the United States; he may require the Opinion, in writing, of the principal Officer in each of the executive Departments, upon any Subject relating to the Duties of their respective Offices, and he shall have Power to grant Reprieves and Pardons for Offences against the United States, except in Cases of Impeachment.

He shall have Power, by and with the Advice and Consent of the Senate, to make Treaties, provided two thirds of the Senators present concur; and he shall nominate, and by and with the Advice and Consent of the Senate, shall appoint Ambassadors, other public Ministers and Consuls, Judges of the supreme Court, and all other Officers of the United States, whose Appointments are not herein otherwise provided for, and which shall be established by Law: but the Congress may by Law vest the Appointment of such inferior Officers, as they think proper, in the President alone, in the Courts of Law, or in the Heads of Departments.

The President shall have Power to fill up all Vacancies that may happen during the Recess of the Senate, by granting Commissions which shall expire at the End of their next Session.

Section. 3. He shall from time to time give to the Congress Information of the State of the Union, and recommend to their Consideration such Measures as he shall judge necessary and expedient; he may, on extraordinary Occasions, convene both Houses, or either of them, and in Case of Disagreement between them, with Respect to the Time of Adjournment, he may adjourn them to such Time as he shall think proper; he shall receive Ambassadors and other public Ministers; he shall take Care that the Laws be faithfully executed, and shall Commission all the Officers of the United States.

Section. 4. The President, Vice President and all civil Ofiicers of the United States, shall be removed from Office on Impeachment for, and Conviction of, Treason, Bribery, or other high Crimes and Misdemeanors.

Article III.

Section. 1. The judicial Power of the United States, shall be vested in one supreme Court, and in such inferior Courts as the Congress may from time to time ordain and establish. The judges, both of the supreme and inferior Courts, shall hold their Offices during good Behaviour, and shall, at stated Times, receive for their Services, a Compensation, which shall not be diminished during their Continuance in Office.

Section. 2. The judicial Power shall extend to all Cases, in Law and Equity, arising under this Constitution, the Laws of the United States, and Treaties made, or which shall be made, under their Authority;—to all Cases affecting Ambassadors, other public Ministers and Consuls;—to all Cases of admiralty and maritime Jurisdiction;—to Controversies to which the United States shall be a Party;—to, Controversies between two or more States;—between a State and Citizens of another State;—between Citizens of different States;—between Citizens of the same State claiming Lands under Grants of different States, and between a State, or the Citizens thereof, and foreign States, Citizens or Subjects.

In all Cases affecting Ambassadors, other public Ministers and Consuls, and those in which a State shall be Party, the supreme Court shall have original Jurisdiction. In all the other Cases before mentioned, the supreme Court shall have appellate Jurisdiction, both as to Law and Fact, with such Exceptions, and under such Regulations as the Congress shall make.

The Trial of all Crimes, except in Cases of Impeachment, shall be by Jury; and such Trial shall be held in the State where the said Crimes shall have been committed; but when not committed within any State, the Trial shall be at such Place or Places as the Congress may by Law have directed.

Section. 3. Treason against the United States, shall consist only in levying War against them, or in adhering to their Enemies, giving them Aid and Comfort. No Person shall be convicted of Treason unless on the Testimony of two Witnesses to the same overt Act, or on Confession in open Court.

The Congress shall have Power to declare the Punishment of Treason, but no Attainder of Treason shall work Corruption of Blood, or Forfeiture except during the Life of the Person attainted.

Article. IV.

Section. 1. Full Faith and Credit shall be given in each State to the public Acts, Records, and judicial Proceedings of every other State. And the Congress may by general Laws prescribe the Manner in which such Acts, Records and Proceedings shall be proved, and the Effect thereof.

Section. 2. The Citizens of each State shall be entitled to all Privileges and Immunities of citizens in the several States.

A Person charged in any State with Treason, Felony, or other Crime, who shall flee from Justice, and be found in another State, shall on Demand of the executive Authority of the State from which he fled, be delivered up, to be removed to the State having Jurisdiction of the Crime.

No Person held to Service or Labour in one State, under the Laws thereof, escaping into another, shall, in Consequence of any Law or Regulation therein, be discharged from such Service or Labour, but shall be delivered up on Claim of the Party to whom such Service or Labour may be due.

Section. 3. New States may be admitted by the Congress into this Union; but no new State shall be formed or erected within the Jurisdiction of any other State; nor any State be formed by the Junction of two or more States, or Parts of States, without the Consent of the Legislatures of the States concerned as well as of the Congress.

The Congress shall have Power to dispose of and make all needful Rules and Regulations respecting the Territory or other Property belonging to the United States; and nothing in this Constitution shall be so construed as to Prejudice any Claims of the United States, or of any particular State.

Section. 4. The United States shall guarantee to every State in this Union a Republican Form of Government, and shall protect each of them against Invasion; and on Application of the Legislature, or of the Executive (when the Legislature cannot be convened) against domestic Violence.

Article. V.

The Congress, whenever two thirds of both Houses shall deem it necessary, shall propose Amendments to this Constitution, or, on the Application of the Legislatures of two thirds of the several States, shall call a Convention for proposing Amendments, which, in either Case, shall be valid to all Intents and Purposes, as Part of this Constitution, when ratified by the Legislatures of three fourths of the several States, or by Conventions in three fourths thereof, as the one or the other Mode of Ratification may be proposed by the Congress; Provided that no Amendment which may be made prior to the Year One thousand eight hundred and eight shall in any Manner affect the first and fourth Clauses in the Ninth Section of the first Article; and that no State, without its Consent, shall be deprived of its equal Suffrage in the Senate.

Article. VI.

All Debts contracted and Engagements entered into, before the Adoption of this Constitution, shall be as valid against the United States under this Constitution, as under the Confederation.

This Constitution, and the Laws of the United States which shall be made in Pursuance thereof; and all Treaties made, or which shall be made, under the Authority of the United States, shall be the supreme Law of the Land; and the Judges in every State shall be bound thereby, any Thing in the Constitution or Laws of any State to the Contrary notwithstanding.

The Senators and Representatives before mentioned, and the Members of the several State Legislatures, and all executive and judicial Officers, both of the United States and of the several States, shall be bound by Oath or Affirmation, to support this Constitution; but no religious Test shall ever be required as a Qualification to any Office or public Trust under the United States.

Article. VII.

The Ratification of the Conventions of nine States, shall be sufficient for the Establishment of this Constitution between the States so ratifying the Same.

The Word, "the," being interlined between the seventh and eighth Lines of the first Page. The word "Thirty" being partly written on an Erazure in the fifteenth Line of the first Page. The Words "is tried" being interlined between the thirty second and thirty third Lines of the first Page and the Word "the" being interlined between the forty third and forty fourth Lines of the second Page.

done in Convention by the Unanimous Consent of the States present the Seventeenth Day of September in the Year of our Lord one thousand seven hundred and Eighty seven and of the Independance of the United States of America the Twelfth. In witness whereof We have hereunto subscribed our Names,

Attest WILLIAM JACKSON Secretary

G⁰ WASHINGTON—Presdt
and deputy from Virginia

Delaware	New Hampshire
GEO: READ	JOHN LANGDON
GUNNING BEDFORD jun	NICHOLAS GILMAN
JOHN DICKINSON	
RICHARD BASSETT	Massachusetts
JACO: BROOM	NATHANIEL GORHAM
	RUFUS KING

Delaware
- GEO: READ
- GUNNING BEDFORD jun
- JOHN DICKINSON
- RICHARD BASSETT
- JACO: BROOM

Maryland
- JAMES MᶜHENRY
- DAN OF Sᵀ THOˢ JENIFER
- DANˡ CARROLL

Virginia
- JOHN BLAIR—
- JAMES MADISON JR.

North Carolina
- Wᴹ BLOUNT
- RICHᴰ DOBBS SPAIGHT.
- HU WILLIAMSON

South Carolina
- J. RUTLEDGE
- CHARLES COTESWORTH PINCKNEY
- CHARLES PINCKNEY
- PIERCE BUTLER.

Georgia
- WILLIAM FEW
- ABR BALDWIN

New Hampshire
- JOHN LANGDON
- NICHOLAS GILMAN

Massachusetts
- NATHANIEL GORHAM
- RUFUS KING

Connecticut
- Wᴹ SAMˡ JOHNSON
- ROGER SHERMAN

New York . . ALEXANDER HAMILTON

New Jersey
- WIL: LIVINGSTON
- DAVID BREARLEY.
- Wᴹ PATERSON.
- JONA: DAYTON

Pensylvania
- B FRANKLIN
- THOMAS MIFFLIN
- ROBᵀ MORRIS
- GEO. CLYMER
- THOˢ FITZSIMONS
- JARED INGERSOLL
- JAMES WILSON
- GOUV MORRIS

[77]

In Convention Monday, September 17th, 1787.

Present

The States of

New Hampshire, Massachusetts, Connecticut, Mr. Hamilton from New York, New Jersey, Pennsylvania, Delaware, Maryland, Virginia, North Carolina, South Carolina and Georgia.

Resolved,

That the preceding Constitution be laid before the United States in Congress assembled, and that it is the Opinion of this Convention, that it should afterwards he submitted to a Convention of Delegates, chosen in each State by the People thereof, under the Recommendation of its Legislature, for their Assent and Ratification; and that each Convention assenting to, and ratifying the Same, should give Notice thereof to the United States in Congress assembled. Resolved, That it is the Opinion of this Convention, that as soon as the Conventions of nine States shall have ratified this Constitution, the United States in Congress assembled should fix a Day on which Electors should be appointed by the States which shall have ratified the same, and a Day on which the Electors should assemble to vote for the President, and the Time and Place for commencing Proceedings under this Constitution. That after such Publication the Electors should be appointed, and the Senators and Representatives elected: That the Electors should meet on the Day fixed for the Election of the President, and should transmit their Votes certified, signed, sealed and directed, as the Constitution requires, to the Secretary of the United States in Congress assembled, that the Senators and Representatives should convene at the Time and Place assigned; that the Senators should appoint a President of the Senate, for the sole Purpose of receiving, opening and counting the Votes for President; and, that after he shall be chosen, the Congress, together with the President, should, without Delay, proceed to execute this Constitution.

By the Unanimous Order of the Convention.

G. WASHINGTON Presd^t

W. Jackson, Secretary.

[78]

Sir,

We have now the honor to submit to the consideration of the United States in Congress assembled, that Constitution which has appeared to us the most adviseable.

The friends of our country have long seen and desired, that the power of making war, peace, and treaties, that of levying money and regulating commerce, and the correspondent executive and judicial authorities should be fully and effectually vested in the general government of the Union: But the impropriety of delegating such extensive trust to one body of men is evident—Hence results the necessity of a different organization.

It is obviously impracticable in the federal government of these states, to secure all rights of independent sovereignty to each, and yet provide for the interest and safety of all: Individuals entering into society, must give up a share of liberty to preserve the rest. The magnitude of the sacrifice must depend as well on situation and circumstance, as on the object to be obtained. It is at all times difficult to draw with precision the line between those rights which must be surrendered, and those which may be reserved; and on the present occasion this difficulty was encreased by a difference among the several states as to their situation, extent, habits, and particular interests.

In all our deliberations on this subject we kept steadily in our view, that which appears to us the greatest interest of every true American, the consolidation of our Union, in which is involved our prosperity, felicity, safety, perhaps our national existence. This important consideration, seriously and deeply impressed on our minds, led each state in the Convention to be less rigid on points of inferior magnitude, than might have been otherwise expected; and thus the Constitution, which we now present, is the result of a spirit of amity, and of that mutual deference and concession which the peculiarity of our political situation rendered indispensable.

That it will meet the full and entire approbation of every state is not perhaps to be expected; but each will doubtless consider, that had her interest been alone consulted, the consequences might have been particularly disagreeable or injurious to others; that it is liable to as few exceptions as could reasonably have been expected, we hope and believe; that it may promote the lasting welfare of that country so dear to us all, and secure her freedom and happiness, is our most ardent wish.

With great respect, We have the honor to be. Sir,

Your Excellency's

most obedient and humble servants,

GEORGE WASHINGTON, President.

By unanimous Order of the Convention.

His Excellency the President of Congress.

IN CONGRESS
FRIDAY, SEPTEMBER 28, 1787.

Congress assembled present New Hampshire, Massachusetts, Connecticut, New York, New Jersey, Pennsylvania, Delaware, Virginia, North Carolina, South Carolina, and Georgia and from Maryland, Mr. Ross.

Congress having received the report of the Convention lately assembled in Philadelphia.

Resolved Unanimously that the said Report with the resolutions and letter accompanying the same be transmitted to the several legislatures in Order to be submitted to a convention of Delegates chosen in each state by the people thereof in conformity to the resolves of the Convention made and provided in that case.

SATURDAY, SEPTEMBER 13, 1788

Congress assembled present New Hampshire, Massachusetts, Connecticut, New York, New Jersey, Pennsylvania, Virginia, North Carolina, South Carolina, and Georgia and from Rhode Island Mr. Arnold, and from Delaware Mr. Kearny.

Whereas the Convention assembled in Philadelphia pursuant to the resolution of Congress of the 21st of Feby. 1787 did on the 17th of Sept in the same year report to the United States in Congress assembled a constitution for the people of the United States, Whereupon Congress on the 28 of the same Sept did resolve unanimously "That the said report with the resolutions and letter accompanying the same be transmitted to the several legislatures in order to be submitted to a convention of Delegates chosen in each state by the people thereof in conformity to the resolves of the convention made and provided in that case" And whereas the constitution so reported by the Convention and bv Congress transmitted to the several legislatures has been ratified in the manner therein declared to be sufficient for the establishment of the same

[80]

and such ratifications duly authenticated have been received by Congress and are filed in the Office of the Secretary therefore

Resolved That the first Wednesday in January, next be the day for appointing Electors in the several states, which before the said day shall have ratified the said constitution; that the first Wednesday in February, next be the day for the electors to assemble in their respective states and vote for a president; and that the first Wednesday in March next be the time and the present seat of Congress the place for commencing proceedings under the said Constitution.

AMENDMENTS TO THE CONSTITUTION.

[AMENDMENT I]
Congress shall make no law respecting an establishment of religion, or prohibiting the free exercise thereof; or abridging the freedom of speech, or of the press; or the right of the people peaceably to assemble, and to petition the Government for a redress of grievances.

[AMENDMENT II]
A well regulated Militia, being necessary to the security of a free State, the right of the people to keep and bear Arms.shall not be infringed.

[AMENDMENT III]
No Soldier shall, in time of peace be quartered in any house, without the consent of the Owner, nor in time of war, but in a manner to be prescribed by law.

[AMENDMENT IV]
The right of the people to be secure in their persons, houses, papers, and effects, against unreasonable searches and seizures, shall not be violated, and no Warrants shall issue, but upon probable cause, supported by Oath or affirmation and particularly describing the place to be searched, and the persons or things to be seized.

[AMENDMENT V]
No person shall be held to answer for a capital. Or otherwise infamous crime, unless on a presentment or indictment of Grand Jury,

except in cases arising in the land or naval forces, or in the Militia, when in actual service in time of War or public danger; nor shall any person be subject for the same offence to be twice put in jeopardy of life or limb, nor shall be compelled in any criminal case to be a witness against himself, nor be deprived of life, liberty, or property, without due process of law; nor shall private property be taken for public use, without just compensation.

[AMENDMENT VI]

In all criminal prosecutions, the accused shall enjoy the right to a speedy and public trial, by an impartial jury of the State and district wherein the crime shall have been committed, which district shall have been previously ascertained by law, and to be informed of the nature and cause of the accusation; to be confronted with the witnesses against him; to have compulsory process for obtaining Witnesses in his favor, and to have the Assistance of Counsel for his defence.

[AMENDMENT VII]

In Suits at common law, where the value in controversy shall exceed twenty dollars, the right of trial by jury shall be preserved, and no fact tried by a jury, shall be otherwise re-examined in any Court of the United States, than according to the rules of the common law.

[AMENDMENT VIII]

Excessive bail shall not be required, nor excessive fines imposed, nor cruel and unusual punishments inflicted.

[AMENDEMENT IX]

The enumeration in the Constitution, of certain rights, shall not be construed to deny or disparage others retained by the people.

[AMENDMENT X]

The powers not delegated to the United States by the Constitution, nor prohibited by it to the States, are reserved to the States respectively, or to the people.

[AMENDMENT XI]

The Judicial power of the United States shall not be construed to extend to any suit in law or equity, commenced or prosecuted against one of the United States by Citizens of another State, or by Citizens or Subjects of any Foreign State.

[AMENDMENT XII]

The Electors shall meet in their respective states, and vote by ballot for President and Vice-President, one of whom, at least, shall not be an inhabitant of the same state with themselves; they shall name in their ballots the person voted for, as President, and in distinct ballots the person voted for as Vice President, and they shall make distinct lists of all persons voted for as President, and of all persons voted for as Vice-President, and of the number of votes for each, which lists they shall sign and certify, and transmit sealed to the seat of the government of the United States, directed to the President of the Senate;—The President of the Senate shall, in the presence of the Senate and House of Representatives, open all the certificates and the votes shall then be counted;—The person having the greatest number of votes for President, shall be the President, if such number be a majority of the whole number of Electors appointed; and if no person have such majority, then from the persons having the highest numbers not exceeding three on the list of those voted for as President, the House of Representatives shall choose immediately, by ballot, the President. But in choosing the President, the votes shall be taken by states, the representation from each state having one vote; a quorum for this purpose shall consist of a member or members from two-thirds of the states, and a majority of all the states shall be necessary to a choice. And if the House of Representatives shall not choose a President whenever the right of choice shall devolve upon them, before the fourth day of March next following, then the Vice-President shall act as President, as in the case of the death or other constitutional disability of the President;—The person having the greatest number of votes as Vice-President, shall be the Vice-President, if such number be a majority of the whole number of Electors appointed, and if no person have a majority, then from the two highest numbers on the list, the Senate shall choose the Vice-President; a quorum for the purpose shall consist of two thirds of the whole number of Senators, and a majority of the whole number shall be necessary to a choice. But no person constitutionally ineligible to the oflice of President shall be eligible to that of Vice-President of the United States.

[AMENDMENT XIII]
Section 1. Neither slavery nor involuntary servitude, except as a punishment for crime whereof the party shall have been duly

convicted, shall exist within the United States, or any place subject to their jurisdiction.

Section 2. Congress shall have power to enforce this article by appropriate legislation.

[AMENDMENT XIV]

Section 1. All persons born or naturalized in the United States, and subject to the jurisdiction thereof, are citizens of the United States and of the State wherein they reside. No State shall make or enforce any law which shall abridge the privileges or immunities of citizens of the United States; nor shall any State deprive any person of life, liberty, or property, without due process of law; not deny to any person within its jurisdiction the equal protection of the laws.

Section 2. Representatives shall be apportioned among the several States according to their respective numbers, counting the whole number of persons in each State, excluding Indians not taxed. But when the right to vote at any election for the choice of electors for President and Vice President of the United States, Representatives in Congress, the Executive and Judicial officers of a State, or the members of the Legislature thereof, is denied to any of the male inhabitants of such State, being twenty-one years of age, and citizens of the United States, or in any way abridged, except for participation in rebellion, or other crime, the basis of representation therein shall be reduced in the proportion which the number of such male citizens shall bear to the whole number of male citizens twenty-one years of age in such State.

Section 3. No person shall be a Senator or Representative in Congress, or elector of President and Vice President, or hold any office, civil or military, under the United States, or under any State, who, having previously taken an oath, as a member of Congress, or as an officer of the United States, or as a member of any State legislature, or as an executive or judicial officer of any State, to support the Constitution of the United States, shall have engaged in insurrection or rebellion against the same, or given aid or comfort to the enemies thereof. But Congress may by a vote of two-thirds of each House, remove such disability.

Section 4. The validity of the public debt of the United States, authorized by law, including debts incurred for payment of pensions and bounties for services in suppressing insurrection or rebellion, shall not be questioned. But neither the United States nor any State shall assume or pay any debt or obligation incurred in aid of insurrection or rebellion against the United States, or any claim for the loss or emancipation of any slave; but all such debts, obligations and claims shall be held illegal and void.

Section 5. The Congress shall have power to enforce, by appropriate legislation, the provisions of this article.

[AMENDMENT XV]

Section I. The right of citizens of the United States to vote shall not be denied or abridged by the United States or by any State on account of race, color, or previous condition of servitude.—

Section 2. The Congress shall have power to enforce this article by appropriate legislation.—

[AMENDMENT XVI]

The Congress shall have power to lay and collect taxes on incomes, from whatever source derived, without apportionment among the several States, and without regard to any census or enumeration.

[AMENDMENT XVII]

The Senate of the United States shall be composed of two Senators from each State, elected by the people thereof, for six years; and each Senator shall have one vote. The electors in each State shall have the qualifications requisite for electors of the most numerous branch of the State legislatures.

When vacancies happen in the representation of any State in the Senate, the executive authority of such State shall issue writs of election to fill such vacancies: Provided, That the legislature of any State may empower the executive thereof to make temporary appointments until the people fill the vacancies by election as the legislature may direct.

This amendment shall not be so construed as to affect the election or term of any Senator chosen before it becomes valid as part of the Constitution.

[AMENDMENT XVIII]

Section 1. After one year from the ratification of this article the manufacture, sale, or transportation of intoxicating liquors within, the importation thereof into, or the exportation thereof from the United States and all territory subject to the jurisdiction thereof for beverage purposes is hereby prohibited.

Section 2. The Congress and the several States shall have concurrent power to enforce this article by appropriate legislation.

Section. 3. This article shall be inoperative unless it shall have been ratified as an amendment to the Constitution by the legislatures of the several States, as provided in the Constitution, within seven years from the date of the submission hereof to the States by the Congress.

[AMENDMENT XIX]

The right of citizens of the United States to vote shall not be denied or abridged by the United States or by any State on account of sex.

Congress shall have power to enforce this article by appropriate legislation.

[AMENDMENT XX]

Section 1. The terms of the President and Vice President shall end at noon on the 20th day of January, and the terms of Senators and Representatives at noon on the 3d day of January, of the years in which such terms would have ended if this article had not been ratified; and the terms of their successors shall then begin.

Section. 2. The Congress shall assemble at least once in every year, and such meeting shall begin at noon on the 3d day of January, unless they shall by law appoint a different day.

Section. 3. If, at the time fixed for the beginning of the term of the President, the President elect shall have died, the Vice President elect shall become President. If a President shall not have been chosen before the time fixed for the beginning of his term, or if the President elect shall have failed to qualify, then the Vice President elect shall act as President until a President shall have qualified; and the Congress may by law provide for the case wherein neither a President elect not a Vice President elect shall have qualified, declaring who shall then act as President, or the manner in which one who is to act shall be selected, and such person shall act accordingly until a President or Vice President shall have qualified.

Section. 4. The Congress may by law provide for the case of the death of any of the persons from whom the House of Representatives may choose a President whenever the right of choice shall have devolved upon them, and for the case of the death of any of the persons from whom the Senate may choose a Vice President whenever the right of choice shall have devolved upon them.

Section. 5. Sections 1 and 2 shall take effect on the 15th day of October following the ratification of this article.

Section. 6. This article shall be inoperative unless it shall have been ratified as an amendment to the Constitution by the legislatures of three-fourths of the several States within seven years from the date of its submission.

[AMENDMENT XXI]

Section 1. The eighteenth article of amendment to the Constitution of the United States is hereby repealed.

Section. 2. The transportation or importation into any State Territory, or possession of the United States for delivery or use therein of intoxicating liquors, in violation of the laws thereof, is hereby prohibited.

Section. 3. This article shall be inoperative unless it shall have been ratified as an amendment to the Constitution by conventions in the several States, as provided in the Constitution, within seven years from the date of the submission hereof to the States by the Congress.

Ratifications, Admissions, and Possessions

The Constitution was ratified by popular conventions in the several States, in the following order:

Delaware.................. December 7. 1787; Yeas, 30 (unanimous)
Pennsylvania............ December 12, 1787; Yeas, 46; Nays, 2)
New Jersey.............. December 18, 1787; Yeas, 38 (unanimous)
Georgia.................. January 2, 1788; Yeas, 26 (unanimous)
Connecticut............. January 9, 1788; Yeas, 128; Nays, 40
Massachusetts......... February 6, 1788; Yeas. 187; Nays, 168
Maryland................ April 28, 1788; Yeas, 63; Nays, 11
South Carolina......... May 23, 1788; Yeas, 149; Nays, 7}
New Hampshire...... June 21, 1788; Yeas. S7; Nays, 47
Virginia.................. June 26. 1788; Yeas, 89; Nays, 79
New York............... July 26, 1788: Yeas, 30; Nays, 27
North Carolina........ November 21, 1789; Yeas, l94; Nays, 77
Rhode Island and...
Providence Plantations.....May 29, 1790; Yeas, 34; Nays,)2

Later States were admitted as follows:

Vermont	March 4, 1791	Mississippi	Dec. 10, 1817
Kentucky	June 1, 1792	Illinois	Dec. 3, 1818
Tennessee	June 1, 1796	Alabama	Dec. 14, 1819
Ohio	1803	Maine	March 15,1820
Louisiana	April 30, 1812	Missouri	August 10, 1821
Indiana	Dec. 11, 1816	Arkansas	June 19, 1836

Michigan	Jan. 26, 1837	Colorado	August 1. 1876
Florida	March 3, 1845	North Dakota	Nov. 2. 1889
Texas	December 29, 1845	South Dakota	Nov. 2, 1889
Iowa	Dec.mber 28. 1846	Montana	Nov. 8. 1889
Wisconsin	May 29, 1848	Washington	Nov.ber 11, 1889
California	Sept. 9, 1850	Idaho	July 3, 1890
Minnesota	May 11, 1853	Wyoming	July 10, l890
Oregon	February 14. 1859	Utah	January 4, 1896
Kansas	Jan. 29. 1861	Oklahoma	Nov. 16. 1907
West Virginia	June 19. 1863	New Mexico	January 6, l912
Nevada	October 31, 1864	Arizona	Feb. 14. 1912
Nebraska	March 1, 1867	Hawaii	Aug. 21, 1959 ***
Alaska	Jan. 3, 1959 ***		

Territories of the United States:

Alaska, acquired from Russia Mar. 30, 1867; territory. Aug. 24. 1912. **[Now state]**
Hawaii, annexed on July 7, 1898; territory. April 30, 1900. **[Now state]**

Possessions of the United States:

Puerto Rico, acquired from Spain, December 10, l893.
Guam, acquired from Spain, December 10, 1898.
Philippine Islands, ceded by Spain, December 10, 1898.
American Samoa. acquired by tripartite treaty with Germany and Great Britain. Dec. 2, 1899.
Canal Zone, acquired by treaty with Panama, November 18, 1903
[On September 7, 1977, President Jimmy Carter signed the Panama Canal Treaty and Neutrality Treaty promising to give control of the canal to the Panamanians by the year 2000.]
Virgin Islands, bought from Denmark, August 4, 1916.

RATIFICATION OF AMENDMENTS

Article V of the National Constitution is as follows:
"The Congress, whenever two thirds of both Houses shall deem it necessary, shall propose Amendments to this Constitution, or, on the Application of the Legislatures of two thirds of the several States, shall call a Convention for proposing Amendments, which, in either Case, shall be valid to all Intents and Purposes, as part of this Constitution, when ratified by the Legislatures of three fourths of the several States, or by Conventions in three fourths thereof, as the one or the other Mode of Ratification may be proposed by the Congress;
Until Amendment XXI State ratification was by the legislatures; this last one was submitted to conventions.
It has been usual to date the ratification of all amendments to the National Constitution from the certification of the Secretary of State that a sufficient number of States had approved of it. On May 16, 1921, however, the Supreme Court of the United States announced in Dillon v. Gloss 256 U.S. 368, 376) that an amendment was in effect on the day when the legislature of the last necessary State ratified.

Post 1937 Amendments in Summary
This text (88A-D] is not included in Bloom's 1937 book.
Amendment XXII: Limit of Presidential terms.
Amendment XXIII: Election rules for the District of Columbia
Amendment XXIV: Taxes and the right to vote.
Amendment XXV: Rules of Presidential succession.
Amendment XXVI: Age and the right to vote.
Amendment XXVII: Pay raises and Congress

Post 1937 Amendments As Written with Ratification Dates

Back on page 88 (the prior page) according to Sol Bloom's original numbering, we began an original Bloom section called Ratification of Amendments before we took a natural page break to squeeze in the Twenty-Second through Twenty-Seventh Amendments. We numbered these new pages 88A through 88D. This page is 88A.

Following these four pages with letter suffixes, we resume the original numbering at page 89 and there will be no need for changes to the original numbering scheme until we hit the Alphabetical Analysis. You will see then, that we were compelled to use two pages for every original page while keeping the original Bloom numbering. To help, we add a *part II* designation for the second page.

These new amendments in pages 88B through 88D, will not be included in the continuation of Bloom's Ratification section because we have included their ratification dates in the text of each Amendment. In trying to adhere to the original, we apologize if any of the gyrations necessary have been confusing. Eventually we trust you will find them quite logical.

[AMENDMENT XXII]

Passed by Congress March 21, 1947. Ratified February 27, 1951.

Section 1. No person shall be elected to the office of the President more than twice, and no person who has held the office of President, or acted as President, for more than two years of a term to which some other person was elected President shall be elected to the office of President more than once. But this Article shall not apply to any person holding the office of President when this Article was proposed by Congress, and shall not prevent any person who may be holding the office of President, or acting as President, during the term within which this Article becomes operative from holding the office of President or acting as President during the remainder of such term.

Section 2. This article shall be inoperative unless it shall have been ratified as an amendment to the Constitution by the legislatures of three-fourths of the several States within seven years from the date of its submission to the States by the Congress.

[AMENDMENT XXIII]

Passed by Congress June 16, 1960. Ratified March 29, 1961.

Section 1. The District constituting the seat of Government of the United States shall appoint in such manner as Congress may direct ---A number of electors of President and Vice President equal to the whole number of Senators and Representatives in Congress to which the District would be entitled if it were a State, but in no event more than the least populous State; they shall be in addition to those appointed by the States, but they shall be considered, for the purposes of the election of President and Vice President, to be electors appointed by a State; and they shall meet in the District and perform such duties as provided by the twelfth article of amendment.

Section 2. The Congress shall have power to enforce this article by appropriate legislation.

AMENDMENT XXIV

Passed by Congress August 27, 1962. Ratified January 23, 1964.

Section 1. The right of citizens of the United States to vote in any primary or other election for President or Vice President, for electors for President or Vice President, or for Senator or Representative in Congress, shall not be denied or abridged by the United States or any State by reason of failure to pay poll tax or other tax.

[88B]

Section 2. The Congress shall have power to enforce this article by appropriate legislation.

AMENDMENT XXV

Passed by Congress July 6, 1965. Ratified February 10, 1967.
Note: Article II, sec. 1, of the Constitution affected by 25th amendment.

Section 1. In case of the removal of the President from office or of his death or resignation, the Vice President shall become President.

Section 2. Whenever there is a vacancy in the office of the Vice President, the President shall nominate a Vice President who shall take office upon confirmation by a majority vote of both Houses of Congress.

Section 3. Whenever the President transmits to the President pro tempore of the Senate and the Speaker of the House of Representatives his written declaration that he is unable to discharge the powers and duties of his office, and until he transmits to them a written declaration to the contrary, such powers and duties shall be discharged by the Vice President as Acting President.

Section 4. Whenever the Vice President and a majority of either the principal officers of the executive departments or of such other body as Congress may by law provide, transmit to the President pro tempore of the Senate and the Speaker of the House of Representatives their written declaration that the President is unable to discharge the powers and duties of his office, the Vice President shall immediately assume the powers and duties of the office as Acting President.

---Thereafter, when the President transmits to the President pro tempore of the Senate and the Speaker of the House of Representatives his written declaration that no inability exists, he shall resume the powers and duties of his office unless the Vice President and a majority of either the principal officers of the executive department or of such other body as Congress may by law provide, transmit within four days to the President pro tempore of the Senate and the Speaker of the House of Representatives their written declaration that the President is unable to discharge the powers and duties of his office.

[88C]

Thereupon Congress shall decide the issue, assembling within forty-eight hours for that purpose if not in session. If the Congress, within twenty-one days after receipt of the latter written declaration, or, if Congress is not in session, within twenty-one days after Congress is required to assemble, determines by two-thirds vote of both Houses that the President is unable to discharge the powers and duties of his office, the Vice President shall continue to discharge the same as Acting President; otherwise, the President shall resume the powers and duties of his office.

AMENDMENT XXVI

Passed by Congress March 23, 1971. Ratified July 1, 1971.
Note: Amendment 14, section 2, of the Constitution is modified by section 1 of the 26th amendment.

Section 1. The right of citizens of the United States, who are eighteen years of age or older, to vote shall not be denied or abridged by the United States or by any State on account of age.

Section 2. The Congress shall have power to enforce this article by appropriate legislation.

AMENDMENT XXVII

Originally proposed Sept. 25, 1789. Ratified May 7, 1992.
No law, varying the compensation for the services of the Senators and Representatives, shall take effect, until an election of representatives shall have intervened.

[88D]

Such ratification is entirely apart from State regulations respecting the passage of laws or resolutions. It is based on the higher law of the National Constitution itself, which, as it also did for the election of senators before Amendment XVII, prescribed action by the legislature alone. In consequence, approval or veto of such ratification by the Governor is of no account either as respects the date or the legality of the sanction. The rule that ratification once made may not be withdrawn has been applied in all cases; though a legislature that has rejected may later approve, and this change has been made in the consideration of several amendments.

AMENDMENTS I-X

These passed Congress on September 25, 1789. Eleven States were necessary, since Vermont became a State before the ratification was completed. Virginia was this eleventh State and she agreed to the amendments on December 15, 1791. President Washington announced the action of the States from time to time in messages to Congress. He reported the action of Virginia on December 30, 1791, and that of Vermont on January 18, 1792; but Vermont had ratified on November 3. There is no record of action by Connecticut, Georgia, or Massachusetts. Secretary Jefferson on March 1, 1792, announced the adoption to the Governors of the States. (See pages 81-82.)

AMENDMENT XI

Congress proposed this on March 4, 1794, but the resolution was not enrolled and signed by the Vice President and Speaker until March 11. The records on the adoption are rather meager, and the States were so dilatory in notifying the central government of their sentiments that Congress on March 2, 1797, asked the President to make inquiries to Connecticut, New Jersey, Pennsylvania, Maryland, Virginia, Kentucky, Tennessee, and South Carolina, half of the States then in the Union. On January 8, 1798, he reported that Kentucky having ratified, the amendment was "declared to be a part of the Constitution." But Kentucky had ratified as early as December 17, 1794.

The honor of being the twelfth State to ratify lies between North Carolina and Delaware. Delaware ratified on January 23, 1795.

The legislature of North Carolina passed the ratification as a law on January 19, 1795. In that State the Governor did not possess the power to approve or veto a bill, but the constitution required that each act be signed by the Speakers of the two Houses, and this signature was essential to the validity of the law. All the laws of a session were so signed at that time on the last day; accordingly, this act of ratification bears the date February 7, 1795. It has been considered, therefore, that February 7 was the date of ratification of North Carolina, because the action, as required by State regulations, was not completed until that day. However, at that time in that State the rule of common law was in force which made a statute retroactive to the beginning of the session in which it was enacted, which in this case was December 30, 1794. In Tennessee there was a similar requirement of signature by the Speakers, and there the State Supreme Court declared that though the signing was essential to the validity of the measure, yet it was of a ministerial and not of a legislative character, and being done the "law takes effect from the date of its passage by relation." Because of the contradictory character of the State regulations, and because they are also opposed to the principle of the Dillon v. Gloss decision governing the legislature in the performance of a duty dependent upon the National Constitution only, the ratification by Delaware on January 23, 1795, is here considered as the final necessary one, with the ratification of North Carolina as of January 19. (See page 82.)

AMENDMENT XII

This proposal passed Congress on December 9, 1803, the vote of the Speaker being necessary for it in the House; but it was not enrolled and signed until December 12. James Madison, Secretary of State, declared it in force on September 25, 1804. Thirteen States were then needed to ratify, and Tennessee was supposedly the last necessary State, July 27, 1804. Connecticut and Delaware rejected the proposal; and there is no record for Massachusetts. In New Hampshire the resolution passed on June 15, was vetoed on June 20, was not passed over the veto, and was never certified to the Secretary of State; but since the veto of the Governor was extra-legal, the original action by the legislature of that State really consummated the ratification. (See page 83.)

Amendment XIII
This was submitted on January 31, 1865, by Congress, President Lincoln giving his unnecessary approval also on the next day. It was rejected by Delaware and Kentucky, two of the loyal slave-holding States and the only States which had not already abolished slavery by State action, except Texas. It was also rejected by Mississippi, a slave State that had been one of the Confederate States. The remaining States, including the ten others that had been in the Confederacy, approved. As there were then thirty-six States, ratification by twenty-seven was needed. Georgia was the last necessary State. Her legislature voting on December 6, 1865,. Secretary Seward certified the amendment on December 18, 1865. At this time the southern States had been reorganized under presidential reconstruction and their legislatures, while annulling the ordinances of secession, had also abolished slavery within their limits. Later Congress refused to recognize these reorganized governments, except in Tennessee, but their ratification of the Thirteenth Amendment was nonetheless accepted to make it valid; otherwise, if they were States within the Union, the amendment could not be carried without their approval. If the eleven States that formed the Confederate States were not in the Union, then there were only twenty-five States and nineteen were needed for ratification. On this basis the necessary approval would have been that of New Hampshire, July 1, 1865. (See page 83.)

Amendment XIV
June 13, 1866, was the date on which Congress voted this second of the Civil War amendments. The resolution was signed on June 15 and received by the Secretary of State the next day. There were many complications over the ratification. The southern States were still unreconstructed when it was submitted, and conditions remained unsettled in that region during its consideration, Congress requiring ratification as a condition of reconstruction. Various States rejected the amendment and later accepted it; others, having approved, attempted to withdraw the approval. On the same basis as that under which the Thirteenth Amendment became a part of the Constitution, there were thirty-seven States to vote on it and twenty-eight was the required three-fourths. The legislatures of Louisiana and South Carolina, twenty-seventh and twenty-eighth States, both passed the amendment on July 9, and Alabama on July 13.

Meanwhile, New Jersey and Ohio had withdrawn their acceptance. Secretary Seward made a conditional certification of ratification on July 20, 1868; but on July 21, Congress by concurrent resolution declared that the amendment had been ratified by twenty-nine States and directed Secretary Seward to promulgate it as a part of the Constitution, which he did on July 28 in a lengthy statement showing that he acted under the above order from Congress. Later Oregon also withdrew her acceptance. Delaware. Kentucky, and Maryland rejected the proposal and California ignored it. Four states added their approval after that of Alabama, more than making up the necessary twenty-eight without the three States that had withdrawn. (See page 84.)

AMENDMENT XV
The prohibition of a color limitation on suffrage was offered to the States by Congress on February 26, 1869, and deposited with the Secretary of State on the next day. By this time most of the southern States had been reconstructed; ratification of this amendment was required, however, of the remaining few before they would be readmitted. Georgia was the twenty-eighth State, February 2, 1870, and Secretary Fish announced the approval on March 30. New York withdrew her acceptance on January 5, 1870, but Nebraska added her name on February 17, and Texas on February 18. New Jersey. the last State to vote, did so on February 15, 1871. California, Delaware, Kentucky, Maryland, Oregon, and Tennessee rejected the amendment. (See page 85.)

AMENDMENT XVI
Not until July 12, 1909, did Congress suggest another amendment to the States. The resolution was signed on July 16 and deposited in the Department of State July 21. Before it was ratified the number of States had increased to forty-eight, making thirty-six essential for the incorporation of the amendment into the Constitution. Delaware on February 3, 1913, made up the required number; but New Mexico and Wyoming also accepted the amendment on this day, though probably at later hours. Kentucky is included in the above thirty-six, even though the Governor had vetoed the legislative approval. Secretary Knox issued his certificate on the ratification on February 23, 1913. The amendment was rejected by Connecticut. Florida, Rhode Island, and Utah, and Pennsylvania and Virginia took no action. (See page 85.)

AMENDMENT XVII
The amendment for popular election of senators passed Congress on May 13, 1912, and reached the Secretary of State on the I$tl1. In contrast with the slow progress of the Sixteenth Amendment through the State legislatures, this one was adopted by Connecticut, the thirty-sixth State, on April 8, 1913. Only one other State ratified, that of Louisiana, more than a year later. It was rejected by Delaware and Utah, and no action was taken by Alabama, Florida, Georgia, Kentucky, Maryland, Mississippi, Rhode Island, South Carolina, and Virginia. The Secretary's certification is dated May 31, 1913. (See page 85.)

AMENDMENT XVIII
The enactment of the prohibition amendment was almost as swift as its repeal. The amendment was offered to the States by Congress on December 18, 1917, and deposited with the Department of State on the 19th. On January 16, 1919, it was ratified by Missouri, Nebraska, and Wyoming, probably in this order with Missouri as the thirty-sixth State. Five other States ratified on January 15 and two on January 17. The amendment was promulgated on January 29, and was in effect from January 16, 1920. The California legislature passed the resolution on January 13, 1919, that endorsement being the twenty-first. A referendum was ordered on it, but this did not affect the legality of the enactment. Rhode Island rejected the amendment; Connecticut took no action. (See page 85.)

AMENDMENT XIX
The amendment for female suffrage received the sanction of Congress on June 4, 1919, and was placed with the Secretary of State the next day. The ratification of Tennessee, the thirty-sixth State, was on August 18, 1920. The struggle there for approval of the amendment was a severe one, and on August 31 the House reconsidered and non-concurred; but the Senate refused to recognize this action, as the Governor had not only forwarded to Washington the certificate of adoption but the Secretary of State had announced the inclusion of the amendment in the Constitution on August 26. After Tennessee two other States voted their adherence to the proposal, Connecticut on September 14, and Vermont on February 8, 1921. There was no action by Alabama, Florida, or North Carolina; and rejection by Delaware, Georgia, Louisiana, Maryland, Mississippi, South Carolina, and Virginia. (See page 86.)

AMENDMENT XX

The "lame duck" amendment passed Congress on March 2, 1932, and was signed and deposited on March 3. It was ratified on January 23, 1933, by Georgia, Missouri, Ohio, and Utah, which approvals made up the necessary thirty-six States; of these Utah, because of its most western location, was probably the last. All forty-eight States ratified the amendment, which was certified by the Secretary of State on February 6, 1933. (See page 86.)

AMENDMENT XXI

Congress voted the repeal of the Eighteenth Amendment on February 20, 1933, and it was deposited in the Department of State the same day. Ratification was by State conventions, which required preliminary legislative action to prescribe the election of the delegates and the meetings; and in forty-three States this was done by September 7, but four of the laws put off the conventions until 1934. In North Carolina the people voted on the question of holding a convention, and rejected it. Thirty-eight conventions met in 1933; that of South Carolina rejected the amendment. The conventions of Pennsylvania, Ohio, and Utah ratified on December 5, 1933, in this order. Maine, December 6, was the thirty-seventh State. The certificate of the adoption of the amendment was made by the Acting Secretary of State on December 5, and the President in accordance with a special law also issued his proclamation the same day. (See page 87.)

The table on the next page is amended from one from the Department of State. The chief change is the substitution of January 23, 1795, Delaware, for February 7, 1795, North Carolina, for the date of the ratification of the Eleventh Amendment. The reasons for the substitution are given above in this article. The change to February 2, 1870, Georgia, for February 3, 1870, Iowa, for the Fifteenth Amendment, and the omission of North Carolina from the States that gave the final necessary ratification of the Eighteenth Amendment, are for the same reasons.

AMENDMENTS TO THE CONSTITUTION

	Passed by Congress	Engrossed Received— & Signed	State Dept.	Ratified by last necessary State	Certified—Secy. of State
I (freedom of religion, etc.)	Sept. 25, 1789	Sept. 28	*Sept. 26	Dec. 15, 1791 Virginia, 11th	Mar. 1, 1792
II (right to bear arms)	"	"	"	"	"
III (quartering of soldiers)	"	"	"	"	"
IV (security against search)	"	"	"	"	"
V (due process of law)	"	"	"	"	"
VI (right to speedy trial)	"	"	"	"	"
VII (right to jury trial)	"	"	"	"	"
VIII (no cruel punishments)	"	"	"	"	"
IX (unenumerated rights not denied)	"	"	"	"	"
X (undelegated powers reserved)	"	"	"	"	"
XI (suability of a State)	Mar. 4, 1794	Mar. 11	*Mar. 12	Jan. 23, 1795 Delaware, 12th	Jan. 8, 1798
XII (reform in electoral vote)	Dec. 9, 1803	Dec. 12	*Dec. 12	June 15, 1804 New Hampshire, 13th	Sept. 25, 1804
XIII (abolishing slavery)	Jan. 31, 1865	Feb. 1	Feb. 2	Dec. 6, 1865 Georgia, 27th	Dec. 18, 1865
XIV (rights of citizens)	June 13, 1866	June 15	June 16	July 9, 1868 La., S. C., 28th	July 28, 1868
XV (negro suffrage)	Feb. 26, 1869	Feb. 26	Feb. 27	Feb. 3, 1870 Georgia, 29th	Mar. 30, 1870
XVI (income tax)	July 12, 1909	July 16	July 21	Feb. 3, 1913 Del., N. M., Wyom., 36th	Feb. 25, 1913
XVII (election of Senators)	May 13, 1912	May 15	May 15	April 8, 1913 Connecticut, 36th	May 31, 1913
XVIII (prohibition)	Dec. 18, 1917	Dec. 18	Dec. 19	Jan. 16, 1919 Mo., Neb., Wyom., 36th	Jan. 29, 1919
XIX (woman suffrage)	June 4, 1919	June 5	June 5	Aug. 18, 1920 Tennessee, 36th	Aug. 26, 1920
XX ("lame duck")	Mar. 2, 1932	Mar. 3	Mar. 3	Jan. 23, 1933 Ga., Mo., Ohio, Utah, 36th	Feb. 6, 1933
XXI (repeal of prohibition)	Feb. 20, 1933	Feb. 20	Feb. 20	Dec. 5, 1933 Pa., Ohio, Utah, 36th	Dec. 5, 1933‡

* Resolution of Congress asking President to transmit.

† Date when President informed Congress.

‡ Date also of President's proclamation.

(See note on page 94.)

[95]

Notes on Coming Alphabetical Analysis

What a great book written originally by a great man, Sol Bloom.
Thank you for reading this far. There are more great things to come.

This coming Alphabetic Analysis of the Constitution, Bill of Rights, Amendments, etc. by Sol Bloom, from my observations is a unique notion and it is very helpful for those studying the Constitution, looking for a few easier answers than reading through the entire text each time a question arises.

In this book, I have tried to remain true to the writer's intentions and the writer's words. Most of the book is redone / re-mastered in an easily readable format; and thus this book has more pages than shown in Sol Bloom's page numbering scheme.

In the original book, which is a treasure to possess, and which, I am pleased to possess multiple times, Mr. Bloom squeezed everything he could into every page by reducing the font size and spacing in-between lines. Bloom also added excitement to his formatting by changing the font and he sometimes used the small caps v small letters, and he sprayed italics and all-caps and dark + light to help him make sections stand out. Nice Job!

[95A]

To be true, the official page numbering of this book is Sol Bloom's numbering. However, when your author hit the Alphabetic Analysis below, The font and size would have been semi-indiscernible if I remained true to original page numbering per page. And, so, I use Bloom Page numbering but each page of the original Alphabetical Analysis has been re-mastered to two pages in table form, with the second page being [page # part 2] So, forgive me on the # of pages v. the Bloom listed number.

Last thought… most authors begin sections / chapters on odd pages and on the even pages, they place the book title, with page # to the left, and on odd pages, they put the Chapter or Verse Title with page # to the right. Since we use two pages for each original page, the left and right page numbering gets off a bit so please forgive us on that as we make each page true Enjoy Bloom's Alphabetical Analysis beginning on page 96:

[95B]

ALPHABETICAL ANALYSIS OF THE CONSTITUTION OF THE UNITED STATES AND OF THE AMENDMENTS THERETO

INTRODUCTION

The suggestion for this Alphabetical Analysis appeared originally in William Hickey, Constitution of the United States of America, . . . will) an Alphabetical Analysis (1846) one of the early efforts to make available the exact text of the Constitution, the "fireside companion of the American citizen," as Hickey called it. The book also contained much valuable historical information. Congress purchased large editions of it for distribution, it became a standard text and later editions brought the tabulation through the Fifteenth Amendment. The principle of the compilation requires that the key word shall in each case be explained by the quotation of a sufficient amount of the context, with a reference to its exact place in the Constitution or Amendment.

The original suffered from over-elaboration; words were included in the alphabetical list that were unimportant, or so general throughout the document as to have no special significance. On the other hand, as the plan of the analysis excluded all words not in the text, various matters were not sufficiently indicated; for instance, the word "copyright" did not appear in Hickey's analysis, but it is a word for which the searcher would naturally look. The present compilation, while following Hickey's general plan, is a complete reconstruction, which is down to date, and which tries to exclude the superfluous, to avoid repetitions by the use of cross references, and to add essentials. When the word in the alphabetical list is not itself in the text it is enclosed in [ ] square brackets.

SOL BLOOM,
Director General.

ALPHABETICAL ANALYSIS

TERM / DESCRIPTION	ART	SEC	CL.	PG
ABRIDGE. No State shall make or enforce any law which shall abridge the privileges or immunities of the citizens of the United States......14th Amend				84
ABRIDGED. (See Denied.)				
ABSENCE. The Senate shall chuse . . . a President pro tempore. In the Absence of the Vice President	1	3	5	67
ABSENT Members. . . Majority of each [House] shall constitute a Quorum to do Business; but a smaller Number...... may be authorized to compel the Attendance of absent Members, in such manner, and under such penalties as each house may provide	1	5	1	68

[96]

TERM / DESCRIPTIONI	ART.	SEC.	CL.	PG
ACCOUNT. . . . a regular Statement and Account of the Receipts and Expenditures of all public Money shall be published from time to time.	1	9	7	71
ACCUSATION. In all criminal prosecutions, the accused shall . . . be informed of the nature and cause of the accusation ; . 6th amend.				82
ACCUSED. (See Criminal Prosecutions.)				
ACT. (See Treason.)				
ACT as President. . . . the Congress may by Law provide for the Case of Removal, Death, Resignation or Inability, both of the President and Vice President, declaring what Office shall then act as President, and such Officer shall act accordingly, until the Disability be removed, or a President shall be elected. ACT as President. If a President shall not have been chosen before the time fixed for the beginning of his term, or if the President elect shall have failed to qualify, then the Vice President el-ct shall act as President until a President shall have qualified ; and the Congress may by law pro-vide for the case wherein neither a President elect nor a Vice President elect shall have qualified, declaring who shall then act as President, or the manner in which one who is to act shall be selected, and such person shall act accordingly until a President or Vice President shall have qualified.	2	1	6	72
ACTS. Full Faith and Credit shall be given in each State to the public Acts, Records, and judicial Proceedings of every other State. And the Congress may by general Laws prescribe the Manner in which such Acts, Records and Proceedings shall be proved, and the Effect thereof.	4	1		73
ADJOURN. Neither House, during the Session of Congress, shall, without the Consent of the other, adjourn for more than three days, nor to any other Place than that in which the two Houses shall be sitting.	1	5	4	68
ADJOURN from Day to Day. . . . a Majority of each [House] shall constitute a Quorum to do Business ; but a smaller Number may adjourn from day to day, .. .	1	5	1	63
ADJOURNMENT. If any Bill shall not be returned by the President within ten Days (Sundays excepted) after it shall have been presented to him, the Same shall be a Law, in like Manner as if he had signed it, unless the Congress by their Adjournment prevent its Return, in which Case it shall not be a Law;	1	7	2	69
ADJOURNMENT. Every Order, Resolution, or Vote to which the Concurrence of the Senate and House of Representatives may be necessary (except on a question of Adjournment) shall be presented to the President of the United States ;	1	7	3	69
ADJOURNMENT. [The President] may . . . convene both Houses, or either of them, and in Case of Disagreement between them, with Respect to the Time of Adjournment, he may adjourn them to such Time as he shall think proper ;	2	3		73

ADMIRALTY and Maritime Jurisdiction. The judicial Power shall extend ... to all Cases of admiralty and maritime Jurisdiction ;	3	2	1	74
ADMITTED. New States may be admitted by the Congress into this Union ; . . . (See States	4	3	1	75
ADOPTION of this Constitution. No Person except a natural born Citizen, T,,, or a Citizen of the United States, at the time of the Adoption of this Constitution, shall be eligible to the Office of President ;	2	1	5	72
ADOPTION of this Constitution. All Debts contracted and Engagements m #CY) 0. entered into, before the Adoption of this Constitution, shall be as valid against the United States under this Constitution, as under the Confederation.	6		1	76
ADVICE and Consent of the Senate. (See Senate.)				
AFFIRMATION. (See Oath or Affirmation.)				
AGE. No Person shall be a Representative who shall not have attained to the Age of twenty five Years.	1	2	2	65
AGE. No Person shall be a Senator who shall not have attained to the -Ts in c = Age of thirty Years,	1	3	3	67
AGE. No Person . . . shall be eligible to the Office of President . . . , who shall not have attained to the Age of thirty five Years.	2	1	5	72
AGREEMENT or Compact. No State shall, without the Consent of Congress, . . . enter into any Agreement or Compact with another State or with a foreign Power,	1	10	3	71
AID. (See Treason.)				
[ALIENS.] (See Natural Born Citizen; Naturalization.)				
ALLIANCE. No State shall enter into any . . . Alliance.	1	10	1	71
AMBASSADORS. (See Appointments.)				
AMBASSADORS. [The President] shall receive Ambassadors and other public Ministers ;	2	3		73
AMBASSADORS. The judicial Power shall extend . . . to all Cases affecting Ambassadors, other public Ministers and Consuls	3	2	1	74

[Page 97 part 2]

TERM / DESCRIPTION	DOC	ART.	SEC.	CL.	PG
AMBASSADORS. In all Cases affecting Ambassadors, other public Ministers and Consuls, . . . the supreme Court shall have original Jurisdiction.	3	2	2		74
AMENDMENTS. All Bills for raising Revenue shall originate in the House of Representatives ; but the Senate may propose or concur with Amendments as on other Bills.	1	7	1		68
AMENDMENTS. The Congress, whenever two thirds of both Houses shall deem it necessary, shall propose Amendments to this Constitution, or, on the Application of the Legislatures of two thirds of the several States, shall call a Convention for proposing Amendments, which, in either Case, shall be valid to all Intents and Purposes, as Part of this Constitution, when ratified by the Legislatures of three fourths of the several States, or by Conventions in three fourths thereof, as the one or the other Mode of Ratification may be proposed by the Congress ; Pro-vided that no Amendment which may be made prior to the Year One thousand eight hundred and eight shall in any Manner affect the first and fourth Clauses in the Ninth Section of the first Article; and that no State, without its Consent, shall be deprived of it's equal Suffrage in the Senate.	5				76
AMERICA. (See United States.)					
[AMNESTY.] (See Pardons ; Rebellion.)					
APPELLATE Jurisdiction. (See Supreme Court.)					
APPOINTMENT. (See Militia.)					
[APPOINTMENT of Electors.] (See Election of President.)					
APPOINTMENTS. (See Vacancies.)					
APPOINTMENTS. [The President] . . shall nominate, and by and with the Advice and Consent of the Senate, shall appoint Ambassadors, other public Ministers and Consuls, Judges of the supreme Court, and all other Officers of the United States, whose Appointments are not herein other-wise provided for, and which shall be established by Law ; but the Congress may by Law vest the Appointment of such inferior Officers, as they think proper, in the President alone, in the Courts of Law, or in the Heads of Departments.	2	2	2		73
APPORTIONED. (See Representatives.)					
APPORTIONMENT. (See Taxes.)					
[APPRENTICES.] (See Fugitive Slaves.)					
APPROPRIATION. (See Armies.)					
APPROPRIATIONS. No Money shall be drawn from the Treasury, but in Consequence of Appropriations made by Law ;	1	9	7		71
[APPROPRIATIONS.] (See Expenditures.)					
APPROVED. (See Bill; Order.)					
[ARMIES.] No State shall, without the Consent of Congress, . .. keep Troops,	1	10	3		71
ARMIES. (See Quartered.)					

ARMING. (See Militia.)				
ARMS. A well regulated Militia, being necessary to the Security of a free State, the right of the people to keep and bear Arms, shall not be infringed. 2nd Amend	2nd			81
ARMY. The President shall be Commander in Chief of the Army.	2	2	1	73
ARREST. The Senators and Representatives shall . . . in all Cases, except Treason, Felony and Breach of the Peace, be privileged from Arrest during their Attendance at the Session of their respective Houses, and in going to and returning from the same ; . . .	1	6	1	68
ARSENALS. (See Forts.)				
ARTS. (See Science.)				
ASSEMBLE. (See Meeting.)				
ASSEMBLE. Congress shall make no law . . . abridging . . . the right of the people peaceably to assemble, and to petition the Government for -a redress of grievances. 1st amend.	1st			81
ASSUME. (See Debt of the United States.)				
ATTAINDER. No Bill of Attainder . . . shall be passed	1	9	3	70
ATTAINDER. No State shall . . . pass any Bill of Attainder, . . .	1	10	1	71
ATTAINDER of Treason. The Congress shall have Power to declare the Punishment of Treason, but no Attainder of Treason shall work Corruption of Blood, or Forfeiture except during the Life of the Person .	3	3	2	74
ATTENDANCE. (See Absent Members.)				
ATTENDANCE. (See Arrest.)				
AUTHORS. (See Science.)				

[Page 98 part 2]

TERM / DESCRIPTION	DOC	ART.	SEC.	CL.	PG
BAIL. Excessive bail shall not be required, nor excessive fines imposed, nor cruel and unusual. Punishments inflicted. 8th amend.	8th				82
BALLOT. The Electors shall meet in their respective States, and vote by Ballot for two Persons, ...					
BALLOT. The Electors shall meet in their respective states, and vote by ballot for President and Vice-President, . . . they shall name in their ballots the person voted for as President, and in distinct ballots the person voted for as Vice-President, 12th amend.	12th				83
BALLOT. . . . if no person [of those voted for by the Electors] have such majority, then .. . the House of Representatives shall choose immediately, by ballot, the President. 12th amend.	12th				83
BANKRUPTCIES. Congress shall have Power . . . To establish . . . uniform Laws on the subject of Bankruptcies throughout the United States;		1	8	4	69
[BANKS.] (See Implied Powers ; Money.)					
BASIS of Representation. (See Representatives.)					
BASSETT, Richard. Signs the Constitution					77
BEDFORD, Gunning, Jr. Signs the Constitution.					77
BEHAVIOUR. (See Good Behaviour.)					
BEVERAGE Purposes. (See Liquors.)					
BILL. Every Bill which shall have passed the House of Representatives and the Senate, shall, before it become a Law, be presented to the President of the United States ; If he approve he shall sign it, but if not he shall return it, with his Objections to that House in which it shall have originated, who shall enter the Objections at large on their Journal, and proceed to reconsider it. If after such Reconsideration two thirds of that House shall agree to pass the Bill, it shall be sent, together with the Objections, to the other House, by which it shall likewise be reconsidered, and if approved by two thirds of that House, it shall become a Law. But in all such Cases the Votes of both Houses shall be determined by yeas and Nays, and the Names of the Persons voting for and against the Bill shall be entered on the Journal of each House respectively. If any Bill shall not be returned by the President within ten Days (Sundays excepted) after it shall have been presented to him, the Same shall be a Law, in like Manner as if he had signed it, unless the Congress by their Adjournment prevent its Return, in which Case it shall not be a Law.		1	7	2	69
BILL of Attainder. (See Attainder.)					
BILL of Rights. (See Amendments I-X)					
BILLS for Raising Revenue. (See Revenue.)					
BILLS of Credit. No State shall . . . emit Bills of Credit;		1	10	1	71
BLAIR, John. Signs the Constitution.					77
BLOOD. (See Corruption of Blood.)					
BLOUNT, William. Signs the Constitution					77

[BONDS.] (See Securities.)				
BORROW Money. The Congress shall have Power . . . To borrow Money on the credit of the United States;	1	8	2	69
BOUNTIES. (See Pensions.)				
BREACH of the Peace. (See Arrest.)				
BREARLEY, David signs Constitution.				77
BRIBERY. (See Impeachment.)				
BROOM, Jacob. Signs the Constitution.				77
BUILDINGS. (See Forts.)				
BUSINESS. . . . a Majority of each [House] shall constitute a Quorum to do Business;	1	5	1	68
BUTLER, Pierce. Signs the Constitution.				77
[CABINET Officers.] (See Departments.)				
CAPITAL Crime. (See Crime.)				
CAPITATION. (See Tax.)				
CAPTURES. The Congress shall have Power To . . .. make Rules concerning Captures on Land and Water;	1	8	11	70
CARROLL, Daniel. Signs the Constitution.				77
CASES. (See Judicial Power.)				
CAUSE. no Warrants shall issue, but upon probable cause, 4th amend.	4th			81
CENSUS. (See Enumeration.)				
CESSION. The Congress shall have Power . . . To exercise exclusive Legislation in all Cases whatsoever, over such District (not exceeding ten Miles square) as may, by Cession of particular States, and the Acceptance of Congress, become the Seat of the Government of the United States,	1	8	17	70

[Page 99 part 2]

TERM / DESCRIPTION	DOC	ART.	SEC.	CL.	PG
CHIEF Justice. When the President of the United States is tried, the Chief Justice shall preside;	1	3	6		67
CITIZEN. No Person shall be a Representative who shall not have . . . been seven Years a Citizen of the United States, . . . 1 2 2 66	1	2	2		66
CITIZEN. No Person shall be a Senator who shall not have . . . been nine Years a Citizen of the United States.	1	3	3		67
CITIZEN. No Person except a natural born Citizen, or a Citizen of the United States, at the time of the Adoption of this Constitution, shall be eligible to the Office of President;	2	1	6		72
CITIZENS. The judicial Power shall extend to all Cases, . . . between a State and Citizens of another State ;—between Citizens of different States,—between Citizens of the same State claiming Lands under Grants of different States, and between a State, or the Citizens thereof, and foreign States, Citizens or Subjects.	3	2	1		74
CITIZENS. The Citizens of each State shall be entitled to all Privileges and Immunities of Citizens in the several States.	4	2	1		75
CITIZENS. The Judicial power of the United States shall not be construed to extend to any suit in law or equity, commenced or prosecuted against one of the United States by Citizens of another State, or by Citizens or Subjects of any Foreign State. 11th amend.	11TH				82
CITIZENS. All persons born or naturalized in the United States, and subject to the jurisdiction thereof, are citizens of the United States and of the State wherein they reside. No State shall make or enforce any law which shall abridge the privileges or immunities of citizens of the United States; nor shall any State deprive any person of life, liberty, or property, without due process of law; nor deny to any person within its jurisdiction the equal protection of the laws. 14th amend.	14TH				84
CITIZENS. But when the right to vote at any election . . . is denied to any of the male inhabitants of such State, being twenty-one years of age, and citizens of the United States, or in any way abridged, except for participation in rebellion, or other crime, the basis of representation therein shall be reduced in the proportion which the number of such male citizens shall bear to the whole number of male citizens twenty-one years of age in such State 14th amend.	14TH				84
CITIZENS. The right of citizens of the United States to vote shall not be denied or abridged by the United States or by any State on account of race, color, or previous condition of servitude. 15th amend.	15TH				
CITIZENS. The right of citizens of the United States to vote shall not be denied or abridged by the United States or by any State on account of sex. 19th amend.	19TH				86
[CITIZENS.] (See People.)					
CIVIL OFFICERS. (See Officers.)					
[CIVIL Rights.] (See Bill of Rights & 14th Amend.					
CLAIM. But neither the United States nor any State shall assume or pay . . . any claim for the loss or emancipation of any	14TH				84

slave ; but all such debts, obligations and claims shall be held illegal and void. 14ᵗʰ amend.				
CLAIMING Lands. (See Grants.)				
CLAIMS. The Congress shall have Power to dispose of and make all needful Rules and Regulations respecting the Territory or other Property be-longing to the United States ; and nothing in this Constitution shall be so construed as to Prejudice any Claims of the United States, or of any particular State.	4	3	2	75
CLEAR. (See Enter.)				
CLYMER, George. Signs the Constitution.				
[COASTWISE Trade.] (See Enter.)				
COIN. (See Counterfeiting.)				
COIN. No State shall make . . . any Thing but gold and silver Coin a Tender in Payment of Debts;	1	10	1	71
COIN Money. (See Money.)				
COLLECT. (See Taxes.)				
COLOR. (See Race.)				
COMFORT. (See Treason.)				
COMMANDER in Chief. The President shall be Commander in Chief of the Army and Navy of the United States, and of the Militia of the several States, when called into the actual Service of the United States :	2	2	1	73
COMMERCE. The Congress shall have the power to regulate commerce with foreign Nations, and among the several states, and with the Indian Tribes ;	1	8	3	69
COMMERCE. No Preference shall be given by any Regulation of Commerce or Revenue to the Ports of one state over those of another.	1	9	6	70
COMMISSION. The President shall commission all the officers of the United States.	2	3		73

[Page 100 part 2]

TERM / DESCRIPTION	DOC	ART	SEC	CL	PG
COMMISSIONS. The President shall have Power to fill up all Vacancies that may happen during the Recess of the Senate, by granting Commissions which shall expire at the End of their next Session.		2	2	3	73
COMMON Defence. We the People of the United States, in Order to . . . provide for the common defence . . . do ordain and establish this Constitution for the United States of America. Preamble	PRE				66
COMMON Defence. (See Taxes.)					
COMMON Law. In Suits at common law, where the value in controversy shall exceed twenty dollars, the right of trial by jury shall be preserved, and no fact tried by a jury, shall be otherwise re-examined in any Court of the United States, than according to the rules of the common law. 7th amend.	7TH				82
COMPACT. (See Agreement.)					
COMPENSATION. The Senators and Representatives shall receive a Compensation for their Services, to be ascertained by Law, and paid out of the Treasury of the United States.		1	6	1	68
COMPENSATION. The President shall, at stated Times, receive for his Services, a Compensation, which shall neither be encreased nor diminished during the Period for which he shall have been elected, and he shall not receive within that Period any other Emolument from the United States, or any of them.		2	1	7	72
COMPENSATION. The Judges, both of the supreme and inferior Courts, shall . . . at stated Times, receive for their Services, a Compensation, which shall not be diminished during their Continuance in Office.		3	1		74
[COMPENSATION.] (See Emolument ; Emoluments.)					
COMPENSATION. . . . nor shall private property be taken for public use, without just compensation 5th amend.	5TH				82
COMPULSORY Process. In all criminal prosecution, the accused shall enjoy the right . . . to have compulsory process for obtaining Witnesses in his favor. . . . 6th amend.	6TH				82
CONCURRENCE. (See Vote in Congress.) CONCURRENT Power. The Congress and the several States shall have concurrent power to enforce this article by appropriate legislation … 18th amend.	18TH				85
CONFEDERATION. No State shall enter into any . . Confederation;					
CONFEDERATION. All Debts contracted and Engagements entered into, before the Adoption of this Constitution, shall be as valid against the United States under this Constitution, as under the Confederation.		6		1	76
CONFESSION. No Person shall be convicted of Treason unless on the Testimony of two Witnesses to the same overt Act, or on Confession in open Court.		3	3	1	74
[CONFISCATION.] (See Private Property)					
CONFRONTED. In all criminal prosecutions, the accused shall enjoy the right to be confronted with the witnesses against him; 6th amend.	6TH				82

CONGRESS. All legislative Powers herein granted shall be vested in a Congress of the United States, which shall consist of a Senate and House of Representatives	1	1		66
CONGRESS. The actual Enumeration shall be made within three Years after the first Meeting of the Congress of the United States, and within every subsequent Term of ten Years, in such Manner as they shall by Law direct.	1	2	3	66
CONGRESS. The Times, Places and Manner of Holding Elections for Senators and Representatives, shall be prescribed in each State by the Legislature thereof ; but the Congress may at any time by Law make or alter such Regulations, except as to the Places of chusing Senators.	1	4	1	67
CONGRESS of the United States.—Organization: Each House shall be the Judge of the Elections, Returns and Qualifications of its own Members, and a Majority of each shall constitute a Quorum to do Business ; but a smaller Number may adjourn from day to day, and may be authorized to compel the Attendance of absent Members, in such Manner, and under such Penalties as each House may provide.	1	5	1	68
Continued... Each House may determine the Rules of its Proceedings, punish its Member for disorderly Behaviour, and, with the Concurrence of 2/3 expel a member.	1	5	2	68
Continued... Each House shall keep a Journal of its Proceedings, and from time to time publish the same, excepting such Parts as may in their Judgment require Secrecy; and the Yeas and Nays of the Members of either House on any question shall, at the Desire of one fifth of those Present, be entered on the Journal.	1	5	3	68
Continued... Neither House, during the Session of Congress, shall, without the Consent of the other, adjourn for more than three days, nor to any other Place than that in which the two Houses shall be sitting.	1	5	4	68

[Page 101 part 2]

TERM / DESCRIPTION	DOC	ART.	SEC.	CL.	PG
CONGRESS of the United States.—Powers :—The Congress shall have Power To Lay and collect Taxes, Duties, Im-posts and Excises, to pay the Debts and provide for the common Defence and general Welfare of the United States ; but all Duties, Imposts and Excises shall be uniform throughout the United States ;	1	8	1		69
To borrow Money on the credit of the United States;	1	8	2		69
To regulate Commerce with foreign Nations, and among the several States, and with the Indian Tribes ;	1	8	3		69
To establish an uniform Rule of Naturalization, and uniform Laws on the subject of Bankruptcies throughout the United States ;	1	8	4		69
To coin Money, regulate the Value thereof, and of foreign Coin, and fix the Standard of Weights and Measures;	1	8	5		69
To provide for the Punishment of counterfeiting the Securities and current Coin of the United States;	1	8	6		69
To establish Post Offices and post Roads ;	1	8	7		69
To promote the Progress of Science and useful Arts, by securing for limited Times to Authors and Inventors the exclusive Right to their respective Writings and Discoveries;	1	8	8		69
To constitute Tribunals inferior to the supreme Court ;	1	8	9		69
To define and punish Piracies and Felonies committed on the high Seas, and Offences against the Law of Nations;	1	8	10		69
To declare War, grant Letters of Marque and Reprisal, and make Rules concerning Captures on Land and Water ;	1	8	11		70
To raise and support Armies, but no Appropriation of Money to that Use shall be for a longer Term than two Years;	1	8	12		70
To provide and maintain a Navy;	1	8	13		70
To make Rules for the Government and Regulation of the land and naval Forces	1	8	14		70
To provide for calling forth the Militia to execute the Laws of the Union, suppress Insurrections and repel Invasions;	1	8	15		70
To provide for organizing, arming, and disciplining, the Militia, and for governing such Part of them as may be employed in the Service of the United States, reserving to the States respectively, the Appointment of the Officers, and the Authority of training the Militia according to the discipline prescribed by Congress ;	1	8	16		70
To exercise exclusive Legislation in all Cases whatsoever, over such District (not exceeding ten Miles square) as may, by Cession of particular States, and the Acceptance of Congress, become the Seat of the Government of the United States, and to exercise like Authority over all Places Purchased by the Consent of the Legislature of the State in which the Same shall be, for the Erection of Forts, Magazines, Arsenals, dock-Yards, and other needful Buildings;—And	1	8	17		70
To make all Laws which shall be necessary and proper for carrying into Execution the foregoing Powers, and all other Powers vested by this Constitution in the Government of the United States, or in any Department or Officer thereof.	1	8	18		70

Congress shall have power to enforce this article by appropriate legislation. 13th amend.	13TH			84
The Congress shall have power to enforce, by appropriate legislation, the provisions of this article. 14th amend.	14TH			85
The Congress shall have power to enforce this article by appropriate legislation. .. 15th amend.	15TH			85
The Congress shall have power to lay and collect taxes on incomes, m o_ from whatever source derived, without apportionment among the several d. a States, and without regard to any census or enumeration. 16th amend.	16TH			85
The Congress and the several States shall have concurrent power to enforce this article by appropriate legislation. 18th amend.	18TH			85
Congress shall have power to enforce this article by appropriate legislation. 19th amend;	19TH			84
CONGRESS. The Migration or Importation of such Persons as any of the States now existing shall think proper to admit, shall not be prohibited Fs by the Congress prior to the Year one thousand eight hundred and eight but a Tax or duty may be imposed on such Importation, not exceeding ten dollars for each Person.	1	9	1	70
CONGRESS. No Title of Nobility shall be granted by the United States : And no Person holding any Office of Profit or Trust under them, shall, without the Consent of the Congress, accept of any present, Emolument Office, or Title, of any kind whatever, from any King, Prince, or foreign a State.	1	9	8	71
CONGRESS. No State shall, without the Consent of the Congress, lay any . . . Imposts or Duties on Imports or Exports, except what may be absolutely necessary for executing it's inspection Laws; and the net Produce of all Duties and Imposts, laid by any State on Imports or Exports, shall be for Use of the Treasury of the United States; and all such Laws shall be subject to the Revision and Controul of the Congress.	1	10	2	71
CONGRESS. No State shall, without the Consent of Congress, lay any Duty of Tonnage, keep Troops, or Ships of War in time of Peace, enter any Agreement or Compact with another State,	1	10	3	71

[Page 102 part 2]

TERM / DESCRIPTION	DOC	ART.	SEC.	CL.	PG
CONGRESS CONTINUED or with a foreign Power, or engage in War, unless actually invaded, or in such imminent Danger as will not admit of delay.	1	10	3		71
CONGRESS. The Congress may determine the Time of chusing the Electors [of President], and the Day on which they shall give their Votes; which Day shall be the same throughout the United States.	2	1	4		72
CONGRESS. . . . Congress may by Law provide for the Case of Removal, Death, Resignation or Inability, both of the President and Vice President, declaring what Officer shall then act as President, and such Officer shall act accordingly, until the Disability be removed, or a President shall be elected.	2	1	6		72
CONGRESS. . . . the Congress may by Law vest the Appointment of such inferior Officers, as they think proper, in the President alone, in the Courts of Law, or in the Heads of Departments.	2	2	2		73
CONGRESS. [The President] . . . shall from time to time give to the Congress Information of the State of the Union, and recommend to their Consideration such Measures as he shall judge necessary and expedient ; he may, on extraordinary Occasions, convene both Houses, or either of them, and in Case of Disagreement between them, with Respect to the Time of Adjournment, he may adjourn them to such Time as he shall think proper;	2	3			73
CONGRESS. The judicial Power of the United States, shall be vested in one supreme Court, and in such inferior Courts as the Congress may from time to time ordain and establish.	3	1	1		74
CONGRESS. In all the other Cases before mentioned, the supreme Court shall have appellate Jurisdiction, both as to Law and Fact, with such Exceptions, and under such Regulations as the Congress shall make.	3	2	2		74
CONGRESS. The Trial of all Crimes, except in Cases of Impeachment, shall be by Jury ; and such Trial shall be held in the State where the said Crimes shall have been committed ; but when not committed within any State, the Trial shall be at such Place or Places as the Congress may by Law have directed	3	2	3		74
CONGRESS. The Congress shall have Power to declare the Punishment of Treason, but no Attainder of Treason shall work Corruption of Blood, or Forfeiture except during the Life of the Person attainted.	3	3	2		74
CONGRESS. Full Faith and Credit shall be given in each State to the public Acts, Records, and judicial Proceedings of every other State. And the Congress may by general Laws prescribe the Manner in which such Acts, Records and Proceedings shall be proved, and the Effect thereof.	4	1			75
CONGRESS. New States may be admitted by the Congress into this Union ; but no new State shall be formed or erected within the Jurisdiction of any other State ; nor any State be formed by the Junction of two or more States, or Parts of States, without the Consent of the Legislatures of the States concerned as well of the Congress.	4	3	1		75

CONGRESS. The Congress shall have Power to dispose of and make all needful Rules and Regulations respecting the Territory or other Property belonging to the United States;	4	3	2	75
CONGRESS. The Congress, whenever two thirds of both Houses shall deem it necessary, shall propose Amendments to this Constitution, or, on the Application of the Legislatures of two thirds of the several States, shall call a Convention for proposing Amendments, which, in either Case, shall be valid to all Intents and Purposes, as Part of this Constitution, when ratified by the Legislatures of three fourths of the several States, or by Conventions in three fourths thereof, as the one or the other Mode of Ratification may be proposed by the Congress ; Provided that no Amendment which may be made prior to the Year One thousand eight hundred and eight shall in any Manner affect the first and fourth Clauses in the Ninth Section of the first Article ; and that no State, without its Con-sent, shall be deprived of it's equal Suffrage in the Senate.	5			75
CONGRESS. Congress shall make no law respecting an establishment of religion, or prohibiting the free exercise thereof ; or abridging the freedom of speech, or of the press ; or the right of the people peaceably to assemble, and to petition the Government for a redress of grievances. 1st amend.	1ST			81
CONGRESS. No person shall be a Senator or Representative in Congress, or elector of President and Vice President, or hold any office, civil or military, under the United States, or under any State, who, having previously taken an oath, as a member of Congress, or as an officer of the United States, or as a member of any State legislature, or as an executive or judicial officer of any State, to support the Constitution of the United States, shall have engaged in insurrection or rebellion against the same, or given aid or comfort to the enemies thereof. But Congress may by a vote of two-thirds of each House, remove such disability. 14th amend.	14TH			84
CONGRESS. . . . the Congress may by law provide for the case wherein neither a President elect nor a Vice President elect shall have qualified, declaring who shall then act as President, or the manner in which one who is to act shall be selected, and such person shall act accordingly until a President or Vice President shall have qualified. 20th amend.	20TH			86

[Page 103 part 2]

TERM / DESCRIPTION	DOC	ART.	SEC.	CL.	PG
CONGRESS. The Congress may by law provide for the case of the death of any of the persons from whom the House of Representatives may choose a President whenever the right of choice shall have devolved upon them, and for the case of the death of any of the persons from whom the Senate may choose a Vice President whenever the right of choice shall have devolved upon them 20th amend.	20TH				86
[CONGRESSMEN.] (See Representatives.)					
CONNECTICUT. First representation	1	2	3		66
CONNECTICUT. Delegates sign the Constitution					77
CONSENT OF CONGRESS. (See Congress.)					
CONSTITUTION. We the People of the United States, in Order to form a more perfect Union, establish Justice, insure domestic Tranquility, pro-vide for the common defence, promote the general Welfare, and secure the Blessings of Liberty to ourselves and our Posterity, do ordain and establish this Constitution for the United States of America. Preamble	PRE				66
CONSTITUTION. The Congress shall have Power . . . To make all Laws which shall be necessary and proper for carrying into Execution the fore-going Powers, and all other Powers vested by this Constitution in the Government of the United States, or in any Department or Officer thereof.	1	8	18		70
CONSTITUTION. Before he [the President] enter on the Execution of his Office, he shall take the following Oath or Affirmation :—"I do solemnly swear (or affirm) that I will faithfully execute the Office of President of the United States, and will to the best of my Ability, preserve, protect and defend the Constitution of the United States	2	1	8		73
CONSTITUTION. The judicial Power shall extend to all Cases, in Law and Equity, arising under this Constitution.	3	2	1		74
CONSTITUTION. (See Amendments.)					
CONSTITUTION. All Debts contracted and Engagements entered into, before the Adoption of this Constitution, shall be as valid against the United States under this Constitution, as under the Confederation.	6		1		76
CONSTITUTION. This Constitution, and the Laws of the United States which shall be made in Pursuance thereof; and all Treaties made, or which shall be made, under the Authority of the United States, shall be the supreme Law of the Land: and the Judges in every State shall be bound thereby, any Thing in the Constitution or Laws of any State to the Contrary notwithstanding.	6		2		76
CONSTITUTION. The Senators and Representatives before mentioned, and the Members of the several State Legislatures, and all executive and judicial Officers, both of the United States and of the several States, shall be bound by Oath or Affirmation, to support this Constitution ;	6		3		76

Provision	Art.	Sec.	Cl.	Page
CONSTITUTION. The Ratification of the Conventions of nine States, shall be sufficient for the Establishment of this Constitution between the States so ratifying the Same.	7			76
CONSTITUTION. The enumeration in the Constitution, of certain rights, o shall not be construed to deny or disparage others retained by the people. 9th amend.	9TH			82
CONSTITUTION. The powers not delegated to the United States by the Constitution, nor prohibited by it to the States, are reserved to the States CI' CD respectively, or to the people. 10th amend.	10TH			82
CONSULS. (See Ambassadors.)				
CONTRACTS. No State shall . . . pass any . . . Law impairing the Obligation of Contracts.	1	10	1	71
CONTROVERSIES. (See Judicial Power.)				
CONVENE Congress. (See Meeting.)				
CONVENTION. (See Amendments.)				
CONVENTIONS. (See Amendments ; Seven Years				
CONVENTIONS'. (See Ratification of the Constitution.)				
CONVICTED. (See Impeachment ; Treason.)				
[COPYRIGHT.] (See Authors.)				
CORRUPTION of Blood. The Congress shall have Power to declare the -C 1E Punishment of Treason, but no Attainder of Treason shall work Corruption of Blood, or Forfeiture except during the Life of the Person attainted.	3	3	2	74
COUNSEL. In all criminal prosecutions, the accused shall enjoy the right to have the Assistance of Counsel for his defence. 6th amend.	6TH			82
COUNTERFEITING. The Congress shall have Power . .. To provide for the Punishment of counterfeiting the Securities and current Coin of the United States;	1	8	6	69
[COURTS.] The Congress shall have Power . .. To constitute Tribunals inferior to the supreme Court;	1	8	9	69
COURTS. The judicial Power of the United States, shall be vested in one supreme Court, and in such inferior Courts as the Congress may from time to time ordain and establish	3	1		74
[COURTS.] (See Judges ; Judicial ; Supreme Court.)				

TERM / DESCRIPTION	DOC	ART.	SEC.	CL.	PG
COURTS of Law. . ... Congress may by Law vest the Appointment of such inferior Officers, as they think proper, in the President alone, in the Art. sec. cl. pg. Courts of Law, or in the Heads of Departments.	2	2	2		73
CREDIT. Full Faith and Credit shall be given in each State to the public Acts, Records, and judicial Proceedings of every other State. And the Congress may by general Laws prescribe the Manner in which such Acts, Records and Proceedings shall be proved, and the Effect thereof	4	1			75
CREDIT. (See Bills of Credit.) CREDIT of the United States. The Congress shall have Power . . . To borrow Money on the credit of the United States;	1	8	2		69
[CRIME.] (See Fugitive from Justice.)					
CRIME. No person shall be held to answer for a capital, or otherwise infamous crime, unless on a presentment or indictment of a Grand Jury, except in cases arising in the land or naval forces, or in the Militia, when in actual service in time of War or public danger ; 5th amend.	5TH				81
CRIMES. (See Impeachment ; Treason.)					
CRIMES. The Trial of all Crimes, except in Cases of Impeachment, shall be by Jury ; and such Trial shall be held in the State where the said Crimes shall have been committed ; but when not committed within any State, the Trial shall be at such Place or Places as the Congress may by Law have directed.	3	2	3		74
CRIMINAL case. . . . nor shall any person . . .. be compelled in any criminal case to be a witness against himself, . . . 5th amend.	5TH				82
CRIMINAL Prosecutions. In all criminal prosecutions, the accused shall enjoy the right to a speedy and public trial, by an impartial jury of the State and district wherein the crime shall have been committed, which district shall have been previously ascertained by law, and to be informed of the nature and cause of the accusation ; to be confronted with the witnesses against him ; to have compulsory process for obtaining Witnesses in his favor, and to have the Assistance of Counsel for his defence. 6th amend.	6TH				82
CRUEL and Unusual Punishments. (See Bail.)					
DANGER. (See Invaded.)					
DAYTON, Jonathan. Signs the Constitution					
DEATH. In Case of the Removal of the President from Office, or of his Death, Resignation, or Inability to discharge the Powers and Duties of the said Office, the Same shall devolve on the Vice President, and the Congress may by Law provide for the Case of Removal, Death, Resignation or Inability, both of the President and Vice President, declaring what Officer shall then act as President, and such Officer shall act accordingly, until the Disability be removed, or a President shall be elected.	2	1	6		72

[DEATH.] If, at the time fixed for the beginning of the term of the President, the President elect shall have died, the Vice President elect shall o become President. 20th amend.	20TH			86
DEATH. The Congress may by law provide for the case of the death of .4- CD any of the persons from whom the House of Representatives may choose a President whenever the right of choice shall have devolved upon them and for the case of the death of any of the persons from whom the 0 ,-1 -6 Senate may choose a Vice President whenever the right of choice shall have devolved upon them. 20th amend.	20TH			86
DEBATE. The Senators and Representatives . . . for any Speech or Debate in either House... shall not be questioned in any other Place.	1	6	1	68
[DEBT, Public.] The Congress shall have Power . . . To borrow Money N L.) (NJ t-) on the credit of the United States;	1	8	2	69
DEBT of the United States. The validity of the public debt of the United c ° States, authorized by law, including debts incurred for payment of pensions and bounties for services in suppressing insurrection or rebellion, shall not be questioned. But neither the United States nor any State shall assume or pay any debt or obligation incurred in aid of insurrection or rebellion against the United States, or any claim for the loss emancipation of any slave; but all such debts, obligations and claims ..... shall be held illegal and void. 14th amend.	14TH			84
DEBTS. No State shall... make any Thing but gold and silver Coin a Tender in Payment of Debts;	1	10	1	71
DEBTS. All Debts contracted and Engagements entered into, before the (.9 ..... Adoption of this Constitution, shall be as valid against the United States under this Constitution, as under the Confederation.	6		1	76
DEBTS of the United States. (See Taxes.)				
DECEMBER. The Congress shall assemble at least once in every Year, and such Meeting shall be on the first Monday in December, unless they shall by Law appoint a different Day. (See January.)	1	4	2	67

TERM / DESCRIPTION	DOC	ART.	SEC.	CL.	PG
DEFENCE. (See Common Defence.)					
DELAWARE. First Representation.		4	2	3	66
DELAWARE. Delegates sign the Constitution.					77
DELEGATED. The powers not delegated to the United States by the Constitution, nor prohibited by it to the States, are reserved to the States respectively, or to the people. 10th amend.	10TH				82
DELIVERED up. (See Fugitive.)					
DELIVERY. (See Liquors.)					
DEMAND. (See Fugitive.)					
DENIED or Abridged. But when the right to vote . . . is denied to any of the male inhabitants of such State, being twenty-one years of age, and citizens of the United States, or in any way abridged, except for participation in rebellion, or other crime, the basis of representation therein shall be reduced in the proportion which the number of such male citizens shall bear to the whole number of male citizens twenty-one years of age in such State. 14th amend.	14TH				84
DENIED or Abridged. The right of citizens of the United States to vote shall not be denied or abridged by the United States or by any State on account of race, color, or previous condition of servitude. 15th amend.	15TH				85
DENIED or abridged. The right of citizens of the United States to vote shall not be denied or abridged by the United States or by any State on account of sex. 19th amend.	19TH				86
DEPARTMENT. The Congress shall have Power... To make all Laws which shall be necessary and proper for carrying into Execution the fore-going Powers, and all other Powers vested by this Constitution in the Government of the United States, or in any Department or Officer thereof.		1	8	18	70
DEPARTMENTS. The President . . . may require the Opinion, in writing, of the principal Officer in each of the executive Departments, upon any Subject relating to the Duties of their respective Offices, . . .		2	2	1	73
DEPARTMENTS. . . . . the Congress may by Law vest the Appointment of such inferior Officers, as they think proper . . . in the Heads of Departments.		2	2	2	73
[DEPENDENCIES.] (See Possession; Territory.)					
DEPRIVED. . . . . no State, without its Consent, shall be deprived of its equal Suffrage in the Senate.		5			76
DICKINSON, John. Signs the Constitution					77
DIED. (See Death.)					
DIRECT Tax. (See Tax.)					
DIRECT Taxes. (See Representatives.)					
DISABILITY. (See Death.)					
DISCIPLINING the Militia. (See Militia.)					
DISCOVERIES. (See Science.)					
DISORDERLY Behaviour. Each House may.... punish its Members for disorderly Behaviour.		1	5	2	68

DISQUALIFICATION. Judgment in Cases of Impeachment shall not ex-0 tend further than to removal from Office, and disqualification to hold rn and enjoy any Office of honor, Trust or Profit under the United States.		1	3	7	67
DISQUALIFICATION.] (See Rebellion.)					
DISTRICT. In all criminal prosecutions, the accused shall enjoy the right E to a speedy and public trial, by an impartial jury of the State and district wherein the crime shall have been committed, which district shall have been previously ascertained by law. 6th amend.	6TH				82
DISTRICT [of Columbia.] The Congress shall have Power . . . To exercise exclusive Legislation in all Cases whatsoever, over such District (not exceeding ten Miles square) as may, by Cession of particular States, and the Acceptance of Congress, becomes the Seat of the Government of the United States.		1	8	17	70
DOMESTIC Tranquility. We the People of the United States, in Order to insure domestic Tranquility . . . do ordain and establish this Constitution for the United States of America.	PRE				66
DOMESTIC Violence. The United States shall protect each [of the States] .. . on Application of the Legislature, or of the Executive (when t he Legislature cannot be convened) against domestic Violence.		4	4		75
[DOMESTIC Violence.] (See Insurrection: Rebellion)					
DUE Process of Law. . . . nor shall any person be... deprived of life, liberty, or property, without due process of law; 5th amend.	6TH				82
DUE Process of Law. . . . nor shall any State deprive any person of life, CO liberty, or property, without due process of law; 14th amend.	14TH				84
DUTIES. The Congress shall have Power To lay and collect . . . Duties, . . . uniform throughout the United States		1	8	1	69

[Page 106 part 2]

Term / Description	Doc	Art.	Sec.	Cl.	Pg
DUTIES. (See Enter.)					
DUTIES. No State shall, without the Consent of the Congress, lay any Im-posts or Duties on Imports or Exports, except what may be absolutely necessary for executing it's inspection Laws: and the net Produce of all Duties and Imposts, laid by any State on Imports or Exports, shall be for the Use of the Treasury of the United States; and all such Laws shall be subject to the Revision and Controul of the Congress.	1	10	2		71
DUTY, Export. (See Tax.)					77
DUTY of Tonnage. (See Tonnage.)					
EFFECTS. (See Searches.)					
EIGHTEENTH Amendment. . . . The eighteenth article of amendment to the Constitution of the United States is hereby repealed. 21st amend.	21ST				87
ELECTION. (See Vote.)					
[ELECTION of President and Vice President of the United States.] The Executive Power shall be vested in a President of the United States of America. He shall hold his Office during the Term of four Years, and, together with the Vice President, chosen for the same Term, be elected, as follows Each State shall appoint, in such Manner as the Legislature thereof may direct, a Number of Electors, equal to the whole Number of Senators and Representatives to which the State may be entitled in the Congress; but no Senator or Representative, or Person holding an Office of Trust or Profit under the United States, shall be appointed an Elector. The Electors shall meet in their respective States, and vote by Ballot for two Persons, of whom one at least shall not be an Inhabitant of the same State with themselves. And they shall make a List of all the Persons voted for, and of the Number of Votes for each; which List they shall sign and certify, and transmit sealed to the Seat of the Government of the United States, directed to the President of the Senate. The President of the Senate shall, in the Presence of the Senate and House of Representatives, open all the Certificates, and the Votes shall then be counted. The Person having greatest Number of Votes shall be the President, if such Number be a Majority of the whole Number of Electors appointed; and if there be more than one who have such Majority, and have equal Number of Votes, then the House of Representatives shall immediately chuse by Ballot one of them for President; and if no Person have a Majority, then from the five highest on the List the said House shall in like Manner chuse the President. But in chusing the President. the Votes shall be taken by States, the Representation from each State having one Vote ; A quorum for this Purpose shall consist of a Member or Members from two thirds of the States, and a Majority of all the States shall be necessary to a Choice. In every Case, after the Choice of the President, the Person having the greatest Number of Votes of	2	1	1-4		71

the Electors shall be the Vice President. But if there should remain two or more who have equal Votes, the Senate shall chuse from them by Ballot the Vice President.

The Congress may determine the Time of chusing the Electors, and the Day on which they shall give their Votes; which Day shall be same throughout the United States. (See continuance.)

The Electors shall meet in their respective states and vote by ballot for President and Vice-President, one of whom, at least, shall not be an inhabitant of the same state with themselves ; they shall name in their ballots the person voted for as President, and in distinct ballots the per-son voted for as Vice-President, and they shall make distinct lists of all persons voted for as President, and of all persons voted for as Vice-President, and of the number of votes for each, which lists they shall sign and certify, and transmit sealed to the seat of the government of the United States, directed to the President of the Senate :— The President of the Senate shall, in the presence of the Senate and House of Representatives, open all certificates and the votes shall then be counted ;—The per-son having the greatest number of votes for President, shall be the President, if such number be a majority of the whole number of Electors appointed ; and if no person have such majority, then from the per-sons having the highest numbers not exceeding three on the lists of those voted for as President, the House of Representatives shall choose immediately, by ballot, the President. But in choosing the President, the votes shall be taken by states, the representation from each state having one vote ; a quorum for this purpose shall consist of a member or members from two-thirds of the states, and a majority of all the states shall be necessary to a choice. And if the House of Representatives shall not choose a President whenever the right of choice shall devolve upon them. before the fourth day of March next following, then the Vice-President shall act as President, as in the case of the death or other constitutional disability of the President.—The person having the greatest number of votes as Vice-President, shall be the Vice-President, if such number be a majority of the whole number of the Electors appointed, and if no person have a majority, then from the two highest numbers on the list, the Senate shall choose the Vice-President ; a quorum for the purpose shall consist of two-thirds of the whole number of Senators, and a majority of the whole number shall

TERM / DESCRIPTION	DOC	ART.	SEC.	CL.	PG
be necessary to a choice. But no person constitutionally ineligible to the office of President shall be eligible to that of Vice-President of the United States. 12th amend.	12TH				86
If, at the time fixed for the beginning of the term of the President, the President elect shall have died, the Vice President elect shall become President. If a President shall not have been chosen before the time fixed for the beginning of his term, or if the k resident elect shall have failed to qualify, then the Vice President elect shall act as President until a President shall have qualified ; and the Congress may by law provide for the case wherein neither a President elect nor a Vice President elect shall have qualified, declaring who shall then act as President, or the manner in which one who is to act shall be selected, and such person shall act accordingly until a President or Vice President shall have qualified. 20th amend.	20TH				86
The Congress may by law provide for the case of the death of any of the persons from whom the House of Representatives may choose a President whenever the right of choice shall have devolved upon them, and for the case of the death of any of the persons from whom the Senate may choose a Vice President whenever the right of choice shall have devolved upon them. 20th amend.	20TH				86
[ELECTION of Representatives.] The House of Representatives shall be composed of Members chosen every second Year by the People of the several States, and the Electors in each State shall have the Qualifications requisite for Electors of the most numerous Branch of the State Legislature.		1	2	1	66
[ELECTION of Representatives.] (See Vacancies.)					
[ELECTION of Senators.] The Senate of the United States shall be com-posed of two Senators from each State, chosen by the Legislatures thereof, for six Years ; and each Senator shall have one Vote. (See next title.)		1	3	1	67
[ELECTION of Senators.] The Senate of the United States shall be com-posed of two Senators from each State, elected by the people thereof, for six years; and each Senator shall have one vote. The electors in each State shall have the qualifications requisite for electors of the most numerous branch of the State legislatures. . . This amendment shall not be so construed as to affect the election or term of any Senator chosen before it becomes valid as part of the Constitution. 17th amend.	17TH				85
ELECTIONS. The Times, Places and Manner of holding Elections for Senators and Representatives, shall be prescribed in each State by the Legislature thereof ; but the Congress may at any time by Law make or alter each Regulations, except as to the Places of chusing Senators.		1	4	1	67
ELECTIONS. Each House shall be the Judge of the Elections, Returns and Qualifications of its own Members, . . .		1	5	1	68

ELECTOR. (See Rebellion.)				
ELECTORS of President and Vice President. (See Election of President and Vice President.)				
[EMINENT Domain.] (See Private Property.)				
EMOLUMENT. . . . no Person holding any Office of Profit or Trust under them [the United States], shall, without the Consent of the Congress, accept of any present, Emolument, Office, or Title, of any kind whatever, from any King, Prince, or foreign State.	1	9	8	71
EMOLUMENTS. No Senator or Representative shall, during the Time for which he was elected, be appointed to any civil Office under the Authority of the United States, which shall have been created, or the Emoluments whereof shall have been encreased during such time.	1	6	2	68
ENEMIES. (See Treason.)				
ENGAGEMENTS. (See Debts.)				
ENTER. . . . nor shall Vessels bound to, or from, one State, be obliged to enter, clear, or pay Duties in another.	1	9	6	71
ENUMERATION. The actual Enumeration [of the people] shall be made within three Years after the first Meeting of the Congress of the United States, and within every subsequent Term of ten Years, in such Manner as they shall by Law direct	1	2	3	64
ENUMERATION. No Capitation, or other direct, Tax shall be laid, unless in Proportion to the Census or Enumeration herein before directed to be taken. (See next title.)	1	9	4	71
ENUMERATION. The Congress shall have power to lay and collect taxes on incomes, from whatever source derived, without apportionment among the several States, and without regard to any census or enumeration. 16th amend.	16TH			85
ENUMERATION. The enumeration in the Constitution, of certain rights, shall not be construed to deny or disparage others retained by the people. 9th amend.	9TH			82
EQUAL Protection of the Laws. No State shall . . . deny to any person within its jurisdiction the equal protection of the laws. 14th amend.	14TH			84

[Page 108 part 2]

TERM / DESCRIPTION	DOC	ART.	SEC.	CL.	PG
EQUAL Suffrage. . . . no State, without its Consent, shall be deprived of its equal Suffrage in the Senate.	5				76
EQUITY. (See Judicial Power.)					
ESTABLISH. (See Ordain.)					
ESTABLISH Justice. We the People of the United States, in Order to . . . establish Justice. . . do ordain and establish this Constitution for the United States of America. - Preamble	PRE				66
ESTABLISHMENT of Religion. Congress shall make no law respecting an establishment of religion, or prohibiting the free exercise thereof; . . . 1st amend.	1ST				81
ESTABLISHMENT of this Constitution. The Ratification of the Conventions of nine States shall be sufficient for the Establishment of this Constitution between the States so ratifying the Same.	1				76
EXCEPTIONS. (See Supreme Court.)					
EXCISES. (See Taxes.)					
EXCLUSIVE Legislation. (See District of Columbia.)					
EXECUTE. (See Laws.)					
EXECUTIVE. (See President)					
EXECUTIVE [of any State]. . . . if Vacancies happen [in the Senate] by Resignation, or otherwise, during the Recess of the Legislature of any State, the Executive thereof may make temporary Appointments until the next Meeting of the Legislature, which shall then fill such vacancies	1	3	2		67
EXECUTIVE [of any State]. The United States shall guarantee to every State in this Union a Republican Form of Government, and shall protect each of them against Invasion ; and on Application of the Legislature, or of the Executive (when the Legislature cannot be convened) against domestic Violence	4	4			75
EXECUTIVE Authority. When vacancies happen in the Representation from any State [in the House], the Executive Authority thereof shall issue Writs of Election to fill such Vacancies.	1	2	4		66
EXECUTIVE Authority. When vacancies happen in the representation of any State in the Senate. the executive authority of such State shall issue writs of election to fill such vacancies: Provided. That the legislature of any State may empower the executive thereof to make temporary appointments until the people fill the vacancies by election as the legislature may direct. 17th amend.	17TH				85
EXECUTIVE Authority. A Person charged in any State with Treason, Felony, or other Crime, who shall flee from Justice, and be found in another State. shall on Demand of the executive Authority of the State from which he fled, be delivered up, to be removed to the State having Jurisdiction of the Crime.	4	2	2		75
EXECUTIVE Departments. (See Departments.) EXECUTIVE Officers. . . . all executive . . . Officers, both of the United States and of the several States. shall be bound by Oath or Affirmation, o to support this Constitution;	6	3			76

EXECUTIVE Power. The executive Power shall be vested in a President of the United States of America.		2	1	1	71
EXPEL. Each House may . . . with the Concurrence of two-thirds, expel a Member.		1	5	2	68
EXPENDITURES. . . . a regular Statement and Account of the Receipts 0 and Expenditures of all public Money shall be published from time to time.		1	9	7	71
[EXPENDITURES.] (See Appropriations.)					
EXPORT TAX.] No Tax or Duty shall be laid on Articles exported from any State.		1	9	5	70
EXPORTATION. (See Liquors.)					
EXPORTS. No State shall, without the Consent of the Congress, lay any cu o Imposts or Duties on Imports or Exports. except what may be absolutely necessary for executing it's inspection Laws: and the net Produce of all Duties and Imposts, laid by any State on Imports or Exports, shall be for the Use of the Treasury of the United States ; and all such Laws shall be subject to the Revision and Controul of the Congress.		1	10	2	71
EX POST FACTO Law. No . . . ex post facto Law shall be passed.		1	9	3	70
EX POST FACTO Law. No State shall pass any ex post facto Law.		1	10	1	71
[EXTRADITION.] (See Fugitive.)					
EXTRAORDINARY Occasions. [The President] . . . may, on extraordinary Occasions, convene both Houses, or either of them,		2	3		73
FACT. (See Law and Fact.)					
FACT. . . . no fact tried by a jury, shall be otherwise re-examined in any Court of the United States, than according to the rules of the common law. 7th amend.	7TH				82
FAITH. (See Credit.)					
FELONIES. (See Piracies.)					

[Page 109 part 2]

Term / Description	Doc	Art.	Sec.	Cl.	Pg
FELONY. (See Arrest ; Crime; Fugitive.)					
[FEMALE] Citizens. (See Sex.)					
FEW, William. Signs the Constitution.					77
FINES. (See Bail.)					
FITZSIMONS, Thomas. Signs the Constitution.					77
FOREIGN Coin. The Congress shall have Power . . . To coin Money, regulate the Value thereof, and of foreign Coin...		1	8	5	69
FOREIGN Nations. The Congress shall have Power . . . To regulate Commerce with foreign Nations.		1	8	3	69
FOREIGN POWER. No State shall, without the Consent of Congress. . . enter into any Agreement or Compact with another State, or with a foreign Power.		1	10	3	71
[FOREIGN Relations.] (See President of the United States, Powers and Duties.)					
FOREIGN State. (See King.) FOREIGN State. The Judicial Power of the United States shall not be construed to extend to any suit in law or equity, commenced or prosecuted against one of the United States by Citizens of another State, or By Citizens or Subjects of any Foreign State. 11th amend.	11TH				82
FOREIGN States. The judicial Power shall extend to all Cases .... between a State, or the Citizens thereof, and foreign States, Citizens or Subjects.		3	2	1	74
FORFEITURE. The Congress shall have Power to declare the Punishment of Treason, but no Attainder of Treason shall work Corruption of Blood, or Forfeiture except during the Life of the Person attained.		3	3	2	74
FORTS. The Congress shall have Power . . . To exercise exclusive Legislation in all Cases whatsoever, . . . over all Places purchased by the Con-sent of the Legislature of the State in which the Same shall be, for the Erection of Forts, Magazines, Arsenals, dock-Yards, and other needful Buildings .		1	8	17	70
FRANKLIN, Benjamin. Signs the Constitution.					77
FREE State. A well regulated Militia, being necessary to the security of a free State, the right of the people to keep and bear Arms, shall not be infringed. 2nd amend.	2ND				81
[FREEDOM of Speech.] (See Debate.)					
FREEDOM of Speech or of the Press. Congress shall make no law abridging freedom of speech, or of the press. 1st amend.	1ST				81
[FUGITIVE from Justice.] A Person charged in any State with Treason, Felony, or other Crime, who shall flee from Justice, and be found in another State, shall on Demand of the executive Authority of the State from which he fled, he delivered up, to be removed to the State having Jurisdiction of the Crime.		4	2	2	75
[FUGITIVE Slaves.] No Person held to Service or Labour in one State, under the Laws thereof, escaping into another, shall, in Consequence of any Law or Regulation therein, be discharged from such Service or Labour, but shall be delivered up on Claim of the Party to whom such Service or Labour may be due.		4	2	3	75
FULL Faith and Credit. (See Credit.)					

GENERAL LAWS. . . . the Congress may by general Laws prescribe the Manner in which such Acts, Records, and Proceedings [of other States] shall be proved, and the Effect thereof.	4	1		75
GENERAL Welfare. We the People of the United States, in Order to promote the general Welfare, . . . do ordain and establish this Constitution for the United States of America. Preamble	PRE			66
GENERAL Welfare. The Congress shall have Power To lay and collect Taxes, Duties, Imposts and Excises, to pay the Debts and provide for the common Defense and general Welfare of the United States.	1	8	1	69
GEORGIA. Delegates sign the Constitution.				77
GEORGIA. First representation.	1	2	3	66
GILMAN, Nicholas. Signs the Constitution.				77
GOLD and Silver Coin. No State shall . . . make any Thing but gold and silver Coin a Tender in Payment of Debts.	1	10	1	71
GOOD Behaviour. The Judges, both of the supreme and inferior Courts, shall hold their Offices during good Behaviour, .	3	1		74
GORHAM, Nathaniel. Signs the Constitution				77
GOVERNING the Militia. (See Militia.)				
GOVERNMENT, Form of. (See Republican.)				
GOVERNMENT, Seat of. (See District of Columbia.)				
GOVERNMENT of the United States. The Congress shall have Power . . To make all Laws which shall be necessary and proper for carrying into Execution the foregoing Powers, and all other Powers vested by this Constitution in the Government of the United States, or in any Department or office thereof	1	8	18	70

TERM / DESCRIPTION	DOC	ART.	SEC.	CL.	PG
[GOVERNOR.] (See Executive; Executive Authority.)	5				76
GRAND Jury. (See Crime.)					
ESTABLISH. (See Ordain.)					
GRANTED Powers. All legislative Powers herein granted shall be vested in a Congress of the United States, which shall consist of a Senate and Art. sec. cl. pg. House of Representatives. (See Reserved Powers.)		1	1		66
GRANTS of States. The judicial Power shall extend to all Cases. . between Citizens of the same State claiming Lands under Grants of different States.		3	2	1	74
GRIEVANCES. (See Petition)					
GUARANTEE. The United States shall guarantee to every State in this Union a Republican Form of Government.		4	4		75
HABEAS Corpus. The Privilege of the Writ of Habeas Corpus shall not be suspended, unless when in Cases of Rebellion or Invasion the public Safety may require it.		1	9	2	70
HAMILTON, Alexander. Signs the Constitution.					77
HEADS of Departments. (See Departments.)					
HIGH Crimes and Misdemeanors. (See Impeachment.)					
HIGH Seas. (See Piracies.)					
HONOR. (See Office.)					
HOUSE. No Soldier shall, in time of peace be quartered in any house, without the consent of the Owner, nor in time of war, but in a manner to be prescribed by law. 3rd amend.	3RD				81
HOUSE of Representatives. All legislative Powers herein granted shall be vested in a Congress of the United States, which shall consist of a Senate and House of Representatives.		1	1		66
HOUSE of Representatives. The House of Representatives shall be com-posed of Members chosen every second Year by the People of the several States, and the Electors in each State shall have the Qualifications requisite for Electors of the most numerous Branch of the State Legislature.		1	2	1	66
HOUSE of Representatives. The House of Representatives shall chuse their Speaker and other Officers; and shall have the sole Power of Impeachment.		1	2	5	66
HOUSE of Representatives. All Bills for raising Revenue shall originate in the House of Representatives; but the Senate may propose or concur with Amendments as on other Bills.		1	7	1	68
HOUSE of Representatives. The Person having the greatest Number of Votes shall be the President, if such Number be a Majority of the whole Number of Electors appointed ; and if there be more than one who have such Majority, and have an equal Number of Votes, when the House of Represent-atives shall immediately chuse by Ballot one of them for President ; and if no Person have a Majority, then from the five highest on the list the said House shall in like Manner chuse the President. But in chusing the President, the Votes shall be taken by States, the Representation from each State having		2	1	3	72

one Vote ; A quorum for this Purpose shall consist of a Member or Members from two thirds of the States, and a Majority of all the States shall be necessary to a Choice. (See next title.)				
HOUSE of Representatives.. . . if no person have such majority [of the 0- -6 electorial votes for President of the United States], then from the persons m a) 0. having the highest numbers not exceeding three on the list of those voted 6_ a) for as President, the House of Representatives shall choose immediately, -a by ballot, the President. But in choosing the President, the votes shall E be taken by states, the representation from each state having one vote; a quorum for this purpose shall consist of a member or members from o cu u two-thirds of the states, and a majority of all the states shall be necessary to a choice. And if the House of Representatives shall not choose a w a President whenever the right of choice shall devolve upon them, before • o the fourth day of March next following, then the Vice-President shall act as President, as in the case of the death or other constitutional disability of the President. 12th amend.	12TH			83
HOUSE of Representatives. The Congress may by law provide for the case of the death of any of the persons from whom the House of Representatives may choose a President whenever the right of choice shall have devolved upon them. 20th amend.	20TH			86
HOUSE of Representatives, Members of. (See Representatives.)				
HOUSE of Representatives and Senate. (See Congress.)				
HOUSES. (See Searches.)				
[IMMIGRATION.] (See Commerce				
IMMUNITIES. (See Privileges.)				
IMMUNITIES of Members of Congress.] (See Arrest ; Debate.)				

[Page 111 part 2]

Term / Description	Doc	Art.	Sec.	Cl.	Pg
IMPEACHMENT. The House of Representatives . . . shall have the sole Power of Impeachment	1	2	5		67
IMPEACHMENT. The Senate shall have the sole Power to try all Impeachments. When sitting for that Purpose, they shall be on Oath or Affirmation. When the President of the United States is tried, the Chief Justice shall preside: And no Person shall be convicted without the Concurrence of two thirds of the Members present. Judgment in Cases of Impeachment shall not extend further than to removal from Office, and disqualification to hold and enjoy any Office of honor, Trust or Profit under the United States: but the Party convicted shall nevertheless be liable and subject to Indictment, Trial, Judgment and Punishment, according to Law.	1	3	6		67
IMPEACHMENT. The President... shall have Power to grant Reprieves and Pardons for Offences against the United States, except in Cases of Impeachment.	1	3	7		67
IMPEACHMENT. The President, Vice President and all civil Officers of the United States, shall be removed from Office on Impeachment for, and Conviction of, Treason, Bribery, or other high Crimes and Misdemeanors.	2	4			73
IMPEACHMENT. The Trial of all Crimes, except in Cases of Impeachment, shall be by Jury;	3	2	3		74
IMPLIED Powers.] The Congress shall have Power . . . To make all Laws which shall be necessary and proper for carrying into Execution the foregoing Powers, and all other Powers vested by this Constitution in the Government of the United States, or in any Department or Officer thereof.	1	8	18		70
[IMPORTATION. (See Slave Trade.)					
IMPORTATION. (See Liquors.)					
IMPOSTS. (See Duties; Taxes.)					
INABILITY. (See Death.)					
INCOME. (See Taxes.)					
INDIAN Tribes. The Congress shall have Power . . . To regulate Commerce . . . with the Indian Tribes ; . . .	1	8	3		69
INDICTMENT. . . . the Party convicted [following impeachment] shall nevertheless be liable and subject to Indictment, Trial, Judgment and Punishment, according to Law.	1	3	7		67
INDICTMENT. No person shall be held to answer for a capital, or other-wise infamous crime, unless on a presentment or indictment of a Grand Jury, except in cases arising in the land or naval forces, or in the Militia, when in actual service in time of War or public danger ; . . . 5th amend.	5TH				81
INFAMOUS Crime. (See Crime.)					
INFERIOR Courts. (See Judicial Power.)					
INFERIOR Officers. (See Appointments.)					
INGERSOLL, Jared. Signs the Constitution.					77

INHABITANT. No Person shall be a Representative . . . who shall not, when elected, be an Inhabitant of that State in which he shall be chosen.	1	2	2	66
INHABITANT. No Person shall be a Senator . . . who shall not, when elected, be an Inhabitant of that State for which he shall be chosen.	1	3	3	67
INHABITANT. The Electors shall meet in their respective States, and vote by Ballot for two Persons [for President], of whom one at least, shall not be an Inhabitant of the same State with themselves. (See next title.)	2	1	3	71
INHABITANT. The Electors shall . . . vote by ballot for President and Vice-President, one of whom, at least, shall not be an inhabitant of the same state with themselves; 12th amend.	12TH			83
[INHABITANT.] (See Reside; Resident.)				
INOPERATIVE. (See Seven Years.)				
INSPECTION. No State shall, without the Consent of the Congress, lay any Imposts or Duties on Imports or Exports, except what may be absolutely necessary for executing it's inspection Laws.	1	10	2	71
INSURRECTION. (See Debt ; Domestic Violence; Invasions; Rebellion.				
INTERNAL Improvements.] (See Commerce; Post Roads.)				
[INTERNAL Revenue.] (See Taxes.)				
[INTERNATIONAL Law.] (See Law of Nations)				
[INTERSTATE] Agreement. (See Agreement.)				
[INTERSTATE Comity.] (See Credit.)				
[INTERSTATE] Commerce. (See Commerce.)				
INTOXICATING Liquors. (See Liquors.)				
INVADED. No State shall, without the Consent of Congress, engage in War, unless actually invaded, or in such imminent Danger as will not admit of delay.	1	10	3	71
INVASION. The Privilege of the Writ of Habeas Corpus shall not be suspended, unless when in Cases of Rebellion or Invasion the public Safety may require it.	1	9	2	70

[Page 112 part 2]

TERM / DESCRIPTION	DOC	ART.	SEC.	CL.	PG
INVASION. The United States . . . shall protect each [State]... against Invasion;	4	4			75
INVASIONS. The Congress shall have Power . . . To provide for calling forth the Militia to execute the Laws of the Union, suppress Insurrections and repel Invasions;	1	8		15	70
INVENTORS. (See Science.)					
JACKSON, William. Secretary of Constitutional Convention, attests interlineations.					76
JANUARY. The terms of the President and Vice President shall end at noon on the 20th day of January, and the terms of Senators and Representatives at noon on the 3d day of January, of the years in which such terms would have ended if this article had not been ratified; and the terms of their successors shall then begin. 20th amend.	20TH				86
JANUARY. The Congress shall assemble at least once in every Year, and such meeting shall begin at noon on the 3d day of January, unless they shall by law appoint a different day. 20th amend.	20TH				86
JENIFER, Daniel of St. Thomas. Signs the Constitution.					77
JEOPARDY. . . nor shall any person be subject for the same offence to be twice put in jeopardy of life or limb, . . . 5th amend.	5TH				82
JOHNSON, William Samuel. Signs the Constitution.					77
JOURNAL. Each House shall keep a Journal of its Proceedings, and from time to time publish the same, excepting such Parts as may in their Judgment require Secrecy ; and the Yeas and Nays of the Members of either House on any question shall, at the Desire of one-fifth of those Present, be entered on the Journal	1	5	3		68
JOURNAL. (See Bill.)					
JUDGES. The Judges, both of the supreme and inferior Courts, shall hold their Offices during good Behaviour, and shall, at stated Times, receive for their Services, a Compensation, which shall not be diminished during their Continuance in Office.	3	1		74	
JUDGES. This Constitution, and the Laws of the United States which shall be made in Pursuance thereof; and all Treaties made, or which shall be made, under the Authority of the United States, shall be the supreme Law of the Land; and the Judges in every State shall be bound thereby, any Thing in the Constitution or Laws of any State to the Contrary notwithstanding.	6		2		76
JUDGES of the Supreme Court. (See Appointments.)					
JUDGMENT in Cases of Impeachment. (See Impeachment.)					
JUDICIAL Officers. . . . all . . . judicial Officers, both of the United States and of the several States, shall be bound by Oath or Affirmation, to support this Constitution;	6		3		76

JUDICIAL Power. The judicial Power of the United States shall be vested in one supreme Court, and in such inferior Courts as the Congress may from time to time ordain and establish. . . .	3	1		74
The judicial Power shall extend to all Cases, in Law and Equity, arising under this Constitution, the Laws of the United States, and Treaties made, or which shall be made, under their Authority ;—to all Cases affecting Ambassadors, other public Ministers and Consuls ;—to all Cases of admiralty and maritime Jurisdiction ;—to Controversies to which the United States shall be a Party ;—to Controversies between two or more States ;—between a State and Citizens of another State ;—between Citizens of different States,—between Citizens of the same State claiming Lands under Grants of different States, and between a State, or the Citizens thereof, and foreign States, Citizens or Subjects. (See title below.) ...	3	2	1	74
In all Cases affecting Ambassadors, other public Ministers and Consuls, and those in which a State shall be Party, the supreme Court shall have original Jurisdiction. In all the other Cases before mentioned, the supreme Court shall have appellate Jurisdiction, both as to Law and Fact, with such Exceptions, and under such Regulations as the Congress shall make.	3	2	2	74
JUDICIAL Power. The Judicial power of the United States shall not be construed to extend to any suit in law or equity, commenced or prosecuted against one of the United States by Citizens of another State, or by Citizens or Subjects of any Foreign State. 11th amend.	11TH			82
JUDICIAL Proceedings. (See Acts.)				
[JUDICIARY.] (See Courts ; Judicial ; Jurisdiction ; Supreme Court.)				
JURISDICTION. A Person charged in any State with Treason, Felony, or other Crime, who shall flee from Justice, and be found in another State, shall on Demand of the executive Authority of the State from which he fled, be delivered up, to be removed to the State having Jurisdiction of the Crime.	4	2	2	75
JURISDICTION. ... . no new State shall be formed or erected within the Jurisdiction of any other State;	4	3	1	75

[Page 113 part 2]

TERM / DESCRIPTION	DOC	ART.	SEC.	CL.	PG
JURISDICTION. . . . nor shall any State. . . deny to any person within its jurisdiction the equal protection of the laws 14th amend.	14TH				84
JURISDICTION. (See Liquors.)					
JURISDICTION of the Supreme Court. (See Supreme Court.)					
JURY. The Trial of all Crimes, except in Cases of Impeachment, shall be by Jury ;		3	2	3	74
JURY. (See Criminal Prosecutions.)					
JURY. (See Common Law.)					
JUSTICE. We the People of the United States, in Order to ... establish Justice.... do ordain and establish this Constitution for the United States of America. Preamble	PRE				64
JUSTICE. (See Fugitive.)					
KING, Rufus. Signs the Constitution.					77
KING, Prince, or Foreign State. No Title of Nobility shall be granted by the United States: And no Person holding any Office of Profit of Trust under them, shall, without the Consent of the Congress, accept of any present, Emolument, Office, or Title, of any kind whatever, from any King, Prince, or foreign State.		1	9	8	71
LABOUR. (See Fugitive Slaves.)					
[LAND.] (See Captures; Forts; Grants; Territory.)					
LAND and Naval Forces. The Congress shall have Power . . . To make Rules for the Government and Regulation of the land and naval Forces ;		1	8	14	70
[LAND Forces.] (See Armies; Army; Militia.)					
LANDS. The judicial Power shall extend to all Cases... between Citizens of the same State claiming Lands under Grants of different States.		3	2	1	74
LANGDON, John. Signs the Constitution.					77
LAW. (See Congress.)					
LAW The Senators and Representatives shall receive a Compensation for their Services, to be ascertained by Law, and paid out of the Treasury of the United States.		1	6	1	68
LAW. No Money shall be drawn from the Treasury, but in Consequence of Appropriations made by Law.		1	9	7	71
LAW. No Soldier shall, in time of peace be quartered in any house, without the consent of the Owner, nor in time of war, but in a manner to be prescribed by law. 3rd amend.	3RD				81
LAW. In all criminal prosecutions, the accused shall enjoy the right to a speedy and public trial, by an impartial jury of the State and district o wherein the crime shall have been committed, which district shall have been previously ascertained by law, . . . 6th amend.	6TH				82
LAW. The validity of the public debt of the United States, authorized by law, including debts incurred for payment of pensions and bounties for services in suppressing insurrection or rebellion, shall not be questioned._ 14th amend.					84

LAW. No State shall make or enforce any law which shall abridge the privileges or immunities of citizens of the United States. 14th amend.	14TH				84
LAW. . . . the Party convicted [following impeachment] shall nevertheless be liable and subject to Indictment, Trial, Judgment and Punishment, according to Law.	1	3	7	67
LAW. (See Common; Contracts; Due Process ; Ex Post Facto.)				
LAW Supreme. (See Supreme Law.)				
LAW and Equity. (See Judicial Power.)				
LAW and Fact. In all the other Cases before mentioned, the supreme Court -a in c = shall have appellate Jurisdiction, both as to Law and Fact, with such Exceptions, and under such Regulations as the Congress shall make.	3	2	2	74
LAW of Nations. The Congress shall have Power . . . To define and punish Piracies and Felonies committed on the high Seas, and Offences -- against the Law of Nations. 1 8 10 69	1	8	10	69
LAWS. [The President] . . . shall take Care that the Laws be faithfully -executed . . .	2	3		73
LAWS. Full Faith and Credit shall be given in each State to the public a _c Acts, Records, and judicial Proceedings of every other State. And the Congress may by general Laws prescribe the Manner in which such Acts, Records and Proceedings shall be proved, and the Effect thereof.	4	1		75
LAWS. No State shall . . . deny to any person within its jurisdiction a) al the equal protection of the laws 14th amend.	14TH				84
LAWS. The transportation or importation into any State, Territory, or possession of the United States for delivery or use therein of intoxicating liquors, in violation of the laws thereof, is hereby prohibited. 21st amend.	21ST				87

[Page 114 part 2]

Term / Description	Doc	Art.	Sec.	Cl.	Pg
LAWS, Necessary and Proper. (See Implied Powers.)					
LAWS of Any State. This Constitution, and the Laws of the United States which shall be made in Pursuance thereof; and all Treaties made, or which shall be made, under the Authority of the United States, shall be the supreme Law of the Land; and the Judges in every State shall be bound thereby. any Thing in the Constitution or Laws of any State to the Contrary notwithstanding.	6			2	76
LAWS of the Union. The Congress shall have Power . . . To provide for calling forth the Militia to execute the Laws of the Union, . . .	1	8		15	70
LAWS of the United States. The judicial Power shall extend to all Cases, in Law and Equity, arising under this Constitution, the Laws of the United States, and Treaties made, or which shall be made, under their Authority.	3	2		1	74
LEGAL] Tender. (See Tender.)					
[LEGISLATIVE POWERS. All legislative Powers herein granted shall be vested in a Congress of the United States,.	1	1			66
[LEGISLATURE, National.] (See Congress.)					
LEGISLATURE, State. The House of Representatives shall be composed of Members chosen every second Year by the People of the several States, and the Electors in each State shall have the Qualifications requisite for Electors of the most numerous Branch of the State Legislature.	1	2		1	66
LEGISLATURE, State. The Senate of the United States shall be composed of two Senators from each State, chosen by the Legislature thereof, for six Years; ... (See 17th amend.)	17TH				85
LEGISLATURE, State. . . . if Vacancies happen [in the Senate] by Resignation, or otherwise, during the Recess of the Legislature of any State, the Executive thereof may make temporary Appointments until the next Meeting of the Legislature, which shall then fill such Vacancies. (See next title.)	1	3		2	67
LEGISLATURE, State. When vacancies happen in the representation of any State in the Senate, the executive authority of such State shall issue writs of election to fill such vacancies: Provided, That the legislature of any State may empower the executive thereof to make temporary appointments until the people fill the vacancies by election as the legislature may direct. 17th amend.	17TH				85
LEGISLATURE, State. The Times, Places and Manner of holding Elections for Senators and Representatives, Shall be prescribed in each State by the Legislature thereof ; but the Congress may at any time by Law make or alter such Regulations, except as to the Places of chusing Senators. (See 17th amend.)	1	4		1	67
LEGISLATURE, State. The United States shall guarantee to every State in this Union a Republican Form of Government,	4	4			75

and shall protect o each of them against Invasion; and on Application of the Legislature, or of the Executive (when the Legislature cannot be convened) against domestic Violence.				
LEGISLATURES, State. New States may be admitted by the Congress into this Union ; but no new State shall be formed or erected within, the Jurisdiction of any other State; nor any State be formed by the Junction of two or more States, or Parts of States, without the Consent of the Legislatures of the States concerned as well as of the Congress.	4	3	1	75
LEGISLATURES, State. (See Amendments ; Seven Years.)				
LEGISLATURES, State. the Members of the several State Legislatures, shall be bound by Oath or Affirmation, to support this Constitution;	6		3	76
LEGISLATURES, State. The electors [of Senators] in each State shall have the qualifications requisite for electors of the most numerous branch of the State legislatures. 17th amend.	17TH			85
LETTERS of Marque and Reprisal. The Congress shall have Power To declare War, grant Letters of Marque and Reprisal.	1	8	11	70
LETTERS of Marque and Reprisal. No State shall grant Letters of Marque and Reprisal.	1	10	1	71
LIBERTY. We the People of the United States, in Order to . . . secure the Blessings of Liberty to ourselves and our Posterity, do ordain and establish this Constitution for the United States of America. Preamble	PRE			66
LIBERTY. (See Life.) LIFE, Liberty, or Property. . . . nor shall any person be .. . Deprived of life, liberty, or property, without due process of law; . . . 5th amend.	5TH			82
LIFE, Liberty, or Property. No State shall . . . deprive any person of life, liberty, or property, without due process of law; . . . 14th amend.	14TH			84
, LIFE or Limb. . . . nor shall any person be subject for the same offence to be twice put in jeopardy of life or limb, ... 5th amend.	5TH			82
LIMB. (See Life or Limb.)				

[Page 115 part 2]

TERM / DESCRIPTION	DOC	ART.	SEC.	CL.	PG
[LIMITATION on the Ratification of Amendments.] (See Seven Years.)					
[LIMITED Powers.] All legislative Powers herein granted shall be vested in a Congress.		1	1		66
[LIMITED Powers.] The powers not delegated to the United States by the Constitution, nor prohibited by it to the States, are reserved to the States respectively, or to the people. 10th amend.	10TH				82
LIQUORS. After one year from the ratification of this article the manufacture, sale, or transportation of intoxicating liquors within, the importation thereof into, or the exportation thereof from the United States and all territory subject to the jurisdiction thereof for beverage purposes is hereby prohibited. 18th amend.	18TH				85
LIQUORS. The eighteenth article of amendment to the Constitution of the United States is hereby repealed. 21st amend.	21ST				87
The transportation or importation into any State, Territory, or possession of the United States for delivery or use therein of intoxicating liquors, in violation of the laws thereof, is hereby prohibited. 21st amend.	21ST				87
LIVINGSTON, William. Signs the Constitution					77
McHENRY, James.. Signs the Constitution					77
MADISON, James. Signs the Constitution					77
MAGAZINES. (See Forts.)					
MAJORITY. (See Quorum.)					
MAJORITY. The Person having the greatest Number of [electoral] Votes shall be the President, if such Number be a Majority of the whole Number of Electors appointed ; and if there be more than one who have such Majority, and have an equal Number of Votes, then the House of Representatives shall immediately chuse by Ballot one of them for President ; and if no Person have a Majority, then from the five highest on the List—the said House shall in like Manner chuse the President. But . . . the Votes shall be taken by States, the Representation from each State having one Vote; . . . and a Majority of all the States shall be necessary to a Choice. (See next title.)		2	1	3	72
MAJORITY. The person having the greatest number of [electoral.] votes for President, shall be the President, if such number be a majority of the whole number of Electors appointed ; and if no person have such majority, then from the persons having the highest numbers not exceed-ing three on the list of those voted for as President, the House of Representatives shall choose immediately, by ballot, the President. But in choosing the President, the votes shall be taken by states, the	12TH				83

representation from each state having one vote; . . . and a majority of all the states shall be necessary to a choice. . . . The person having the greatest number of votes as Vice-President, shall be the Vice-President, if such number be a majority of the whole number of Electors appointed, and if no person have a majority, then from the two highest numbers on the list, the Senate shall choose the Vice-President ; a quorum for the purpose shall consist of two-thirds of the whole number of Senators, and a majority of the whole number shall be necessary to a choice. 12th amend.				
[MALE] Citizens. (See Vote.)				
MANUFACTURE. (See Liquors.)				
MARITIME Jurisdiction. (See Admiralty.)				
MARYLAND. First representation	1	2	3	66
MARYLAND. Delegates sign the Constitution.				77
MARQUE and Reprisal. (See Letters.)				
MASSACHUSETTS. First representation.	1	2	3	66
MASSACHUSETTS. Delegates sign the Constitution.				77
MEASURES. (See Weights and Measures.)				
MEASURES. [The President] . . . shall from time to time give to the Congress Information of the State of the Union, and recommend to their Consideration such Measures as he shall judge necessary and expedient.	2	3		73
MEETING. The Congress shall assemble at least once in every Year, and such Meeting shall be on the first Monday in December, unless they shall by Law appoint a different Day. (See next title.)	1	4	2	67
MEETING. The Congress shall assemble at least once in every year, and such meeting shall begin at noon on the 3d day of January, unless they shall by law appoint a different day. 20th amend.				86
[MEETING.] (See Adjourn.)				
[MEETING.] [The President]. . . may, on extraordinary Occasions, convene both Houses, or either of them.	2	3		73

[Page 116 part 2]

TERM / DESCRIPTION	DOC	ART.	SEC.	CL.	PG
MEMBERS of the House of Representatives. (See Representatives.)					
MEMBERS of the Senate. (See Senators.)					
[MESSAGES.] (See Measures.)					
MIFFLIN, Thomas. Signs the Constitution					77
MIGRATION. (See Slave Trade.)					
MILITIA. The Congress shall have Power . . . To provide for calling forth the Militia to execute the Laws of the Union, suppress Insurrections and repel Invasions.		1	8	15	70
MILITIA. The Congress shall have Power . . . To provide for organizing, arming, and disciplining. the Militia, and for governing such Part of them as may be employed in the Service of the United States, reserving: to the States respectively, the Appointment of the Officers, and the Authority of training the Militia according to the discipline prescribed by Congress.		1	8	16	70
MILITIA. The President shall be Commander in Chief of the Army and Navy of the United States, and of the Militia of the several States, when called into the actual Service of the United States.		2	2	1	73
MILITIA. A well regulated Militia, being necessary to the security of a free State, the right of the people to keep and bear Arms, shall not be infringed. 2nd amend.	2ND				81
Militia... No person shall be held to answer for a capital, or otherwise infamous crime, unless on a presentment or indictment of a Grand Jury, except in cases arising in the land or naval forces, or in the Militia, when in actual service in time of War or public danger. 5th emend.	5TH				81
MINISTERS, public. (See Ambassadors.)					
MISDEMEANORS. (See Impeachment.)					
MONEY. The Congress shall have Power . . . To borrow Money on the credit of the United States ; . . .		1	8	2	69
MONEY. The Congress shall have Power . . . To coin Money, regulate the Value thereof, and of foreign Coin.		1	8	5	69
MONEY. The Congress shall have Power ... To raise and support Armies, but no Appropriation of Money to that Use shall be for a longer Term than two Years.		1	8	12	70
MONEY. No Money shall be drawn from the Treasury, but in Consequence of Appropriations made by Law ; and a regular Statement and Account of the Receipts and Expenditures of all public Money shall be published from time to time..		1	9	7	71
MONEY. No State shall . . . coin Money		1	10	1	71
[MONEY.] (See Coin ; Counterfeiting.)					
MORRIS, Gouverneur. Signs the Constitution.					
MORRIS, Robert. Signs the Constitution.					
[NAMES.] (See Yeas and Nays.)					
NATURAL Born Citizen. No Person except a natural born Citizen, or a Citizen of the United States, at the time of the		2	1	5	72

Adoption of this Constitution, shall be eligible to the Office of President.				
NATURALIZATION. The Congress shall have Power . . . To establish an uniform Rule of Naturalization, . . . 1 8 4 69	1	8	4	69
NATURALIZED. All persons born or naturalized in the United States, and subject to the jurisdiction thereof, are citizens of the United States and of the State wherein they reside. 14th amend.	14TH			84
NAVAL Forces. The Congress shall have Power . . . To make Rules for the Government and Regulation of the land and naval Forces.	1	8	14	70
NAVAL Forces. No person shall be held to answer for a capital, or otherwise infamous crime, unless on a presentment or indictment of a Grand Jury, except in cases arising in the land or naval forces, 5th amend.	5TH			82
[NAVIGATION.] (See Commerce; Enter.)				
NAVIGATION Laws.] (See Commerce ; Duties ; Export Tax ; Exports.)	1	8	13	70
NAVY. The Congress shall have Power . . . To provide and maintain a Navy.				
[NAVY.] (See Ships of War.)				
NAVY. The President shall be Commander in Chief of the Army and Navy of the United States.	2	2	1	73
NECESSARY and Proper. (See Implied Powers.)				
NEW HAMPSHIRE. First representation. 1 2 3 66	1	2	3	66
NEW HAMPSHIRE. Delegates sign the Constitution.				77
NEW JERSEY. First Representation. 1 2 3 66	1	2	3	66
NEW YORK. First Representation. 1 2 3 66	1	2	3	66
NEW YORK. Delegates sign the Constitution.				77

[Page 117 part 2]

TERM / DESCRIPTION	DOC	ART.	SEC.	CL.	PG
NINE States. (See Ratification of the Constitution.)					
NOBILITY. No Title of Nobility shall be granted by the United States.		1	9	8	71
NOBILITY. No State shall . . . grant any Title of Nobility.		1	10	1	71
NOMINATE. (See Appointments)					
NORTH CAROLINA. First representation		1	2	3	66
CAROLINA. Delegates sign the Constitution.					77
LIVINGSTON, William. Signs the Constitution					77
OATH. No person shall be a Senator or Representative in Congress, or elector of President and Vice President, or hold any office, civil or military, under the United States, or under any State, who, having previously taken an oath, as a member of Congress, or as an officer of the United States, or as a member of any State legislature, or as an executive or judicial officer of any State, to support the Constitution of the United States, shall have engaged in insurrection or rebellion against the same, or given aid or comfort to the enemies thereof. But Congress may by a vote of two-thirds of each House, remove such disability 14th amend.	14TH				84
OATH or Affirmation. The Senate shall have the sole Power to try all Impeachments. When sitting for that Purpose, they shall be on Oath or Affirmation.		1	3	6	67
OATH or Affirmation. The Senators and Representatives before mentioned, and the Members of the several State Legislatures, and all executive and judicial Officers, both of the United States, and of the several States, shall be bound by Oath or Affirmation, to support this Constitution.		6		3	76
OATH or Affirmation. . . . no Warrants shall issue, but upon probable cause, supported by Oath or affirmation... 4th amend.	4TH				81
OATH or Affirmation of the President of the United States. Before he enter on the Execution of his Office, he shall take the following Oath or Affirmation:—"I do solemnly swear (or affirm) that I will faithfully execute the Office of President of the United States, and will to the best of my Ability, preserve, protect and defend the Constitution of the United States."		2	1	8	76
OBJECTIONS of the President to bills. (See Bills.)					
OBLIGATION of Contracts. (See Contracts)					
OCCASIONS. (See Extraordinary Occasions.)					
OCTOBER. Sections 1 and 2 shall take effect on the 15th day of October following the ratification of this article. 20th amend.	20TH				87

OFFENCE. . . . nor shall any person be subject for the same offence be twice put in jeopardy of life or limb, . . . 6th amend.	6ᵀᴴ			82
OFFENCES. The Congress shall have Power . . . To define and punish Piracies and Felonies committed on the high Seas, and Offences against the Law of Nations.	1	8	10	69
OFFENCES. The President . . . shall have Power to grant Reprieves and Pardons for Offences against the United States, except in Cases of Impeachment.	2	2	1	73
OFFICE. Judgment in Cases of Impeachment shall not extend further E1/11 than to removal from Office, and disqualification to hold and enjoy any in Office of honor, Trust or Profit under the United States.	1	3	7	67
OFFICE. No Senator or Representative shall, during the Time for which he was elected. be appointed to any civil Office under the Authority of the United States, which shall have been created, or the Emoluments whereof shall have been encreased during such time; and no Person holding any Office under the United States, shall be a Member of either House during his Constitution in Office.	1	6	2	68
OFFICE. . . . no Person holding any Office of Profit or Trust under [the United States] . . . shall, without the Consent of the Congress, accept of any present, Emolument, Office, or Title, of any kind whatever, from any King, Prince, or foreign State. 1 9 8 71 _c 3 .6.,	1	9	8	71
OFFICE. . . . no Senator or Representative, or Person holding an Office of Trust or Profit under the United States, shall be appointed an Elector.	2	1	2	71
OFFICE, Civil or Military. (See Oath.)				
OFFICERS. The House of Representatives shall chuse their Speaker and any other Officers.	1	2	5	66
OFFICERS. The Senate shall chuse their other Officers, and also a President pro tempore.	1	3	5	66
OFFICERS. . . . all executive and judicial Officers, both of the United States and of the several States, shall be bound by Oath or Affirmation to support this Constitution;	6		3	76

[Page 118 part 2]

TERM / DESCRIPTION	DOC	ART.	SEC.	CL.	PG
OFFICERS [of the Militia.] (See Militia.)					
OFFICERS of the United-States. The President, Vice President and all civil Officers of the United States, shall be removed from Office on Impeachment for, and Conviction of, Treason, Bribery, or other high Crimes and Misdemeanors.	2	4			73
[OFFICERS of the United States.] (See Appointments; Departments; Disqualification; Judges; Qualifications.)					
ONE FIFTH. . . . the Yeas and Nays of the Members of either House on any question shall, at the Desire of one fifth of those Present, be entered on the Journal.— 1 5 3 68	1	5	3		68
OPINION. The President . . . may require the Opinion, in writing, of the principal Officer in each of the executive Departments, upon any Subject relating to the Duties of their respective Offices, . . . 2 1 73	1	2	1		73
ORDAIN. We the People of the United States. . . . do ordain and establish this Constitution for the United States of America. . . Preamble.	PRE				66
ORDAIN. The judicial Power of the United States shall be vested in one supreme Court, and in such inferior Courts as the Congress may from time to time ordain and establish.	3	1			74
ORDER. Resolution, or Vote. Every Order, Resolution, or Vote to which the Concurrence of the Senate and House of Representatives may be necessary (except on a question of Adjournment) shall be presented to the President of the United States; and before the Same shall take Effect, shall be approved by him, or being disapproved by him, shall be re-passed by two thirds of the Senate and House of Representatives, according to the Rules and Limitations prescribed in the case of a Bill. (See Bill.)	1	7	3		69
ORIGINAL jurisdiction. In all Cases affecting Ambassadors, other public Ministers and Consuls, and those in which a State shall be Party, the supreme Court shall have original Jurisdiction.	3	2	2		74
ORIGINATE. All Bills for raising Revenue shall originate in the House of Representatives.	1	7	1		68
OVERT Act. (See Treason.)					
OWNER. No Soldier shall, in time of peace be quartered in any house, without the consent of the Owner, nor in time of war, but in a manner to be prescribed by law. 3rd amend.	3RD				81
[PAPER MONEY.] (See Bills of Credit ; Gold.)					
PAPERS. (See Searches.)					
PARDONS. The President . . . shall have Power to grant Reprieves and Pardons for Offences against the United States, except in Cases of Impeachment.	2	2	1		73
[PARLIAMENTARY] Rules. (See Rules.)					
[PATENTS.] (See Science.)					
PATERSON, William. Signs the Constitution.					77
PAY the Debts. (See Taxes.)					
[PEACE.] (See Treaties.)					

PEACE, Breach of. (See Arrest.)				
PEACE, in Time of. No State shall, without the Consent of Congress, keep Troops, or Ships of War in time of Peace.		1	10	3	71
PEACE, in Time of. No Soldier shall, in time of peace be quartered in any house, without the consent of the Owner, . . . 3rd amend.	3RD				81
PENNSYLVANIA. First representation.		1	2	3	66
PENNSYLVANIA. Delegates sign the Constitution.					77
PENSIONS. The validity of the public debt of the United States, authorized by law, including debts incurred for payment of pensions and bounties for services in suppressing insurrection or rebellion, shall not be questioned. 14th amend.	14TH				84
PEOPLE. We the People of the United States... do ordain and establish this Constitution for the United States of America. Preamble.	PRE				66
PEOPLE. The House of Representatives shall be composed of Members, chosen every second Year by the People of the several States.		1	2	1	66
PEOPLE. Congress shall make no law . . . abridging . . . the right of the people peaceably to assemble, and to petition the Government for a redress of grievances. 1st amend.	1AT				81
PEOPLE. A well regulated Militia, being necessary to the security of a NP free State, the right of the people to keep and bear Arms, shall not be infringed. 2d amend.	2ND				81
PEOPLE. The right of the people to be secure in their persons, houses, papers, and effects, against unreasonable searches and seizures, shall not be violated.... 4th amend.	4TH				81

[Page 119 part 2]

Territory or other Property belonging to the United States; and nothing in this Constitution shall be so construed as to Prejudice any Claims of the United States, or of any particular State.				
PRESENT. .... no Person holding any Office of Profit or Trust under [the United States] ... shall, without the Consent of the Congress, accept of any present, ... from any King, Prince, or foreign State.	1	9	8	71
PRESENTMENT. No person shall be held to answer for a capital, or Ni cu otherwise infamous crime, unless on a presentment or indictment of a Grand Jury, 5th amend.	5TH			81
PRESERVE the Constitution. (See Oath.)				
PRESIDENT of the Senate. (See Senate-)				
PRESIDENT pro tempore. (See Senate.)				
PRESIDENT of the United States. The Senate shall chuse their other Officers, and also a President pro tempore, in the Absence of the Vice President, or when he shall exercise the Office of President of the United States.	1	3	5	67
PRESIDENT of the United States. When the President of the United-States is tried [following Impeachment], the Chief Justice shall preside.	1	3	6	67
PRESIDENT of the United States. (See Bill ; Order.)				
PRESIDENT of the United States. The executive Power shall be vested in a President of the United States of America. He shall hold his Office during the Term of four Years, and, together with the Vice President, chosen for the same Term, be elected, as follows ... (See Election of President and Vice President of the United States.)	2	1	1	71

[Page 120 part 2]

TERM / DESCRIPTION	DOC	ART.	SEC.	CL.	PG
No Person except a natural born Citizen, or a Citizen of the United States, at the time of the Adoption of this Constitution, shall be eligible to the Office of President; neither shall any Person be eligible to that Office who shall not have attained to the Age of thirty five Years, and been fourteen Years a Resident within the United States.		2	1	5	72
The terms of the President and Vice President shall end at noon on the 20th day of January, and the terms of Senators and Representatives at noon on the 3d day of January, of the years in which such terms would have ended if this article had not been ratified; and the terms of their successors shall then begin. 20th amend.	20TH		1		86
[In Case of the Removal of the President from Office, or of his Death, Resignation, or Inability to discharge the Powers and Duties of the said Office, the Same shall devolve on the Vice President, and the Congress may by law provide for the Case of Removal, Death, Resignation or Inability, both of the President and Vice President, declaring what Officer shall then act as President, and such Officer shall act accordingly, until the Disability be removed, or a President shall be elected. _		2	1	6	72
The President shall, at stated Times, receive for his Services, a Compensation, which shall neither be encreased nor diminished during the Period for which he shall have been elected, and he shall not receive within that Period any other Emolument from the United States, or any of them.		2	1	7	72
Before he enter on the Execution of his Office, he shall take the following Oath or Affirmation :—"I do solemnly swear (or affirm) that I will faithfully execute the Office of President of the United States, and will to the best of my Ability, preserve, protect and defend the Constitution of the United States."		2	1	8	73
PRESIDENT of the United States, Powers and Duties:— The President shall be Commander in Chief of the Army and Navy of the United States, and of the Militia of the several States, when called into the actual Service of the United States ; he may require the Opinion, in writing, of the principal Officer in each of the executive Departments, upon any Subject relating to the Duties of their respective Offices, and he shall have Power to grant Reprieves and Pardons for Offences against the United States, except in Cases of Impeachment.		2	2	1	73
He shall have Power, by and with the Advice and Consent of the Senate, to make Treaties, provided two thirds of the Senators present concur ; and he shall nominate, and by and with the Advice and Consent of the Senate, shall appoint Ambassadors, other public Ministers and Consuls, Judges of the supreme Court, and all other Officers of the United States, whose Appointments are not herein otherwise provided for, and which shall be established by Law ; but the Congress may by Law vest the Appointment of such inferior Officers, as they		2	2	2	73

think proper, in the President alone, in the Courts of Law, or in the Heads of Departments.				
The President shall have Power to fill up all Vacancies that may happen during the Recess of the Senate, by granting Commissions which shall expire at the end of their next Session.	2	2	3	73
He shall from time to time give to the Congress Information of the State of the Union, and recommend to their Consideration such Measures as he shall judge necessary and expedient ; he may, on extraordinary Occasions, convene both Houses, or either of them, and in Case of Dis-agreement between them, with Respect to the Time of Adjournment, he may adjourn them to such Time as he shall think proper ; he shall receive Ambassadors and other public Ministers ; he shall take Care that the Laws be faithfully executed, and shall Commission all the Officers of the United States.	2	3		73
PRESIDENT of the United States. The President, Vice President and all civil Officers of the United States, shall be removed from Office on Impeachment for, and Conviction of, Treason, Bribery, or other high Crimes and Misdemeanors	2	4		73
[PRESIDENTIAL Succession.] (See Death.)				
PRESS. (See Freedom.)				
PRINCE. (See King.)				
PRINCIPAL Officer. The President . . . may require the Opinion, in writing, of the principal Officer in each of the executive Departments, upon any Subject relating to the Duties of their respective Offices.	2	2	1	73
PRIVATE Property. . . . nor shall private property be taken for public use, without just compensation. 5th amend.	5TH			82
[PRIVATEERING.] (See Letters of Marque.)				
PRIVILEGE. (See Habeas Corpus.)				
PRIVILEGED. The Senators and Representatives shall . . . be privileged e. from Arrest during their Attendance at the Session of their respective Houses, and in going to and returning from the same.	1	6	1	68
PRIVILEGES and Immunities. The Citizens of each State shall he entitled to all Privileges and Immunities of Citizens in the several States.	4	2	1	75
PRIVILEGES or Immunities. No State shall make or enforce any law which shall abridge the privileges or immunities of citizens the of the United States. 14th amend.	14TH			84

TERM / DESCRIPTION	DOC	ART.	SEC.	CL.	PG
PRIZES.] (See Captures.)					
[PROBABLE Cause. (See Searches and Seizure.)					
PROCEEDINGS. (See Rules.)					
PROCEEDINGS. (See Journals.)					
PROCEEDINGS. (See Acts.)					
PROCESS. (See Compulsory.)					
PROFIT. (See Office.)					
PROHIBITED. (See Liquors.)					
PROHIBITED Powers. The powers not delegated to the United States by this Constitution, nor prohibited by it to the States, are reserved to the States respectively, or to the people. (See State.) 10th amend.	10TH				82
PROPERTY. (See Life.)					
PROPERTY. (See Private Property.)					
[PROPERTY of the United States.] (See Forts.)					
PROPERTY of the United States. The Congress shall have Power to dispose of and make all needful Rules and Regulations respecting the Territory or other Property belonging to the United States.		4	3	2	75
PROSECUTIONS. (See Criminal Prosecutions.)					
PROTECT. The United States shall guarantee to every State in this Union a Republican Form of Government, and shall protect each of them against Invasion ; . . . 4 4 — 75		4	4		75
PROTECT the Constitution. (See Oath.)					
PROTECTION. No State shall . . . deny to any person within its jurisdiction the equal protection of the laws. 14th amend.	14TH				84
[PUBLIC Debts.] (See Debt ; Debts ; Taxes.)					
[PUBLIC Land.] (See Territory.)					
PUBLIC Ministers. (See Ambassadors.)					
PUBLIC Safety. The Privilege of the Writ of Habeas Corpus shall not he suspended, unless when in Cases of Rebellion or Invasion the public Safety may require it.		1	9	2	70
PUBLIC Trust. (See Office.)					
PUBLIC Use. (See Private Property.)					
PUBLISHED. . . a regular Statement and Account of the Receipts and Expenditures of all public Money shall be published from time to time.		1	9	7	71
PUNISH. Each House may . . . punish its Members for disorderly Behaviour.		1	5	2	68
PUNISHMENT. (See Counterfeiting ; Impeachment ; Treason.)					
PUNISHMENTS. (See Bail					
QUALIFICATIONS. (See Election.)					
[QUALIFICATIONS.] (See Disqualification ; President ; Representative; (Senator ; Vice President ; Vote.)					
QUARTERED. No Soldier shall, in time of peace be quartered in any o r-. o house, without the consent of the	3RD				81

Owner, nor in time of war, but in a manner to be prescribed by law. 3d amend.				
QUESTIONED. The Senators and Representatives . . . for any Speech or Debate in either House shall not be questioned in any other Place.	1	6	1	68
QUESTIONED. The validity of the public debt of the United States, E authorized by law, . . . shall not be questioned. 14th amend.	14TH			84
QUORUM. . . . a Majority of each [House] shall constitute a Quorum to do Business • but a smaller Number may adjourn from day to day, and may be authorized to compel the Attendance of absent Members, in such Manner, and under such Penalties as each House may provide.	1	5	1	65
QUORUM. (See Election of President and Vice President.)				
RACE. The right of citizens of the United States to vote shall not be denied or abridged by the United States or by any State on account of color, race, race color or previous condition of servitude. 15th amend.	15TH			85
RATIFICATION of Amendments to the Constitution. (See Amendments.)				
[RATIFICATION of Amendments, Limitation on.] (See Seven Years.)				
RATIFICATION of the Constitution. The Ratification of the Conventions of nine States, shall be sufficient for the Establishment of this Constitution between the States so ratifying the Same.	7			76
REBELLION. The Privilege of the Writ of Habeas Corpus shall not be suspended, unless when in Cases of Rebellion or Invasion the public Safety may require it.	1	9	2	70
REBELLION. No person shall be a Senator or Representative in Congress, or Elector of President and Vice President, or hold any office, civil or military, under the United States, or under any State, who, having previously				

[Page 122 part 2]

TERM / DESCRIPTION	DOC	ART.	SEC.	CL.	PG
taken an oath, as a member of Congress, or as an officer of the United States, or as a member of any State legislature, or as an executive or judicial officer of any State, to support the Constitution of the United States, shall have engaged in insurrection or rebellion against the same, or given aid or comfort to the enemies thereof. But Congress may by a vote of two-thirds of each House, remove such disability. 14th amend.	14TH				84
REBELLION. (See Debt of the United States.)					
RECEIPTS and Expenditures. . . . a regular Statement and Account of the Receipts and Expenditures of all public Money shall be published from time to time .	12	9	7		71
[RECESS.] (See Adjourn.)					
RECESS of the Senate. The President shall have Power to fill up all Vacancies that may happen during the Recess of the Senate, by granting Commissions which shall expire at the End of their next Session.	2	2	3		73
[RECOGNITION of Foreign Nations.] (See Ambassadors.)					
RECOMMEND. [The President.] . . . shall from time to time give to the Congress Information of the State of the Union, and recommend to their Consideration such Measures as he shall judge necessary and expedient.	2	3			73
RECONSIDER a Bill. (See Bill.)					
RECORDS. (See Acts.)					
REDRESS of Grievances. (See Petition.)					
REGULATIONS. (See Supreme Court.)					
RELIGION. Congress shall make no law respecting an establishment of religion, or prohibiting the free exercise thereof. 1st amend.	1ST				
RELIGIOUS Test. . . . no religious Test shall ever be required as a Qualification to any Office or Public Trust under the United States.	6		3		76
[REMOVAL.] (See Expel.)					
REMOVED from Office. The President, Vice President and all civil Officers of the United States, shall be removed from Office on Impeachment for, and Conviction of, Treason, Bribery, or other high Crimes and Misdemeanors. 2 4 — 73	2	4			73
REPEALED. The eighteenth article of amendment to the Constitution of the United States is hereby repealed. 21st amend.	21ST				87
[REPRESENTATION.] (See Representatives.)					
REPRESENTATIVE. No Person shall be a Representative who shall not have attained to the Age of twenty five Years, and been seven Years a Citizen of the United States, and who shall not, when elected, be an Inhabitant of that State in which he shall be chosen.	1	2	2		66
REPRESENTATIVE. No . . . Representative shall, during the Time for which he was elected, be appointed to any civil Office under the Authority of the United States, which shall	1	6	2		68

have been created, or the o Emoluments whereof shall have been encreased during such time; and no Person holding any Office under the United States, shall be a Member of either House during his Continuance in Office				
REPRESENTATIVE.... no ... Representative ... shall be appointed an Elector.	2	1	2	71
REPRESENTATIVE. (See Rebellion.)				
REPRESENTATIVES. Representatives and direct Taxes shall be apportioned among the several States which may be included within this Union, according to their respective Numbers, which shall be determined by adding to the whole Number of free Persons, including those bound to 1/11 Service for a Term of Years, and excluding Indians not taxed, three fifths of all other Persons. The actual Enumeration shall be made within three Years after the first Meeting of the Congress of the United States, and within every subsequent Term of ten Years, in such Manner as they shall be Law direct. The Number of Representatives shall not exceed one for every thirty Thousand, but each State shall have at Least one Representative; and until such enumeration shall be made, the State of New Hampshire shall be entitled to chuse three, Massachusetts eight, Rhode-Island and Providence Plantations one, Connecticut five, New-York six, New Jersey four, Pennsylvania eight, Delaware one, Maryland six, Virginia ten, North Carolina five, South Carolina five, and Georgia three. (See next title.)	1	2	3	66
REPRESENTATIVES. Representatives shall be apportioned among the several States according to their respective numbers, counting the whole number of persons in each State, excluding Indians not taxed. But a -- c when the right to vote at any election... is denied to any of the male inhabitants of such State, being twenty-one years of age, and citizens of the United States, or in any way abridged, except for participation in rebellion, or other crime, the basis of representation therein shall be reduced in the proportion which the number of such male citizens shall bear to the whole number of male citizens twenty-one years of age in such State. 14th amend.	14TH			84

[Page 123 part 2]

TERM / DESCRIPTION	DOC	ART.	SEC.	CL.	PG
REPRESENTATIVES. The Times, Places and Manner of holding Elections for . . . Representatives, shall be prescribed in each State by the Legislature thereof; but the Congress may at any time by Law make or alter such Regulations.		1	4	1	67
REPRESENTATIVES. The . . . Representatives shall receive a Compensation for their Services, to be ascertained by Law, and paid out of the Treasury of the United States. They shall in all Cases, except Treason, Felony and Breach of the Peace, be privileged from Arrest during their Attendance at the Session of their [House] . . ., and in going to and returning from the same ; and for any Speech or Debate in either House, they shall not be questioned in any other Place.		1	6	1	68
REPRESENTATIVES. The . . . Representatives . . . shall be bound by Oath or Affirmation, to support this Constitution.		6		3	76
REPRESENTATIVES. The terms of [Representatives]. . . shall end at noon on the . . . 3rd day of January, of the years in which such terms would have ended if this article had not been ratified ; and the terms of their successors shall then begin. 20th amend.	20TH				86
REPRESENTATIVES, House of. (See House of Representatives.)					
REPRIEVES. (See Pardons.)					
REPRISAL. (See Letters of Marque.)					
REPUBLICAN. The United States shall guarantee to every State in the Union a Republican Form of Government.		4	4		75
RESERVED Powers. The powers not delegated to the United States by this Constitution, nor prohibited by it to the States, are reserved to the States respectively, or to the people. 10th amend.	10TH				82
RESIDE. All persons born or naturalized in the United States, or subject to the jurisdiction thereof, are citizens of the United States and of the State wherein they reside. 14th amend.	14TH				84
[RESIDE.] (See Inhabitant.)					
RESIDENT. No Person . . . shall be eligible to the Office of President . . . who shall not have . . . been fourteen Years a Resident within the United States.		2	1	5	72
RESIGNATION. (See Death.)					
RESOLUTION. (See Order.)					
RETAINED Rights. The enumeration in the Constitution, of certain rights, shall not be construed to deny or disparage others retained by the people. 9th amend.	9TH				82
RETURNS. (See Elections.)					
REVENUE. All Bills for raising Revenue shall originate in the House of Representatives; but the Senate may propose or concur with Amendments as on other Bills.		1	7	1	68

REVENUE. No Preference shall be given by any Regulation of Commerce or Revenue to the Ports of one State over those of another:		1	9	6	70
[R E V E N U E.] (See Receipts.)					
RHODE ISLAND. First representation		1	2	3	66
RIGHTS. The enumeration in the Constitution, of certain rights, shall not be construed to deny or disparage others retained by the people. 9th amend.	9TH				82
ROADS. (See Post Offices.)					
RULES. Each House may determine the Rules of its Proceedings.		1	5	2	68
RULES. The Congress shall have Power . . . To . . . make Rules concerning Captures on Land and Water.		1	8	11	70
RULES. The Congress shall have Power . . . To make Rules for the Government and Regulation of the land and naval Forces.		1	8	14	70
RUTLEDGE, John. Signs the Constitution.					77
SAFETY. (See Public Safety.)					
[SALARY.] (See Compensation.)					
SALE. (See Liquors.)					
SCIENCE and Useful Arts. The Congress shall have Power promote the Progress of Science and useful Arts, by securing for limited Times to Authors and Inventors the exclusive Right to their respective Writings and Discoveries.		1	8	8	69
SEARCHES and Seizures. The right of the people to be secure in their persons, houses, papers, and effects, against unreasonable searches and seizures, shall not be violated, and no Warrants shall issue, but upon probable cause, supported by Oath or affirmation, and particularly describing the place to be searched, and the persons or things to be seized. 4th amend.	4TH				81
SEAT of the Government. (See District of Columbia.)					
SECRECY. Each House shall keep a Journal of its Proceedings, and from time to time publish the same, excepting such Parts as may in their Judgment require Secrecy.		1	5	3	68

[Page 124 part 2]

TERM / DESCRIPTION	DOC	ART.	SEC.	CL.	PG
[SECURITIES.] (See Credit.)					
SECURITIES. (See Counterfeiting.)					
SEIZURES. (See Searches and Seizures.)					
[SENATE. All legislative Powers herein granted shall be vested in a Congress of the United States, which shall consist of a Senate and House of Representatives.		1	1		66
SENATE. The Senate of the United States shall be composed of two Senators from each State, chosen by the Legislature thereof, for six Years; and each Senator shall have one Vote.		1	3	1	67
Immediately after they shall be assembled in Consequence of the first Election, they shall be divided as equally as may be into three Classes. The Seats of the Senators of the first Class shall be vacated at the Expiration of the second Year, of the second Class at the Expiration of the fourth Year, and of the third Class at the Expiration of the sixth Year, so that one third may be chosen every second Year ; and if Vacancies happen by Resignation, or otherwise, during the Recess of the Legislature of any State, the Executive thereof may make temporary Appointments until the next Meeting of the Legislature, which shall then fill such Vacancies. (See next title.)		1	3	2	67
SENATE. The Senate of the United States shall be composed of two Senators from each State, elected by the people thereof, for six years ; and each Senator shall have one vote. The electors in each State shall have the qualifications requisite for electors of the most numerous branch of the State legislatures. 17th amend.	17TH				85
When vacancies happen in the representation of any State in the Senate, the executive authority of such State shall issue writs of election to fill such vacancies: Provided, That the legislature of any State may empower the executive thereof to make temporary appointments until the people fill the vacancies by election as the legislature may direct. 17th amend.	17TH				85
SENATE. The Vice President of the United States shall be President of the Senate. but shall have no Vote, unless they be equally divided		1	3	4	67
SENATE. The Senate shall chuse their other Officers, and also a President pro tempore, in the Absence of the Vice President, or when he shall exercise the Office of President of the United States.		1	3	5	67
SENATE. The Senate shall have the sole Power to try all Impeachment.		1	3	6	61
SENATE. (See Congress ; Senators.)					
SENATE. All Bills for raising Revenue shall originate in the House of Representatives but the Senate may propose or concur with Amendments as on other Bills. 1 7 1 68		1	7	1	68
SENATE. (See Election of President and Vice President.)					
SENATE. [The President] . . . shall have Power, by and with the Advice and Consent of the Senate, to make Treaties, provided two thirds of the Senators present concur; and he		2	2	2	73

shall nominate, and by and with the Advice and Consent of the Senate, shall appoint Ambassadors, other public Ministers and Consuls, Judges of the supreme Court, and all other Officers of the United States, whose Appointments are not herein otherwise provided for, and which shall be established by Law : but the Congress may by Law vest the Appointment of such inferior Officers, as they think proper, in the President alone, in the Courts of Law, or in the Heads of Departments.				
The President shall have Power to fill up all Vacancies that may happen during the Recess of the Senate, by granting Commissions which shall expire at the End of their next Session.	2	2	3	73
SENATE. . . . no State, without its Consent, shall be deprived of it's equal Suffrage in the Senate.	5			76
[SENATE, Executive Sessions.] (See Secrecy.)				
SENATOR. . . . each Senator shall have one Vote	1	3	1	67
SENATOR. No Person shall be a Senator who shall not have attained to the Age of thirty Years, and been nine Years a Citizen of the United States, and who shall not, when elected, be an Inhabitant of that State for which he shall be chosen. 1 3 3 67	1	3	3	67
SENATOR. No Senator . . . shall, during the Time for which he was elected, be appointed to any civil Office under the Authority of the United States, which shall have been created, or the Emoluments whereof shall have been encreased during such time ; and no Person holding any Office under the United States, shall be a Member of either House during his Continuance in Office.	1	6	2	68
SENATOR. . . . no Senator . . . shall be appointed an Elector. 2 1 2 71	2	1	2	71
SENATOR. (See Rebellion.)				
SENATORS. Senators . thereof but Regulations, amend.)				
SENATORS. Services, to The Times, Places and Manner of holding Elections for Senators shall be prescribed in each State by the Legislature thereof. . . but the Congress may at any time by law make or alter such except as to the Places of chusing Senators. (See 17th amend.)	1	4	1	67
SENATORS. The Senators . . . shall receive a Compensation for their be ascertained by Law, and paid out of the Treasury of the United States.	1	6	1	68

TERM / DESCRIPTION	DOC	ART.	SEC.	CL.	PG
They shall in all Cases, except Treason, Felony and Breach of the Peace, be privileged from Arrest during their Attendance at the Session of their House—and in going to and returning from the same; and for any Speech or Debate in either House, they shall not be questioned in any other Place.		1	6	1	68
SENATORS. The Senators . . . shall be bound by Oath or Affirmation, to support this Constitution; . . .		6		3	76
SENATORS. The terms of [Senators] . . . shall end . . . at noon on the 3rd day of January, of the years in which such terms would have ended if this article had not been ratified; and the terms of their successors shall then begin. 20th amend.	20TH				86
[SERVANTS.] (See Fugitive Slaves.) SERVICE. (See Fugitive Slaves.)					
SERVICE. of the United States. The Congress shall have Power . . . To provide for organizing, arming, and disciplining, the Militia, and for governing such Part of them as may be employed in the Service of the United States.		1	8	16	70
SERVICE of the United States. The President shall be Commander in Chief . . . of the Militia of the several States, when called into the actual Service of the United States.		2	2	1	73
SERVICES. (See Compensation.)					
SERVITUDE. (See Race.)					
SERVITUDE. (See Slavery.)					
SESSION. (See Meeting.)					
SEVEN Years. This article shall be inoperative unless it shall have been ratified as an amendment to the Constitution by the legislatures of the Several States, as provided in the Constitution, within seven years from the date of the submission hereof to the States by the Congress. 18th amend.	18TH				86
SEVEN Years. This article shall be inoperative unless it shall have been ratified as an amendment to the Constitution by the legislatures of three-fourths of the several States within seven years from the date of its submission. 20th amend.	20TH				87
SEVEN Years. This article shall be inoperative unless it shall have been ratified as an amendment to the Constitution by conventions in the several States, as provided in the Constitution, within seven years from the date of the submission hereof to the States by the Congress. 21st amend.	21ST				87
SEX. The right of citizens of the United States to vote shall not be denied or abridged by the United States or by any State on account of sex. 19th amend.	19TH				86
SHERMAN, Roger. Signs the Constitution.					77
SHIPS of War. No State shall, without the Consent of Congress, . keep Troops, or Ships of War in time of Peace		1	10	3	71
[SHIPS of War.] (See Navy.)					

SIGNED by the President. (See Bill; Order.)				
SILVER. (See Gold.)				
SLAVE. But neither the United States nor any State shall assume or pay . . . any claim for the loss or emancipation of any slave; but all such . . . claims shall be held illegal and void. 14th amend.	14TH			85
[SLAVE Trade.] The Migration or Importation of such Persons as any of the States now existing shall think proper to admit, shall not be prohibited by the Congress prior to the Year one thousand eight hundred and eight, but a Tax or duty may be imposed on such Importation, not exceeding ten dollars for each Person.	1	9	1	70
[SLAVE Trade.] . . . no Amendment which may be made prior to the Year One thousand eight hundred and eight shall in any manner affect the first and fourth Clauses in the Ninth Section of the first Article.	5			76
SLAVERY. Neither slavery nor involuntary servitude, except as a punishment for crime whereof the party shall have been duly convicted, shall exist within the United States, or any place subject to their jurisdiction. 13th amend.	13TH			83
[SLAVES.] (See Fugitive Slaves.)				
SOLDIER. (See Quartered.)				
[SOLDIERS.] (See Armies.)				
SOUTH CAROLINA. First representation. 1 2 3	1	2	3	66
SOUTH CAROLINA. Delegates sign the Constitution.				77
SPAIGHT, Richard Dobbs. Signs the Constitution.				77
SPEAKER. The House of Representatives shall chuse their Speaker	1	2	5	66
SPEECH. (See Freedom.)				
STANDARD. (See Weights and Measures.)				

[Page 126 part 2]

TERM / DESCRIPTION	DOC	ART.	SEC.	CL.	PG
STATE each State shall have at Least one Representative in Congress	1	2	3		66
STATE. The Senate of the United States shall be composed of two Senators from each State.	1	3	1		67
STATE. No Preference shall be given by any Regulation of Commerce or Revenue to the Ports of one State over those of another: nor shall Vessels bound to, or from, one State, be obliged to enter, clear, or pay Duties in another.	1	9	6		70
[SENATE. All legislative Powers herein granted shall be vested in a Congress of the United States, which shall consist of a Senate and House of Representatives.	1	1			66
SENATE. The Senate of the United States shall be composed of two Senators from each State, chosen by the Legislature thereof, for six Years ; and each Senator shall have one Vote.	1	3	1		67
STATE. No State shall enter into any Treaty, Alliance, or Confederation; grant Letters of Marque and Reprisal; coin Money ; emit Bills of Credit; make any Thing but gold and silver Coin a Tender in Payment of Debts; Pass any Bill of Attainder, ex post facto Law, or Law impairing the Obligation of Contracts, or grant any Title of Nobility.	1	10	1		71
No State shall, without the Consent of the Congress, lay any Im-posts or Duties on Imports or Exports, except what may be absolutely necessary for executing it's inspection Laws: and the net Produce of all Duties and Imposts, laid by any State on Imports or Exports, shall be for the Use of the Treasury of the United States ; and all such Laws shall be subject to the Revision and Controul of the Congress-	1	10	2		71
No State shall, without the Consent of Congress, lay any Duty of Tonnage, keep Troops, or Ships of War in time of Peace, enter into any Agreement or Compact with another State, or with a foreign Power, or engage in War, unless actually invaded, or in such imminent Danger as will not admit of delay.	1	10	3		71
STATE. The judicial Power shall extend . . . to Controversies between two or more States ;—between a State and Citizens of another State ;— between Citizens of different States,— between Citizens of the same State claiming Lands under Grants of different States, and between a State, or the Citizens thereof, and foreign States, Citizens or Subjects. (See next title.)	3	2	1		74
STATE. The Judicial power of the United States shall not be construed to extend to any suit in law or equity, commenced or prosecuted against one of the United States by Citizens of another State, or by Citizens or Subjects of any Foreign State. 11th amend.	11TH				82
STATE. . . . In all Cases . . . in which a State shall be Party, the supreme Court shall have original Jurisdiction	3	3	2		74
STATE. The Trial of all Crimes, except in Cases of Impeachment, shall be by Jury; and such Trial shall be held in the State where the said Crimes shall have been committed; but when not committed within any State, the Trial shall be at	3	2	3		74

such Place or Places as the Congress may by Law have directed.				
STATE. Full Faith and Credit shall be given in each State to the public Acts, Records, and judicial Proceedings of every other State. And the Congress may by general Laws prescribe the Manner in which such Acts, Records and Proceedings shall be proved, and the Effect thereof.	4	1		75
STATE. The Citizens of each State shall be entitled to all Privileges and Immunities of Citizens in the several States.	4	2	1	75
STATE. (See Fugitive.)				
STATE. The Congress shall have Power to dispose of and make all Rules and Regulations respecting the Territory or other Property belonging to the United States; and nothing in this Constitution shall be so construed as to Prejudice any Claims of the United States, or of any particular State.	4	3	2	75
STATE. The United States shall guarantee to every State in this Union m a Republican Form of Government, and shall protect each of them against Invasion; and on Application of the Legislature, or of the El Executive (when the Legislature cannot be convened) against domestic Violence.	4	4		75
STATE. . . . no State, without its Consent, shall be deprived of it's equal Suffrage in the Senate.	5			75
STATE. This Constitution, and the Laws of the United States which shall be made in Pursuance thereof ; and all Treaties made, or which shall be made, under the Authority of the United States, shall be the supreme Law of the Land ; and the Judges in every State shall be bound thereby, and Thing in the Constitution or Laws of any State to the Contrary notwithstanding.	6		2	76
STATE. In all criminal prosecutions, the accused shall enjoy the right to a speedy and public trial, by an impartial jury of the State and district wherein the crime shall have been committed. .. 6th amend.	6TH			82
STATE. All persons born or naturalized in the United States, and subject to the jurisdiction thereof, are citizens of the United States and of a -- c the State wherein they reside. No State shall make or enforce any law which shall abridge the privileges or immunities of citizens of the United States; nor shall any State deprive any person of life, liberty, or property without due process of law ; nor deny to any person within its jurisdiction the equal protection of the laws- 14th amend.	14TH			84
STATE. The right of citizens of the United States to vote shall not be denied or abridged by the United States or by any State on account of race, color, or previous condition of servitude. 13th amend.	13TH	1		85

[Page 127 part 2]

Term / Description	Doc	Art.	Sec.	Cl.	Pg
STATE. The right of citizens of the United States to vote shall not be denied or abridged by the United States or by any State on account of sex. 19th amend.	19TH				86
STATE. The transportation or importation into any State. Territory, or possession of the United States for delivery or use therein of intoxicating liquors, in violation of the laws thereof, is hereby prohibited.	21ST				87
STATE Legislature. (See Legislature; Legislatures.)					
STATEMENT. (See Accounts.)					
STATES. The House of Representatives shall be composed of Members chosen every second Year by the People of the several States.	1	2	1		66
STATES. Representatives and direct Taxes shall be apportioned among the several States. (See Representatives.)	1	2	3		66
STATES. The Congress shall have Power...To regulate Commerce . . . among the several States.	1	8	3		69
STATES. The Congress shall have Power . . . To provide for organizing, arming, and disciplining, the Militia, and for governing such Part of them as may be employed in the Service of the United States, reserving to the States respectively, the Appointment of the Officers, and the Authority of training the Militia according to the discipline prescribed by Congress.	4	8	1		75
STATES. The Congress shall have Power . . . To provide for organizing, arming, and disciplining, the Militia, and for governing such Part of them as may be employed in the Service of the United States, reserving to the States respectively, the Appointment of the Officers, and the Authority of training the Militia according to the discipline prescribed by Congress.	1	8	16	70	
STATES. (See Slave Trade.)					
STATES. New States may be admitted by the Congress into this Union ; but no new State shall be formed or erected within the Jurisdiction of any State ; nor any State be formed by the Junction of two or more States, or Parts of States, without the Consent of the Legislatures of the States concerned as well as of the Congress.	4	3	1		75
STATES. (See Amendments ; Seven Years.)					
STATES. . . . the Members of the several State Legislatures, and all executive and judicial Officers, . . . of the several States, shall be bound by Oath or Affirmation, to support this Constitution.	6		3		76
STATES. (See Ratification of the Constitution.)					
STATES. The powers not delegated to the United States by the Constitution, nor prohibited by it to the States, are reserved to the States respectively, or to the people. 10th amend.	10TH				82

STATES. The Congress shall have power to lay and collect taxes on incomes, from whatever source derived, without apportionment among the several States, and without regard to any census or enumeration. 16th amend.	16TH			85
STATES. The Congress and the several States shall have concurrent power to enforce this article by appropriate legislation. 18th amend.	18TH			85
SUBJECTS. (See Foreign State; Foreign States.)				
[SUBPENA.] (See Compulsory Process.)				
[SUCCESSION to the Presidency.] (See Death.)				
SUFFRAGE. . . . no State, without its Consent, shall be deprived of its equal Suffrage in the Senate.	5			76
[SUFFRAGE.] (See Vote.)				
SUITS at Common Law. (See Common Law.)				
SUITS in Law or Equity. (See Judicial Power.)				
SUNDAYS excepted. (See Bill.)				
SUPPORT this Constitution. (See Oath.)				
SUPREME COURT. The judicial Power of the United States, shall be vested in one supreme Court, and in such inferior Courts as the Congress may from time to time ordain and establish. The Judges, both of the supreme and inferior Courts, shall hold their Offices during good Behaviour, and shall, at stated Times, receive for their Services, a Compensation, which shall not be diminished during their Continuance in Office.	3	1		74
SUPREME COURT. In all Cases affecting Ambassadors, other public Ministers and Consuls, and those in which a State shall be Party, the supreme Court shall have original Jurisdiction. In all the other Cases before mentioned, the supreme Court shall have appellate Jurisdiction, both as to Law and Fact, with such Exceptions, and under such Regulations as the Congress shall make.	3	2	2	74
SUPREME COURT, Judges of. (See Appointments.)				
SUPREME Law of the Land. This Constitution, and the Laws of the United States which shall be made in Pursuance thereof ; and all Treaties made, or which shall be made, under the Authority of the United States, shall be the supreme Law of the Land ; and the Judges in every State shall be bound thereby, any Thing in the Constitution or Laws of any State to the Contrary notwithstanding.	6		2	76

TERM / DESCRIPTION	DOC	ART.	SEC.	CL.	PG
[TARIFF.] (See Duties.)					
TAX. No Capitation, or other direct, Tax shall be laid, unless in Proportion to the Census or Enumeration herein before directed to be taken. (See 16th amendment.)		1	9	4	70
TAX. No Tax or Duty shall be laid on Articles exported from any State.		1	9	5	70
TAX. (See Duties; Slave Trade.)					
TAXES. Representation and direct Taxes. (See Representatives.)					
TAXES. The Congress shall have Power To lay and collect Taxes, Duties, Imposts and Excises, to pay the Debts and provide for the common Defence and general Welfare of the United States.		1	8	1	69
TAXES. The Congress shall have power to lay and collect taxes on incomes, from whatever source derived, without apportionment among the several States, and without regard to any census or enumeration... 16th amend.	16TH				85
TENDER. No State shall . . . make any Thing but gold and silver Coin a Tender in Payment of Debts.		1	10	1	71
[TERM] of Judges. The Judges, both of the supreme and inferior Courts, shall hold their Offices during good Behaviour,		3	1		74
[TERM] of Representatives. The House of Representatives shall be com-posed of Members chosen every second Year by the People of the several States.		1	2	1	66
[TERM] of Senators. The Senate of the United States shall be com-posed of two Senators from each State, chosen . . . • for six Years.		1	3	1	67
TERM of the President and Vice President. . . . [The] President . . . shall hold his Office during the Term of four Years—with the Vice President, chosen for the same Term.		2	1	1	71
[TERMS.] (See Impeachment; Removal.)					
TERMS. The terms of the President and Vice President shall end at noon on the 20th day of January, and the terms of Senators and Representatives at noon on the 3rd day of January, of the years in which such terms would have ended if this article had not been ratified; and the terms of their successors shall then begin. 20th amend.	20TH				86
[TERRITORIES.] (See Territory.)					
TERRITORY. The Congress shall have Power to dispose of and make all needful Rules and Regulations respecting the Territory or other Property belonging to the United States.		4	3	2	75
TERRITORY. After one year from the ratification of this article the manufacture, sale, or transportation of intoxicating liquors within, the importation thereof into, or the exportation thereof from the United States and all territory subject to the jurisdiction thereof for beverage purposes is hereby prohibited. (See 21st amend.) 18th amend.	18TH		1		85
TERRITORY. The transportation or importation into any State, Territory, or possession of the United States for	21ST		2		87

delivery or use therein of intoxicating liquors, in violation of the laws thereof, is hereby prohibited. 21st amend.				
TEST. (See Religious.)				
TESTIMONY. (See Treason; Witness; Witnesses.)				
THINGS. (See Searches.)				
THREE FOURTHS. (See Amendments.)				
TITLE of Nobility. (See Nobility.)				
TONNAGE. No State shall, without the Consent of Congress, lay any Duty of Tonnage.	1	10	3	71
[TONNAGE.] (See Enter.)				
[TRAFFIC.] (See Commerce.)				
[TRADEMARK.] (See Commerce				
TRAINING the Militia. (See Militia.)				
TRANQUILITY. (See Domestic.)				
[TRANSPORTATION.] (See Commerce				
TRANSPORTATION. (See Liquors.)				
TREASON. (See Arrest; Fugitive; Impeachment.)				
TREASON. Treason against the United States shall consist only in levying War against them, or in adhering to their Enemies, giving them Aid and Comfort. No Person shall be convicted of Treason unless on the Testimony of two Witnesses to the same overt Act, or on Confession in open Court.	3	3	1	74
The Congress shall have Power to declare the Punishment of Treason, but no Attainder of Treason shall work Corruption of Blood, or Forfeiture except during the life of the Person attainted.	3	3	2	74
TREASURY. The Senators and Representatives shall receive a Compensation for their Services, . . . paid out of the Treasury of the United States.	1	6	1	68
TREASURY. (See Appropriations.)				
TREASURY of the United States. . . . and the net Produce of all Duties and Imposts, laid by any State on Imports or Exports, shall be for the Use of the Treasury of the United States	1	10	2	71

[Page 129 part 2]

UNUSUAL Punishments. (See Punishments.)				
USE. (See Liquors.)				
VACANCIES. When vacancies happen in the Representation from any o State, the Executive Authority thereof shall issue Writs of Election to fill such Vacancies.	1	2	4	66
VACANCIES. . . . if Vacancies happen by Resignation, or otherwise [in -a the Senate], during the Recess of the Legislature of any State, the Executive thereof may make temporary Appointments until the next cu Meeting of the Legislature, which shall then fill such Vacancies. (See next title.)	1	3	2	67
VACANCIES. When vacancies happen in the representation of any cu En State in the Senate, the executive authority of such State shall issue writs of election to fill such vacancies; Provided, That the legislature of any State may empower the executive thereof to make temporary appointments until the people fill the vacancies by election as the legislature may direct....17th amend.	17TH			86
VACANCIES. The President shall have Power to fill up all Vacancies that may happen during the Recess of the Senate, by granting Com-a 3 missions which shall expire at the End of their next Session	2	2	3	73
[VACANCY in the Presidency.] (See Death.)				
VALUE. The Congress shall Have Power . . . To coin Money, regulate the Value thereof, and of foreign Coin.				
VESSELS. (See Enter.)				
[VESTED Powers.] (See Congress; Judicial Power; President.)				
[VETO.] (See Bill.)				
VICE PRESIDENT. The Vice President of the United States shall be President of the Senate, but shall have no Vote, unless they be equally divided.	1	3	4	67

[Page 130 part 2]

TERM / DESCRIPTION	DOC	ART.	SEC.	CL.	PG
VICE PRESIDENT. The Senate shall chuse their other Officers, and also a President pro tempore, in the Absence of the Vice President, or when he shall exercise the Office of President of the United States.		1	3	5	67
VICE PRESIDENT. In Case of the Removal of the President from Office, or of his Death. Resignation, or Inability to discharge the Powers and Duties of the said Office, the Same shall devolve on the Vice President, and the Congress may by Law provide for the Case of Removal. Death, Resignation or Inability, both of the President and Vice President, declaring what Officer shall then act as President, . . .		2	1	6	72
VICE PRESIDENT. The . . . Vice President . . . shall be removed from Office on Impeachment for, and Conviction of, Treason, Bribery, or other high Crimes and Misdemeanors		2	4		73
VICE PRESIDENT, Election of. (See Election of President and Vice President.)					
VICE PRESIDENT, [Qualifications of.] But no person constitutionally ineligible to the office of President shall be eligible to that of Vice-President of the United States. 12th amend.	12TH				83
VIOLENCE. (See Domestic.)					
VOTE. (See Election ; Order.)					
VOTE. But when the right to vote at any election for the choice of electors for President and Vice President of the United States, Representatives in Congress, the Executive and Judicial officers of a State, or the members of the Legislature thereof is denied to any of the male inhabitants of such State, being twenty-one years of age, and citizens of the United States, or in any way abridged, except for participation in rebellion. or other crime, the basis of representation therein shall be reduced in the proportion which the number of such male citizens shall bear the whole number of male citizens twenty-one years of age in such State. 14th amend.	14TH				84
VOTE. The right of citizens of the United States to vote shall not be denied or abridged by the United States or by any State on account of race, color, or previous condition of servitude. 15th amend.	15TH				85
VOTE. The right of citizens of the United States to vote shall not be 1 denied or abridged by the United States or by any State on account of sex. 19th amend.	19TH				86
[VOTES in Congress.] (See Bill ; Order ; Two-Thirds ; Yeas and Nays.)					
VOTES of Electors. (See Election of President and Vice President.)					
WAR. The Congress shall have Power . . . To declare War, . . .		1	8	11	70
WAR. No State shall, without the Consent of Congress, . . . engage in War, unless actually invaded, or in such imminent Danger as will not admit of delay.		1	10	3	71
WAR. Treason against the United States, shall consist only in levying War against them.		3	3	1	74

WAR. No Soldier shall, in time of peace be quartered in any house, without the consent of the Owner, nor in time of war, but in a manner to be prescribed by law 3rd amend.	3RD			81
WARRANTS. (See Searches.)				
WASHINGTON, George. Signs the Constitution.				77
WATER. (See Captures.)				
WEIGHTS and Measures. The Congress shall have Power . . . To . . . fix the Standard of Weights and Measures ; . . .	1	8	5	69
WELFARE. (See General Welfare.)				
WESTERN Claims.] (See Claims.)				
WILLIAMSON Hugh. Signs the Constitution				77
WILSON, James. Signs the Constitution.				77
WITNESS. . . .. nor shall any person . . . be compelled in any criminal case to be a witness against himself, . . . 5th amend.	5TH			82
WITNESSES. No Person shall be convicted of Treason unless on the Testimony of two Witnesses to the same overt Act, or on Confession in open Court.	3	3	1	74
WITNESSES. In all criminal prosecutions, the accused shall enjoy the right to be confronted with the witnesses against him; to have compulsory process for obtaining Witnesses in his favor. . 6th amend.	6TH			82
WRIT of Habeas Corpus. (See Habeas Corpus.)				
WRITING. (See Departments.)				
WRITINGS. (See Science.)				
YEAS and Nays. . . . the Yeas and Nays of the Members of either House on any question shall, at the Desire of one fifth of those Present, be entered on the Journal.	1	5	3	68
YEAS and Nays. (See Bill.)				

[Page 131 part 2]

[Page 131 part 3]

This page not in original
Available for light note-taking
This page left intentionally blank

In CONGRESS, July 4, 1776.
The unanimous Declaration of the thirteen united
States of America,

When in the Course of human events, it becomes necessary for one people to dissolve the political bands which have connected them with another, and to assume among the powers of the earth, the separate and equal station to which the Laws of Nature and of Nature's God entitle them, a decent respect to the opinions of mankind requires that they should declare the causes which impel them to the separation. We hold these truths to be self-evident, that all men are created equal, that they are endowed by their Creator with certain unalienable Rights, that among these are Life, Liberty and the pursuit of Happiness. — That to secure these rights, Governments are instituted among Men, deriving their just powers from the consent of the governed, — That whenever any Form of Government becomes destructive of these ends, it is the Right of the People to alter or to abolish it, and to institute new Government, laying its foundation on such principles and organizing its powers in such form, as to them shall seem most likely to effect their Safety and Happiness. Prudence, indeed, will dictate that Governments long established should not be changed for light and transient causes; and accordingly all experience bath shewn, that mankind are more disposed to suffer, while evils are sufferable, than to right themselves by abolishing the forms to which they are accustomed. But when a long train of abuses and usurpations, pursuing invariably the same Object evinces a design to reduce them under absolute Despotism, it is their right, it is their duty, to throw off such Government, and to provide new Guards for their future security. — Such has been the patient sufferance of these Colonies; and such is now the necessity which constrains them to alter their former Systems of Government. The history of the present King of Great Britain is a history of repeated injuries and usurpations, all having in direct object the establishment of an absolute Tyranny over these States. To prove this, let Facts be submitted to a candid world. He has refused his Assent to Laws, the most wholesome and necessary for the public good.
—He has forbidden his Governors to pass Laws of immediate and pressing importance, unless suspended in their operation till his Assent should be obtained; and when so suspended, he has utterly neglected to attend to them. — He has refused to pass other Laws for the accommodation of large districts of people, unless those people would relinquish the right of Representation in the Legislature, a right inestimable to them and formidable to tyrants only. — He has called together legislative bodies at places unusual, uncomfortable, and distant from the depository of their public Records, for the sole purpose of fatiguing them into compliance with his measures. — He has dissolved Representative Houses repeatedly, for opposing with manly firmness his invasions on the rights of the people. — He has refused for a long time, after such dissolutions, to cause others to be elected; whereby the Legislative powers, incapable of Annihilation, have returned to the People at large for their exercise; the State remaining in the mean time exposed to all the dangers of invasion from without, and convulsions within. — He has endeavoured to prevent the population of these States; for that purpose obstructing the Laws for Naturalization of Foreigners; refusing to pass others to encourage their migrations hither, and raising the conditions of new Appropriations of Lands.

[132]

— He has obstructed the Administration of Justice, by refusing his Assent to Laws for establishing Judiciary powers. He has made Judges dependent on his Will alone, for the tenure of their offices, and the amount and payment of their salaries. — He has erected a multitude of New Offices, and sent hither swarms of Officers to harrass our people, and eat out their sub-stance. — He has kept among us, in times of peace, Standing Armies without the Consent of our legislatures. — He has affected to render the Military independent of and superior to the Civil power. — He has combined with others to subject us to a jurisdiction foreign to our constitution, and unacknowledged by our laws; giving his Assent to their Acts of pre-tended Legislation: — For quartering large bodies of armed troops among us: — For protecting them, by a mock Trial, from punishment for any Murders which they should commit on the Inhabitants of these States: —For cutting off our Trade with all parts of the world: — For imposing Taxes on us without our Consent: — For depriving us in many cases, of the benefits of Trial by Jury: — For transporting us beyond Seas to be tried for pre-tended offences: — For abolishing the free System of English Laws in a neighbouring Province, establishing therein an Arbitrary government, and enlarging its Boundaries so as to render it at once an example and fit instrument for introducing the same absolute rule into these Colonies: — For taking away our Charters, abolishing our most valuable Laws, and altering fundamentally the Forms of our Governments: — For suspending our own Legislatures, and declaring themselves invested with power to legislate for us in all cases whatsoever. — He has abdicated Government here, by declaring us out of his Protection and waging War against us. — He has plundered our seas, ravaged our Coasts, burnt our towns, and destroyed the lives of our people. — He is at this time transporting large Armies of foreign Mercenaries to compleat the works of death, desolation and tyranny, already begun with circumstances of Cruelty & perfidy scarcely paralleled in the most barbarous ages, and totally unworthy the Head of a civilized nation. — He has constrained our fellow Citizens taken Captive on the high Seas to bear Arms against their Country, to become the executioners of their friends and Brethren, or to fall themselves by their Hands. — He has excited domestic insurrections amongst us, and has endeavoured to bring on the inhabitants of our frontiers, the merciless Indian Savages, whose known rule of warfare, is an undistinguished destruction of all ages, sexes and conditions. In every stage of these Oppressions We have Petitioned for Redress in the most humble terms: Our repeated Petitions have been answered only by repeated injury. A Prince, whose character is thus marked by every act which may define a Tyrant, is unfit to be the ruler of a free people. Nor have We been wanting in attentions to our British brethren. We have warned them from time to time of attempts by their legislature to extend an unwarrantable jurisdiction over us. We have reminded them of the circumstances of our emigration and settlement here. We have appealed to their native justice and magnanimity, and we have conjured them by the ties of our common kindred to disavow these usurpations, which, would inevitably interrupt our connections and correspondence They too have been deaf to the voice of justice and of consanguinity. We must, therefore, acquiesce in the necessity, which denounces our Separation, and hold them, as we hold the rest of mankind, Enemies in War, in Peace Friends. We, therefore, the Representatives of the united States of America, in General Congress, Assembled, appealing to the

Supreme Judge of the world for the rectitude of our intentions, do, in the Name, and by Authority of the good People of these Colonies, solemnly publish and declare, That these United Colonies are, and of Right ought to be Free and Independent States; that they are Absolved from all Alle-giance to the British Crown, and that all political connection between them and the State of Great Britain, is and ought to be totally dissolved; and that as Free and Independent States, they have full Power to levy War, conclude Peace, contract Alliances, establish Commerce, and to do all other Acts and Things which Independent States may of right do. — And for the support of this Declaration, with a firm reliance on the protection of Divine Providence, we mutually pledge to each other our Lives, our For-tunes and our sacred Honor.

John Hancock

Button Gwinnett	Benjᵃ Harrison	Richᵈ Stockton
Lyman Hall	Thoˢ Nelson jr.	Jnᵒ Witherspoon
Geo Walton.	Francis Lightfoot Lee	Fraˢ Hopkinson
	Carter Braxton	John Hart
Wᵐ Hooper		Abra Clark
Joseph Hewes,	Robᵗ Morris	
John Penn	Benjamin Rush	
	Benj· Franklin	Josiah Bartlett
Edward Rutledge.	John Morton	Wᵐ Whipple
Thoˢ Heyward Junʳ	Geo Clymer	
Thomas Lynch Junʳ	Jaˢ Smith.	Samˡ Adams
Arthur Middleton	Geo. Taylor	John Adams
	James Wilson	Robᵗ Treat Paine
Samuel Chase	Geo. Ross	Elbridge Gerry
Wᵐ Paca		
Thoˢ Stone	Caesar Rodney	Step. Hopkins
Charles Carroll	Geo Read	William Ellery
of Carrollton	Tho M: Kean	
	Wᵐ Floyd	Roger Sherman
George Wythe	Phil. Livingston	Samˡ Huntington
Richard Henry Lee.	Franˢ Lewis	Wᵐ Williams
Th Jefferson	Lewis Morris	Oliver Wolcott
		Matthew Thornton

NOTE: This reprint is from the copperplate facsimile made in 1823. It involves in a few cases the same doubt respecting capitals that is found in the original Constitution. The signatures in the original are in six columns by States without names, except that Matthew Thornton should be under New Hampshire. The groups here are in the same order, as follows: first column, Georgia, North Carolina, South Carolina, Maryland, Virginia; second column, Virginia (continued), Pennsylvania, Delaware, New York; third column, New Jersey, New Hampshire, Massachusetts, Rhode Island, Connecticut. John Hancock signs as President of the Congress.

George Washington's Farewell Address to the People of the United States

This Address was written primarily to eliminate himself as a candidate for a third term. It was never read by the President in public, but printed in Claypoole's AMERICAN DAILY ADVERTISER, Philadelphia, September 19, 1796. The address is in two parts: In the first, Washington definitely declines a third term, gives reasons, and acknowledges a debt of gratitude for the honors conferred upon him and for the confident support of the people. In the second more important part, he presents, as a result of his experience and as a last legacy of advice, thoughts upon the government.

This reprint is from a facsimile of the manuscript which Washington gave to Claypoole as his "copy." After Claypoole's death, the manuscript was ordered to be sold at auction on February 12, 1850. Senator Henry Clay on January 24 offered a joint resolution for its purchase by the government, but the resolution was not signed by President Taylor until the day of the sale. The manuscript was sold to James Lenox for $2,300, and passed, with his library, to the New York Public Library. There is no evidence of any bid on behalf of the national government.

Friends, & Fellow-Citizens

The period for a new election of a Citizen, to administer the Executive government of the United States, being not far distant, and the time actually arrived, when your thoughts must be employed in designating the person, who is to be cloathed with that important trust, it appears to me proper, especially as it may conduce to a more distinct expression of the public voice, that I should now apprise you of the resolution I have formed, to decline being considered among the number of those, out of whom a choice is to be made.—

I beg you, at the same time, to do me the justice to be assured, that this resolution has not been taken, without a strict regard to all the considerations appertaining to the relation, which binds a dutiful citizen to his country—and that, in withdrawing the tender of service which silence in my situation might imply, I am influenced by no diminution of zeal for your future interest, no deficiency of grateful respect for your past kindness; but am supported by a full conviction that the step is compatible with both.

The acceptance of, & continuance hitherto in, the office to which your suffrages have twice called me, have been a uniform sacrifice of inclination to the opinion of duty, and to a deference for what appeared to be your desire.—I constantly hoped, that it would have been much earlier in my power, consistently with motives, which I was not at liberty to disregard, to return to that retirement, from which I had been reluctantly drawn.—The strength of my inclination to do this, previous to the last election, had even led to the preparation of an address to declare it to you; but mature reflection on the then perplexed & critical posture of our affairs with foreign Nations, and the unanimous advice of persons entitled to my confidence, impelled me to abandon the idea.—

I rejoice, that the state of your concerns, external as well as internal, no longer renders the pursuit of inclination incompatible with the sentiment of duty, or propriety; & am persuaded whatever partiality may be retained for my services, that in the present circumstances of our country, you will not disapprove my determination to retire.—

The impressions, with which, I first undertook the arduous trust, were explained on the proper occasion.—In the discharge of this trust, I will only say, that I have, with good intentions, contributed towards the organization and administration of the government, the best exertions of which a very fallible judgment was capable.—Not unconscious, in the outset, of the inferiority of my qualifications, experience in my own eyes, perhaps still more in the eyes of others, has strengthened the motives to diffidence of myself; and every day the encreasing weight of years admonishes me more and more, that the shade of retirement is as necessary to me as it will be welcome.—Satisfied that if any circumstances have given peculiar value to my services, they were temporary, I have the consolation to believe, that while choice and prudence invite me to quit the political scene, patriotism does not for-bid it.—

In looking forward to the moment, which is intended to terminate the career of my public life, my feelings do not permit me to suspend the deep acknowledgment of that debt of gratitude which I owe to my beloved country,—for the many honors it has conferred upon me; still more for the stedfast confidence with which it has supported me; and for the opportunities I have thence enjoyed of manifesting my inviolable attachment, by services faithful & persevering, though in usefulness unequal to my zeal.—If benefits have resulted to our country from these services, let it always be remembered to your praise, and as an instructive example in our annals, that under circumstances in which the Passions agitated in every direction were liable to mislead, amidst appearances sometimes dubious, —vicissitudes of fortune often discouraging,—in situations in which not infrequently want of success has countenanced the spirit of criticism,—the constancy of your support was the essential prop of the efforts, and a guarantee of the plans by which they were effected.—Profoundly penetrated with this idea, I shall carry it with me to my grave, as a strong incitement to unceasing vows that Heaven may continue to you the choicest tokens of its beneficence—that your union & brotherly affection may be perpetual—that the free constitution, which is the work of your hands, may be sacredly maintained—that its administration in every department may be stamped with wisdom and virtue—that, in fine, the happiness of the people of these States, under the auspices of liberty, may be made complete, by so careful a preservation and so prudent a use of this blessing as will acquire to them the glory of recommending it to the applause, the affection—and adoption of every nation which is yet a stranger to it.

Here, perhaps, I ought to stop. But a solicitude for your welfare, which cannot end but with my life, and the apprehension of danger, natural to that solicitude, urge me on an occasion like the present, to offer to your solemn contemplation, and to recommend to your frequent review, some sentiments; which are the result of much reflection, of no inconsiderable observation, and which appear to me all important to the permanency of your felicity as a People. These will be offered to you with the more freedom, as you can only see in them the disinterested warnings of a parting friend, who can possibly have no personal motive to bias his counsel. Nor can I forget, as an encouragement to it, your endulgent reception of my sentiments on a former and not dissimilar occasion.

Interwoven as is the love of liberty with every ligament of your hearts, no recommendation of mine is necessary to fortify or confirm the attachment.—

The Unity of Government which constitutes you one people is also now dear to you.—It is justly so;—for it is a main Pillar in the Edifice of your real independence, the support of your tranquility at home; your peace abroad; of your safety;—of your prosperity;—of that very Liberty which you so highly prize.—But as it is easy to foresee, that from different causes & from different quarters, much pains will be taken, many artifices employed, to weaken in your minds the conviction of this truth;—as this is the point in your political fortress against which the batteries of internal & external enemies will be most constantly and actively (though often covertly & insidiously) directed, it is of infinite moment, that you should properly estimate the immense value of your national union to your collective & individual happiness;—that you should cherish a cordial, habitual & immoveable attachment to it; accustoming yourself to think and speak of it as of the Palladium of your political safety and prosperity; watching for its preservation with jealous anxiety; discountenancing whatever may suggest even a suspicion that it can in any event be abandoned, and indignantly frowning upon the first dawning of every attempt to alienate any portion of our Country from the rest, or to enfeeble the sacred ties which now link together the various parts.

For this you have every inducement of sympathy and interest.— Citizens by birth or choice, of a common country, that country has a right to concentrate your affections.—The name of AMERICAN, which belongs to you, in your national capacity, must always exalt the just pride of Patriotism, more than any appellation derived from local discriminations.—With slight shades of difference, you have the same Religion, Manners, Habits & political Principles.—You have in a common cause fought & triumphed together—The independence & liberty you possess are the work of joint councils, and joint efforts—of common dangers, sufferings and successes.—

But these considerations, however powerfully they address themselves to your sensibility are greatly outweighed by those which apply more immediately to your Interest.—Here every portion of our country finds the most commanding motives for carefully guarding & preserving the union of the whole.

The North, in an unrestrained intercourse with the South, protected by the equal Laws of a common government, finds in the productions of the latter, great additional resources of maratime & commercial enterprise—and precious materials of manufacturing industry.—The South in the same Intercourse, benefitting by the agency of the North, sees its agriculture grow & its commerce expand. Turning partly into its own channels the sea-men of the North, it finds its particular navigation envigorated;—and while it contributes, in different ways, to nourish & increase the general mass of the national navigation, it looks forward to the protection of a maratime strength, to which itself is unequally adapted.—The East, in a like intercourse with the West, already finds, and in the progressive improvement of interior communications, by land & water, will more & more find a valuable vent for the commodities which it brings from abroad, or manufactures at home.—The West derives from the East supplies requisite to its growth and comfort,—and what is perhaps of still greater consequence, it must of necessity owe the secure enjoyment of indispensable outlets for its own productions to the weight, influence, and the future maritime strength of the Atlantic side of the Union, directed by an indissoluble community of Interest as one Nation.—Any other tenure by which the West can hold this essential advantage, whether derived from its own separate strength, or from an apostate & unnatural connection with any foreign Power, must be intrinsically precarious;—

While then every part of our country thus feels an immediate & particular Interest in union, all the parts combined cannot fail to find in the united mass of means & efforts greater strength, greater resource, proportionably greater security from external danger, a less frequent interruption of their Peace by foreign Nations;—and, what is of inestimable value! they must derive from union an exemption from those broils and Wars between themselves, which so frequently afflict neighbouring countries, not tied together by the same government; which their own rivalships alone would be sufficient to produce, but which opposite foreign alliances, attachments & intriegues would stimulate and imbitter.—Hence likewise they will avoid the necessity of those overgrown military establishments, which under any form of Government are inauspicious to liberty, and which are to be regarded as particularly hostile to Republican Liberty: In this sense it is, that your union ought to be considered as a main prop of your liberty, and that the love of the one ought to endear to you the preservation of the other.—

These considerations speak a persuasive language to every reflecting & virtuous mind,—and exhibit the continuance of the UNION as a primary object of Patriotic desire.—Is there a doubt, whether a common government can embrace so large a sphere?—Let experience solve it.—To listen to mere speculation in such a case were criminal.—We are authorized to hope that a proper organization of the whole, with the auxiliary agency of governments for the respective Subdivisions, will afford a happy issue to the experiment.—'Tis well worth a fair and full experiment With such powerful and obvious motives to union, affecting all parts of our country, while experience shall not have demonstrated its impracticability, there will always be reason to distrust the patriotism of those, who in any quarter may endeavor to weaken its bands.—

In contemplating the causes which may disturb our Union, it occurs as matter of serious concern, that any ground should have been furnished for characterizing parties by *Geographical* discriminations—*Northern and Southern—Atlantic and Western*; whence designing men may endeavour to excite a belief that there is a real difference of local interests and views. One of the expedients of Party to acquire influence, within particular districts, is to misrepresent the opinions & aims of other Districts.—You cannot shield yourselves too much against the jealousies & heart burnings which spring from these misrepresentations.—They tend to render alien to each other those who ought to be bound together by fraternal affection.—The Inhabitants of our Western country have lately had a useful lesson on this head.—

They have seen, in the Negociation by the Executive, and in the unanimous ratification by the Senate, of the Treaty with Spain, and in the universal satisfaction at that event, throughout the United States, a decisive proof how unfounded were the suspicions propagated among them of a policy in the General Government and in the Atlantic States unfriendly to their Interests in regard to the Mississippi—They have been witnesses to the formation of two Treaties, that with G: Britain, and that with Spain, which secure to them every thing they could desire, in respect to our Foreign relations, towards confirming their prosperity.—Will it not be their wisdom to rely for the preservation of of these advantages on the UNION by which they were procured?—Will they not henceforth be deaf to those advisers, if such there are, who would sever them from their Brethren and connect them with Aliens?—

To the efficacy and permanency of Your Union, a Government for the whole is indispensable.--No alliances however strict between the parts can be an adequate substitute.—They must inevitably experience the infractions & interruptions which all alliances in all times have experienced.—Sensible of this momentous truth, you have improved upon your first essay, by the adoption of a Constitution of Government, better calculated than your former for an intimate Union, and for the efficacious management of your common concerns.—This government, the offspring of our own choice uninfluenced and unawed, adopted upon full investigation & mature deliberation, completely free in its principles, in the distribution of its powers, uniting security with energy, and containing within itself a pro-vision for its own amendment, has a just claim to your confidence and your support.—Respect for its authority, compliance with its Laws, acquiescence in its measures, are duties enjoined by the fundamental maxims of true Liberty.—The basis of our political systems is the right of the people to make and to alter their Constitutions of Government.—But the Constitution which at any time exists, 'till changed by an explicit and authentic act of the whole People, is sacredly obligatory upon all.—The very idea of the power and the right of the People to establish Government presupposes the duty of every individual to obey the established Government.

All obstructions to the execution of the Laws, all combinations and associations, under whatever plausible character, with the real design to direct, controul counteract, or awe the regular deliberation and action of the constituted authorities are destructive of this fundamental principle and of fatal tendency.—They serve to organize faction, to give it an artificial and extraordinary force—to put in the place of the delegated will of the Nation, the will of a party;—often a small but artful and enterprising minority of the community;—and, according to the alternate triumphs of different parties, to make the public administration the mirror of the ill concerted and incongruous projects of faction, rather than the Organ of consistent and wholesome plans digested by common councils and modified by mutual interests.—However combinations or associations of the above description may now & then answer popular ends, they are likely, in the course of time and things, to become potent engines, by which cunning, ambitious and unprincipled men will be enabled to subvert the Power of the People, & to usurp for themselves the reins of Government; destroying afterwards the very engines which have lifted them to unjust dominion.—

Towards the preservation of your Government and the permanency of your present happy state, it is requisite, not only that you steadily discountenance irregular oppositions to its acknowledged authority, but also that you resist with care the spirit of innovation upon its principles however specious the pretexts.—One method of assault may be to effect, in the forms of the Constitution, alterations which will impair the energy of the system, and thus to undermine what cannot be directly overthrown.—In all the changes to which you may be invited, remember that time and habit are at least as necessary to fix the true character of Governments, as of other human institutions—that experience is the surest standard, by which to test the real tendency of the existing Constitution of a country—that facility in changes upon the credit of mere hypotheses & opinion exposes to perpetual change, from the endless variety of hypotheses and opinion:—and remember, especially, that for the efficient management of your common interests, in a country so extensive as ours, a Government of as much vigour as is consistent with the perfect security of Liberty is indispensable—Liberty itself will find in such a Government, with powers properly distributed and adjusted, its surest Guardian.—It is indeed little else than a name, where the Government is too feeble to withstand the enterprises of faction, to confine each member of the Society within the limits prescribed by the laws & to maintain all in the secure & tranquil enjoyment of the rights of person & property.—

I have already intimated to you the danger of Parties in the State, with particular reference to the founding of them on Geographical discriminations.— Let me now take a more comprehensive view, & warn you in the most solemn manner against the baneful effects of the Spirit of Party, generally

This Spirit, unfortunately, is inseperable from our nature, having its root in the strongest passions of the human mind.—It exists under different shapes in all Governments, more or less stifled, controuled, or repressed; but in those of the popular form it is seen in its greatest rankness and is truly their worst enemy.—

The alternate domination of one faction over another, sharpened by the spirit of revenge natural to party dissention, which in different ages & countries has perpetrated the most horrid enormities, is itself a frightful despotism.—But this leads at length to a more formal and permanent despotism.—The disorders & miseries, which result, gradually incline the minds of men to seek security & repose in the absolute power of an Individual: and sooner or later the chief of some prevailing faction more able or more fortunate than his competitors, turns this disposition to the purposes of his own elevation, on the ruins of Public Liberty.—

Without looking forward to an extremity of this kind (which nevertheless ought not to be entirely out of sight) the common & continual mischiefs of the spirit of Party are sufficient to make it the interest and the duty of a wise People to discourage and restrain it.—

It serves always to distract the Public councils and enfeeble the Public administration.—It agitates the Community with ill founded jealousies and false alarms, kindles the animosity of one part against another, foments occasionally riot & insurrection.—It opens the doors to foreign influence & corruption, which find a facilitated access to the government itself.

through the channels of party passions. Thus the policy and and the will of one country, arc subjected to the policy and will of another.—

There is an opinion that parties in free countries are useful checks upon the administration of the Government and serve to keep alive the spirit of Liberty.—This within certain limits is probably true—and in Governments of a Monarchical cast Patriotism may look with endulgence, if not with favour, upon the spirit of party.—But in those of the popular character, in Governments purely elective, it is a spirit not to be encouraged.—From their natural tendency, it is certain there will always be enough of that spirit for every salutary purpose.—and there being constant danger of excess, the effort ought to be, by force of public opinion, to mitigate & assuage it.—A fire not to be quenched; it demands a uniform vigilance to prevent its bursting into a flame, lest instead of warming it should consume.—

It is important, likewise, that the habits of thinking in a free Country should inspire caution in those entrusted with its administration, to confine themselves within their respective Constitutional spheres; avoiding in the exercise of the Powers of one department to encroach upon another.—The spirit of encroachment tends to consolidate the powers of all the departments in one, and thus to create whatever the form of government, a real despotism.—A just estimate of that love of power, and proneness to abuse it, which predominates in the human heart, is sufficient to satisfy us of the truth of this position.—The necessity of reciprocal checks in the exercise of political power; by dividing and distributing it into different depositories, & constituting each the Guardian of the Public Weal against invasions by the others, has been evinced by experiments ancient & modern; —some of them in our country & under our own eyes.—To preserve them must be as necessary as to institute them.—If in the opinion of the People, the distribution or modification of the Constitutional powers be in any particular wrong, let it be corrected by an amendment in the way which the Constitution designates.—But let there be no change by usurpation; for though this, in one instance, may be the instrument of good, it is the customary weapon by which free governments are destroyed.—The precedent must always greatly overbalance in permanent evil any partial or transient benefit which the use can at any time yield.—

Of all the dispositions and habits which lead to political prosperity, Religion and morality are indispensable supports.—In vain would that man claim the tribute of Patriotism, who should labour to subvert these great Pillars of human happiness, these firmest props of the duties of Men & citizens.—The mere Politician, equally with the pious man ought to respect & to cherish them.—A volume could not trace all their connections with private & public felicity.—Let it simply be asked where is the security for property, for reputation, for life, if the sense of religious obligation desert the oaths, which are the instruments of investigation in Courts of Justice? —And let us with caution indulge the supposition, that morality can be maintained without religion.— Whatever may be conceded to the influence of refined education on minds of peculiar structure—reason & experience both forbid us to expect that national morality can prevail in exclusion of religious principle.—

'Tis substantially true, that virtue or morality is a necessary spring of popular government.—The rule indeed extends with more or less force to every species of Free Government.—Who that is a sincere friend to it, can look with indifference upon attempts to shake the foundation of the fabric

Promote then as an object of primary importance, Institutions for the general diffusion of knowledge.—In proportion as the structure of a government gives force to public opinion, it is essential that public opinion should be enlightened

As a very important source of strength & security, cherish public credit.—One method of preserving it is to use it as sparingly as possible:— avoiding occasions of expence by cultivating peace, but remembering also that timely disbursements to prepare for danger frequently prevent much greater disbursements to repel it—avoiding likewise the accumulation of debt, not only by shunning occasions of expence, but by vigorous exertions in time of Peace to discharge the Debts which unavoidable wars may have occasioned, not ungenerously throwing upon posterity the burthen which we ourselves ought to bear. The execution of these maxims belongs to your Representatives, but it is necessary that public opinion should cooperate.—To facilitate to them the performance of their duty, it is essential that you should practically bear in mind, that towards the payment of debts there must be Revenue—that to have Revenue there must be taxes—that no taxes can be devised which are not more or less inconvenient and unpleasant—that the intrinsic embarrassment inseperable from the selection of the proper objects (which is always a choice of difficulties) ought to be a decisive motive for a candid construction of the conduct of the Government in making it, and for a spirit of acquiescence in the measures for obtaining Revenue which the public exigencies may at any time dictate.—

Observe good faith & justice towards all Nations Cultivate peace and harmony with all—Religion & morality enjoin this conduct; and can it be that good policy does not equally enjoin it?—It will be worthy of a free, enlightened, and, at no distant period, a great Nation, to give to mankind the magnanimous and too novel example of a People always guided by an exalted justice & benevolence.—Who can doubt that in the course of time and things the fruits of such a plan would richly repay any temporary advantages which might be lost by a steady adherence to it? Can it be, that Providence has not corrected the permanent felicity of a Nation with its virtue?—The experiment, at least, is recommended by every sentiment which ennobles human nature.—Alas! is it rendered impossible by its vices?

In the execution of such a plan nothing is more essential than that permanent, inveterate antipathies against particular Nations and passionate attachments for others should be excluded;—and that in place of them just & amicable feelings towards all should be cultivated.—The Nation, which indulges towards another an habitual hatred, or an habitual fondness, is in some degree a slave.—It is a slave to its animosity or to its affection, either of which is sufficient to lead it astray from its duty and its interest.—Antipathy in one Nation against another—disposes each more readily to offer insult and injury, to lay hold of slight causes of umbrage, and to be haughty and intractable, when accidental or trifling occasions of dispute occur.—Hence frequent collisions, obstinate envenomed and bloody contests.—The Nation, prompted by ill will & resentment sometimes impels to War the Government, contrary to the best calculations of policy.—The Government sometimes participates in the national propensity, and adopts through passion what reason would reject;—at other times, it makes the animosity of the Nation subservient to projects of hostility instigated by pride, ambition and other sinister & pernicious motives.—The peace often, sometimes perhaps the Liberty, of Nations has been the victim.—

So likewise, a passionate attachment of one Nation for another produces a variety of evils.—Sympathy for the favourite nation, facilitating the illusion of an imaginary common interest, in cases where no real common interest exists, and infusing into one the enmities of the other, betrays the former into a participation in the quarrels & Wars of the latter, without adequate inducement or justification:—It leads also to concessions to the favourite Nation of privileges denied to others, which is apt doubly to injure the Nation making the concessions—by unnecessarily parting with what ought to have been retained—& by exciting jealousy, ill will, and a disposition to retaliate, in the parties from whom equal privileges are with-held: And it gives to ambitious, corrupted, or deluded citizens (who devote themselves to the favourite Nation) facility to betray, or sacrifice the interests of their own country, without odium, sometimes even with popularity;—gilding with the appearances of a virtuous sense of obligation a commendable deference for public opinion, or a laudable zeal for public good, the base or foolish compliances of ambition corruption or infatuation.—

As avenues to foreign influence in innumerable ways, such attachments are particularly alarming to the truly enlightened and independent Patriot.—How many opportunities do they afford to tamper with domestic factions, to practise the arts of seduction, to mislead public opinion, to influence or awe the public councils!—Such an attachment of a small or weak, towards a great & powerful Nation, dooms the former to be the satellite of the latter.—

Against the insidious wiles of foreign influence, (I conjure you to believe me fellow-citizens,) the jealousy of a free people ought to be constantly awake; since history and experience prove that foreign influence is one of the most baneful foes of Republican Government.—But that jealousy to be useful must be impartial; else it becomes the instrument of the very influence to be avoided, instead of a defence against it.—Excessive partiality for one foreign nation and excessive dislike of another, cause those whom they actuate to see danger only on one side, and serve to veil and even second the arts of influence on the other.—Real Patriots, who may resist the intriegues of the favourite, are liable to become suspected and odious; while its tools and dupes usurp the applause & confidence of the people, to surrender their interests.—

The Great rule of conduct for us, in regard to foreign Nations is in extending our commercial relations to have with them as little political connection as possible.—So far as we have already formed engagements let them be fulfilled, with perfect good faith.—Here let us stop.—

Europe has a set of primary interests, which to us have none, or a very remote relation.—Hence she must be engaged in frequent controversies, the causes of which are essentially foreign to our concerns.—Hence therefore it must be unwise in us to implicate ourselves, by artificial ties, in the ordinary vicissitudes of her politics, or the ordinary combinations & collisions of her friendships, or enmities:—

Our detached & distant situation invites and enables us to pursue a different course.—If we remain one People, under an efficient government, the period is not far off, when we may defy material injury from external annoyance;—when we may take such an attitude as will cause the neutrality we may at any time resolve upon to be scrupulously respected;—when belligerent nations, under the impossibility of making acquisitions upon us, will not lightly hazard the giving us provocation;—when we may choose peace or War, as our interest guided by justice shall counsel.—

Why forego the advantages of so peculiar a situation?—Why quit our own to stand upon foreign ground?—Why, by interweaving our destiny with that of any part of Europe, entangle our peace and prosperity in the toils of European Ambition, Rivalship, Interest, Humour or Caprice?—

'Tis our true policy to steer clear of permanent alliances, with any portion of the foreign world—so far, I mean, as we are now at liberty to do it—for let me not be understood as capable of patronising infidelity to existing engagements (I hold the maxim no less applicable to public than to private affairs that honesty is always the best policy) .—I repeat it therefore, let those engagements be observed in their genuine sense.—But in my opinion, it is unnecessary and would be unwise to extend them.—

Taking care always to keep ourselves, by suitable establishments, on a respectably defensive posture, we may safely trust to temporary alliances for extraordinary emergencies.—

Harmony, liberal intercourse with all Nations, are recommended by policy, humanity and interest.—But even our commercial policy should hold an equal and impartial hand:—neither seeking nor granting exclusive favours or preferences;—consulting the natural course of things;—diffusing & deversifying by gentle means the streams of commerce, but forcing nothing; —establishing with Powers so disposed—in order to give to trade a stable course, to define the rights of our Merchants, and to enable the Government to support them—conventional rules of intercourse; the best that present circumstances and mutual opinion will permit, but temporary, & liable to be from time to time abandoned or varied, as experience and circum-stances shall dictate; constantly keeping in view, that 'tis folly in one Nation to look for disinterested favors from another—that it must pay with a portion of its Independence for whatever it may accept under that character—that by such acceptance, it may place itself in the condition of having given equivalents for nominal favours and yet of being reproached with ingratitude for not giving more.—There can be no greater error than to expect, or calculate upon real favours from Nation to Nation.—'Tis an illusion which experience must cure, which a just pride ought to discard.—

In offering to you, my Countrymen, these counsels of an old and affectionate friend, I dare not hope they will make the strong and lasting impression, I could wish—that they will controul the usual current of the passions, or prevent our Nation from running the course which has hitherto marked the Destiny of Nations:—But if I may even flatter myself, that they may be productive of some partial benefit, some occasional good; —that they may now & then recur to moderate the fury of party spirit, to warn against the mischiefs of foreign Intrigue, to guard against the Impostures of pretended patriotism—this hope will be a full recompence for the solicitude for your welfare, by which they have been dictated.—

How far in the discharge of my official duties, I have been guided by the principles which have been delineated, the public Records and other evidences of my conduct must witness to You and to the world.—To myself, the assurance of my own conscience is, that I have at least believed myself to be guided by them.

In relation to the still subsisting War in Europe, my Proclamation of the 22d of April 1793 is the index to my Plan.—Sanctioned by your approving voice and by that of Your Representatives in both Houses of Congress, the spirit of that measure has continually governed me:—uninfluenced by any attempts to deter or divert me from it.—

After deliberate examination with the aid of the best lights I could obtain I was well satisfied that our country, under all the circumstances of the case, had a right to take, and was bound in duty and interest, to take a neutral position.—Having taken it, I determined, as far as should depend upon me, to maintain it, with moderation, perseverence & firmness.—

The considerations, which respect the right to hold this conduct, it is not necessary on this occasion to detail.—I will only observe, that according to my understanding of the matter, that right, so far from being denied by any of the Belligerent Powers has been virtually admitted by all.—

The duty of holding a neutral conduct may be inferred, without any thing more, from the obligation which justice and humanity impose on every Nation, in cases in which it is free to act, to maintain inviolate the relations of Peace and amity towards other Nations.—

The inducements of interest for observing that conduct will best be referred to your own reflections & experience.—With me, a predominant motive has been to endeavour to gain time to our country to settle & mature its yet recent institutions, and to progress without interruption, to that degree of strength & consistency, which is necessary to give it, humanly speaking, the command of its own fortunes.—

Though in reviewing the incidents of my Administration, I am un-conscious of intentional error—I am nevertheless too sensible of my defects not to think it probable that I may have committed many errors.—What-ever they may be I fervently beseech the Almighty to avert or mitigate the evils to which they may tend.—I shall also carry with me the hope that my Country will never cease to view them with indulgence; and that after forty five years of my life dedicated to its service, with an upright zeal, the faults of incompetent abilities will be consigned to oblivion, as myself must soon be to the mansions of rest.

Relying on its kindness in this as in other things, and actuated by that fervent love towards it, which is so natural to a man, who views in it the native soil of himself and his progenitors for several Generations;—I anticipate with pleasing expectation that retreat, in which I promise myself to realize, without alloy, the sweet enjoyment of partaking, in the midst of my fellow Citizens, the benign influence of good Laws under a free Government—the ever favourite object of my heart, and the happy reward, as I trust, of our mutual cares, labours and dangers

United States

19th September } 1796
     Gᵉᵒ. WASHINGTON

THE NATION OF 1790

THE NATION OF 1790 When the Constitution went into operation the United States consisted of thirteen States between the Atlantic Ocean and the Appalachian Mountains and additional territory running through to the Mississippi River. This western territory had been claimed by various States as within the bounds of their colonial charters. By 1789 the claims to most of the region north of the Ohio River had been ceded to the central government, and the claims south of the Ohio were soon after given up, as was also the claim to what soon became Vermont, the fourteenth State. Thereafter the thirteen original States had their present boundaries, except that Maine was a part of Massachusetts until 1820 and West Virginia a part of Virginia until 1863. In 1787 the northern part of the western territory had been placed under a territorial government, a plan which became the model for such temporary organization for regions on their way to statehood and a sharing by their inhabitants in the general government; and during the early years under the Constitution territorial governments were formed for the southwestern region. Settlement west of the Appalachians began in colonial times, Kentucky being admitted as a State in 1792; but in general the western region was still frontier. It was plagued by Indian wars; largely still virgin forests or prairies, or with small settlements along the main waterways that were almost the only means of travel or transportation. It was far distant from the coast cities that were the centers of trade; and with crude economic and social conditions that made such backwoods life foreign to the civilization that had grown up on the Atlantic slope in colonial times and come to have a definite aristocratic trend. Pioneer life promoted democratic spirit.

EXPANSION TO1860

By 1848 all of this territorial country east of the Mississippi, except the northeastern part of what is now Minnesota, had be-come States, and Florida had also been acquired and given statehood. This region was considerably larger than the terri-tory of the Thirteen States, for the people of whom the Constitution had been originally framed; and it had increased in

CANADA

NORTHWEST TERRITORY

SPANISH LOUISIANA

PART OF MASS

VT Adm '9'

N.H. 6

Gloucester
Marblehead
Salem MASS Boston
Providence CONN. Newport
R.I. 4

NEW YORK 12

PENNSYLVANIA 15

Northern Liberties
Southwark
Philadelphia
N.J. 7

New York City

MD. 8
Baltimore

DEL. 3

VIRGINIA 21

KENTUCKY Adm 1792 4

TERRITORY SOUTH OF THE OHIO

NORTH CAROLINA 12

SOUTH CAROLINA 8

CLAIMED BY GEORGIA

GEORGIA 4

Charleston

CLAIMED BY SPAIN

SPANISH FLORIDA

ATLANTIC OCEAN

• Towns of 8,000 or more population
9 Electoral vote in 1792

UNITED STATES IN 1790

[147]

population from 110,000 in 1790 to 8,000,000 in 1850. More-over, it had grown up entirely under the aegis of the Constitution, it was essentially the child of the Union and had never known such conditions as those which, in colonial times, had led finally to the American Revolution and had developed the theory of State sovereignty. The democracy of its infancy continued fundamental in its maturing years. In 1850 this region had 76 representatives and 20 senators and the original States plus Vermont and Maine 140 representatives and 30 senators. Three Presidents had come from the western land.

Meanwhile, between 1789 and 1850 the territory of the nation had increased to its present continental dimensions, except for a slice in southern New Mexico and Arizona, added in 1853. This was done by the Louisiana Purchase in 1803 of the valley of the Mississippi west of the main stream; the annexation of Texas in 1845; the division of the Oregon Country with Great Britain in 1846; and the cession of California and the rest of the trans-Rocky region by Mexico in 1848. The nation of 892,000 square miles in 1790 had become one of 3,027,000 by 1860; while the story of pioneer settlement, territorial govern-ment, and statehood had already begun west of the "Father of Waters." Indeed, by the latter date eight states out of this new territory had been added to the Union; though much of this far western region was still unsettled or under frontier conditions. In 1860 the thirteen original States with Vermont and Maine had only half of the 31,000,000 inhabitants, and in the presidential election of that year 164 electors to the 139 of the rest of the country.

ECONOMIC AND SOCIAL CONDITIONS IN 1790

This increase in territory and population and the consequent shifting of political balance was only one phase in the change in the character of the nation under the Constitution. Economic and social alterations had been scarcely less. In 1790 the country was almost entirely rural and agricultural and each section largely self-supporting. The largest city, New York, had but 33,000 inhabitants., and there were only twelve cities or towns of 5,000 or more people, with a total number of 156,- 000 out of a general population of 3,900,000, which was 4 per-cent. Foreign trade came next to agriculture in economic importance, but imports were only $23,000,000 in value and ex-ports $20,000,000. Most of the imports were of manufactured

tured goods, for manufacturing was still in its infancy in the United States and what little existed was purely home work. Machinery was practically unknown; water furnished the only power; "Labor" was never spelled with a capital; corporations an almost non-existent element in business. Travel and transportation were in a wretched condition. Coastwise trade in small ships was, where possible, the most convenient method; the larger rivers were also navigable in their lower reaches. There were no good roads and few of any kind to connect a population scattered over a coast line of some twelve hundred miles and running inland for perhaps half as far. Travel was by horseback, private carriage, or stage; transportation by packsaddle or heavy freight wagons; all slow and often perilous. It took a week to go from Boston to New York.

Isolation and the development of localism and sectional prejudice had been natural results of such conditions. Education was not the privilege of the many; except in New Eng-land there was no system of primary public schools, and the right to secondary training was even less regarded. There were fewer than ten colleges throughout the whole country and their courses were rigidly classical; technical and professional schools were almost unknown. In most of the colonies there had been established churches; and though religious freedom was a Revolutionary cry, the barriers of creed and ethical outlook were still formidable in 1790. The ministry was, as it had been in colonial times, the chief profession; but lawyers had pushed themselves to the front in Revolutionary times. Medicine was crude; bleeding was a general remedy; prevention and sanitation measures considered contrary to the will of Providence. Newspapers had existed in the colonies since 1704 and they had grown steadily in number and influence; and their practice of clipping a large part of their contents from exchanges made them even in 1789 of more general influence than their usually highly partisan editors probably realized. The Revolutionary, era had given birth to many valuable state papers; but Ameri-can literature and art in recognizable form was a later product. Amusements were few; the theater struggling for foothold and frowned upon by conservative elements; music of limited ap-peal; outdoor life in occasional evidence, such as riding or skating, but leisure and the cultivation of the spirit of unconsidered value in the scheme of life.

At the outbreak of the Revolution slavery existed in all of the colonies, but the leaders were general in deprecating its presence as contrary to the spirit of the movement. During the next decade or two in the North, where it was economically un-important, slavery was directly abolished or gradual abolition begun. In the South, except in South Carolina and Georgia, it was believed to be justly dying out. In these two most southern States it was deemed necessary for the cultivation of rice, and the deputies from these States in the Constitutional Convention had insisted upon, and prevailed in, a demand for recognition of slavery in representation, upon a provision for the return of fugitives, and upon a postponement of the abolition of foreign slave trade.

CONDITIONS IN 1860

The contrast in 1860 with the economic and social conditions noticed above as prevalent in 1790 was marked. The country remained prevailingly rural and agricultural but in a markedly less degree. There were nine cities with over 100,000 inhabitants; the largest, New York, had 806,000. There were 26 with a population larger than the largest in 1790, and 316 cities and towns containing 5,000 or more people. This urban population of 6,200,000 was 20 percent of the whole. These cities were already centers of large manufacturing and fast becoming ever greater ones. The factory system had developed and labor was finding its voice. Business had become specialized and there were great banking houses and accumulations of cap-ital under corporate control. The imports of merchandise had increased to $354,000,000 and the exports to $334,000,000. The steamship went into practical operation in 1807 and this not only facilitated ocean navigation but made possible the ascension of the great western rivers and the circuit of transportation over them. Improved roads, turnpikes, canals, and finally railroads had wrought a revolution in land travel and transportation. By 1860 one could travel from Bangor in Maine to New Orleans by train, or from Philadelphia by way of Chicago or St. Louis to the Missouri River. A similar revolution in communication had been made by the introduction of the telegraph, though in 1866 there were only about 40,000 miles of line. Isolation was no longer possible; localism and sectional prejudice were results of a political or economic point of view and

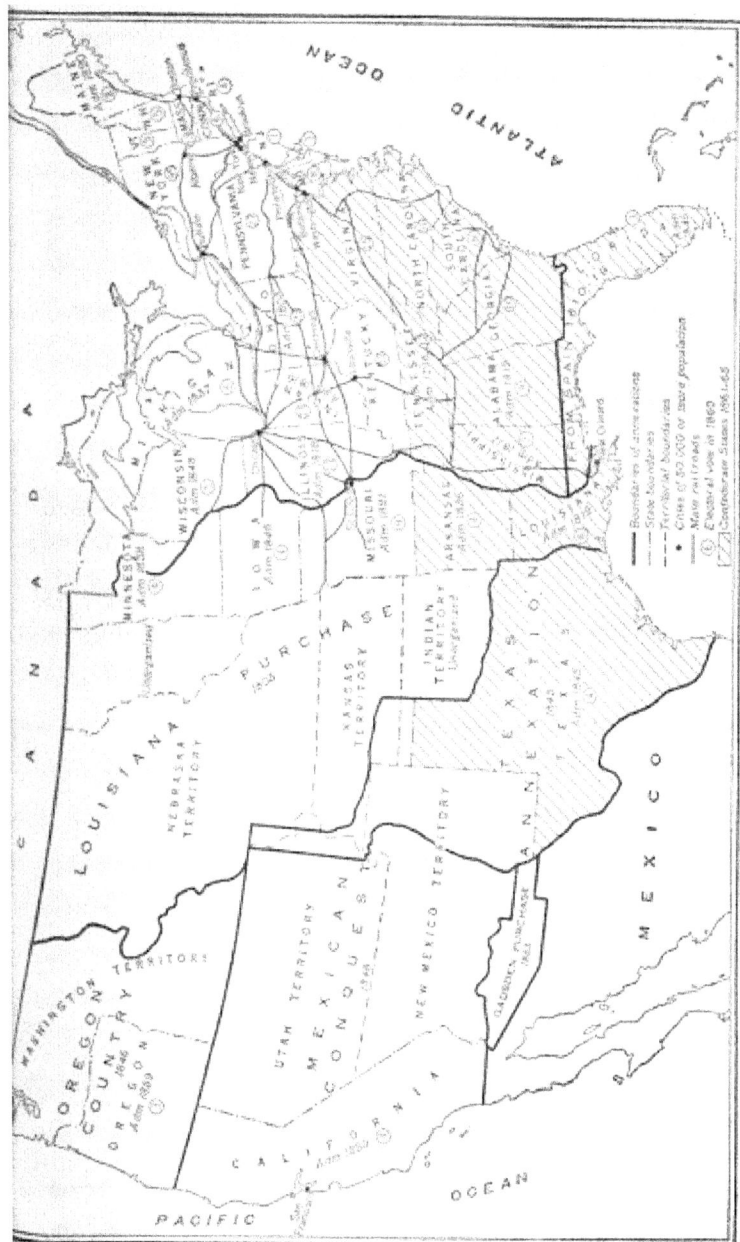

UNITED STATES IN 1860

not mainly of ignorance. Fostered by grants of public land, the school system in much of the country was a matter of just-fiable pride; and higher education on both private and public foundations, and professional schools, were well established wherever flourished the public-school system upon which they fed. Religious freedom was recognized throughout the land. Newspapers had become a stupendous organ of public opinion. The chief papers, such as the New York Tribune, circulated widely and no town of any size was without its own newspaper, or rival ones. The native literature, the arts, music, theater, and other amusements were recognized elements of national life. The people were learning to live; and the accumulation of wealth was developing a leisure class and culture.

IMMIGRATION

The great growth of population was not the result of natural increase only. Beginning about 1820, each year saw the arrival of a host of immigrants. In 1854 there were 428,000 of them. The number varied widely from year to year, but in 1860 4,000,000 of the population, being 13 percent of the whole, were of foreign birth. These were for the most part up to 1860 of the British, Irish, and German stock which had formed the most appreciable elements of the colonial people, and they did not make any marked ethnic change in the character of the population as a whole.

INDUSTRIAL TREND

The contrast between conditions in 1790 and 1860 has been noticed because it was at the end of this period that the nation entered upon its great struggle for continued existence as a whole, and the localism that had hindered and almost prevented the formation of the Union had still to bear the burden of the blame. The manifestation was the same, but the underlying causes had now become distinctly economic, whereas the differences inherited from colonial times were more social and directly political. The spread of the nation and the unparalleled development of industry were of necessity accompanied by an increasing unevenness in their economic effects. The sterile soil of New England could not long compete with the deep fertility of the prairies, especially when the development of transportation brought grain that was cheap to grow, cheap to even distant markets; and more than ever that region turned to its fisheries and foreign trade and also to manufactures. Throughout the Middle States there was this same trend toward industrialism. The West was still essentially agricultural; but even here there were 10 cities of 25,000 inhabitants or more, and a sufficient beginning of manufacturing to warrant the belief that the Old Northwest at least would become diversified in its economic foundations.

THE SOUTH AND SLAVERY

But the South, which now included the States of the South-west, was not only distinctly agricultural, but was confined to two crops, tobacco and cotton. After the invention of the cotton gin, which made it easy to extract the seeds from the lint, the growing of cotton received an enormous impulse, and spread over all the newer lands where climate and soil made its growth profitable. The South became cotton grower for the industrial world; not only did it furnish the supply for the northern mills, but the value of the export of cotton in 1860 was $192,000,000 or 57 percent of the whole export. And the cultivation of cotton was by slave labor; as also, though with much less importance, was the cultivation of tobacco; so that as slavery died out in the rest of the Union it became a chief factor in the economic well-being of the South. In 1790 there were 700,000 slaves in a total population of 3,900,000, which was 18 percent. In 1860 there were 4,000,000 in a population of 31,000,000, or less than 13 percent; but in the eleven States that seceded from the Union to form the Confederate States, there were 3,500,000 slaves in a total population of 8,900,000, which was 89 percent of all the slaves and 40 percent of the population of these seceding States.

SECESSION AND WAR

Such an enormous mass of servile laborers concentrated in one portion of the Union and bound up with the economic development of that region could not but have an influence upon social aspects and also upon the political point of view. Moreover, the conditions set the slave-holding section, a region that was a third in size and 40 percent of the population of the whole, apart from the rest, where slavery was forbidden or un-profitable; and checked the participation of that region in the general development described above. The political effect of this divergence was to keep alive in the South the spirit of localism and belief that the nation was under the new Constitution, as it had been under the Articles of Confederation, a Union of sovereign States, under the Articles of Confederation, a Union of sovereign States, each of which retained the right to withdraw from the government, of which through its ratification or later admission as a State it had become a member.

It is not necessary here to consider the legality of such action. Secession was not a new theory in 1860; the idea was as old as the government and movements for State action in disobedience to national measures had appeared several times in the history of the United States since 1789, and in various sections. But by 1860 the rest of the nation, developed as described above during the 70 years of life under the Constitution, had arrived at a disbelief in this theory. The result was war; and the effect of the defeat of the Confederate States, which the seceding States had formed, was to abolish forever the idea that the States had any rights except such as they possessed under the Constitution of the United States—the Constitution of an in-dissoluble Union as well as one of indestructible States.

THE NATION OF 1937

The third of the maps which accompany this sketch shows how the tale of the forty-eight States has been completed since 1860. During this period there has been also an addition of outlying dependencies, including Alaska, Hawaii, Puerto Rico, Canal Zone, and the Philippines, the last being held in preparation for independence. The number of inhabitants in the continental region increased from 31,000,000 to 128,000,000. The continuance of the change in relative density of population and the shifting of political balance is shown on the maps by the number of electoral votes in each State at the different periods.

CHARACTER OF DEVELOPMENT, 1865-1937

The national growth after the end of the Civil War in 1865 accentuated the development of industrialism, with all its problems of capital and labor, of individual rights and rights of combination, of working conditions and the steadily increasing substitution of machines for human toil. Agriculture, still the most important element in our economic life, but hard pressed to hold its position, has also changed greatly. The regions of chief production have altered with the development of the frontier; products have become more varied, and more attention has been given to horticulture and fresh vegetables. Machines have multiplied and increased the possible

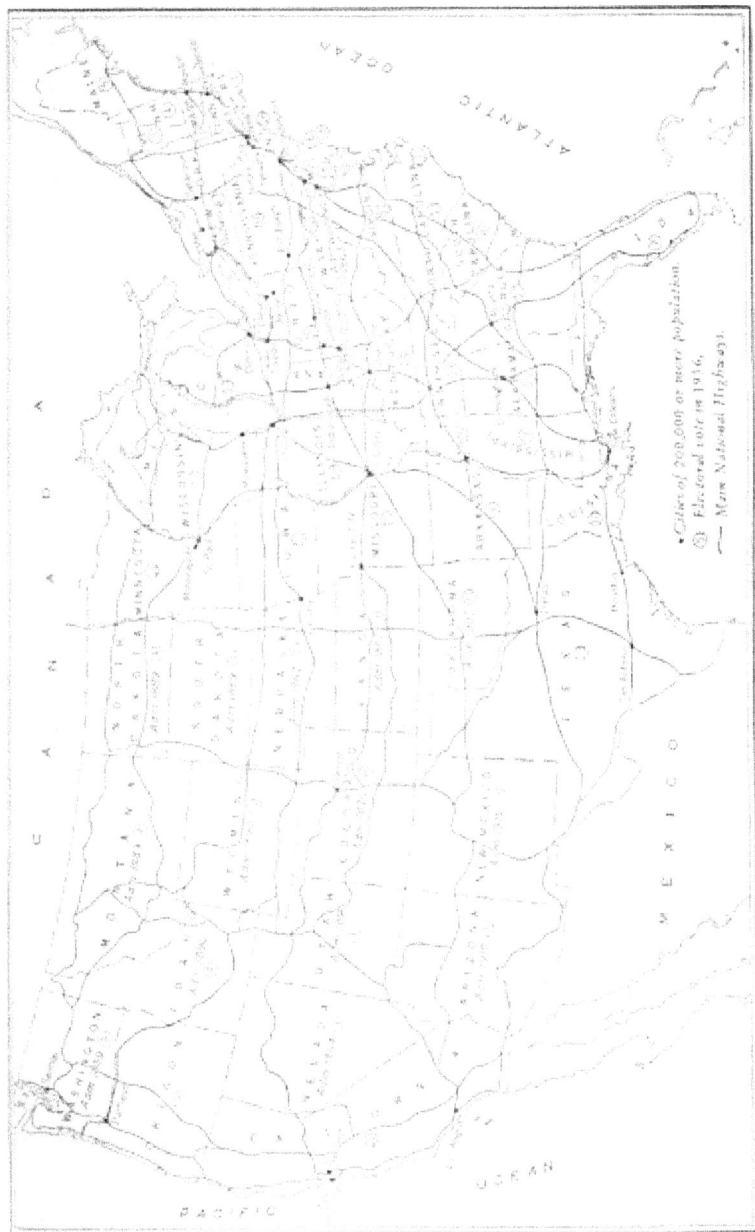

UNITED STATES IN 1937

• Cities of 250,000 or more population
⊙ Electoral vote in 1936,
— Main National Highways

[155]

area of cultivation, while diminishing the need of hand labor and relative employment. Agricultural schools and State and national bureaus have introduced science to agriculture; while the Grange and similar organizations, the gasoline engines, automobiles, telephones, rural delivery, electric light, and radio have wrought against the isolation and social dreariness that formerly surrounded rural life.

While the population has grown and become more and more urban, its character as a whole has been much influenced by postbellum immigration. This has included vast numbers of Latin and Slavic people, not previously an influential factor, and having in many respects behind them generations of habits and culture quite different from those of the earlier growth of the country. Of great importance in postbellum development has been the effect in the South of the abolition of slavery and the consequent growth there of industrialism and share in the new principles of agriculture.

MODERN PROBLEMS

The cross-hatching of the whole country with railroad lines, the universality of the telegraph and later of the telephone and radio, the unparalleled development of automobiles and the paved roads they require, and the introduction of aviation have all added to the complexity of American life, keyed it to the idea of haste, whether in the rush of business or the pursuit of pleasure, and tended also toward the elimination of localism and the prejudices of its ignorance, and toward the primacy of nationalism. Public supervision and control over private affairs, sharp consideration of the rights of the individual and the welfare of the many or the whole, of the claims of property and of humanity, of material and human conservation and reclamation, of the right and requirement of education, of representation and more direct control by the people, of the right to a healthful life and sufficient leisure, of the justifiable place of amusements, indoors and out—these also are phases of our present life. The youthful pioneer spirit died down with the disappearance of the frontier and the end of free land. The nation approached maturity; took on dignity and international responsibility as it became a world power, and faced the teeming problems of greatness, of many aspects of which the Framers had no conception.

Portraits and Sketches of the Chief Justices of the United States

INTRODUCTION

The Constitution does not directly authorize a Chief Justice, but only "Judges, both of the supreme and inferior Courts." Article I, sec. 3, cl. 6, however, says that when "the President is tried [under impeach-ment], the Chief Justice shall preside"; and this was evidently taken by Congress to mean that there should be a Justice with that title, rather than that the presiding officer at the trial should be the Justice who was the head of the Court. The Judiciary Act of September 24, 1789, provided for a Chief Justice and five Associate Justices.

The Chief Justice of the United States, to give him his correct title, is probably the most exalted judicial officer in the world. During the 147 years since the Judiciary Act became law, only eleven men have held the position; and it is even allowable to disregard one of these in the count, since Rutledge, although he presided for one term, was rejected by the Senate. The service of two of them, Marshall and Taney, covered almost sixty-four years. They have been, however, usually of mature years before they assumed the office. Jay, the youngest, was 43, and Marshall 45; the rest have been over 50, and the last three over 60. Disregarding fractions, Jay served 5 years, Rutledge one term, Ellsworth 4 years, Marshall 34, Taney 28, Chase 8, Waite 14, Fuller 21, White 10, Taft 8, and Chief Justice Hughes was appointed in 1930. With one or two exceptions they were prominent in public life before they were elevated to the bench; and this, in some cases, rather than legal preeminence, influenced the appointment. All of them from Marshall on had been admitted to practice before the Supreme Court, and Taney had been Attorney General of the United States and Taft Solicitor General.

In only one case, that of White, has an Associate Justice been promoted; but two of the men, Rutledge and Hughes, had had earlier office as such, though Rutledge attended no terms of the court, and a third, Taney, had been appointed but rejected by the Senate. The first three Chief Justices retired, but beginning with Marshall all have died in office except Taft, who resigned about a month before his decease.

On September 24, 1789, the day he signed the Judiciary Act, President Washington sent to the Senate the nominations of Jay as Chief Justice; and of Rutledge, James Wilson of Pennsylvania, William Cushing of Massachusetts, Robert H. Harrison of Maryland, and John Blair of Virginia as Associate "Judges." The Senate confirmed the appointments on September 26; and Jay's commission was made out that day, Cushing's on the 27th, Wilson's on the 29th, and Blair's on the 30th. Harrison declined and James Iredell of North Carolina was nominated on February 8, 1790, and confirmed and commissioned on February 10. He did not sit until the second term of the court.

In accordance with the Judiciary Act the Supreme Court was to organize on February 1, 1790; but only three Justices attended that day at the Royal Exchange at the foot of Broad Street in New York City. Organization was effected the next day, with Jay, Wilson, Cushing, and Blair on the bench. Rut-ledge, who resigned as Associate Justice in 1791, never attended any of the terms in that capacity. The court sat for a week, but heard no cases. Their commissions were read the first day, a crier and clerk were appointed, a seal authorized, rules formulated, and some nineteen counselors and seven attorneys ad-mitted to practice before the court. There is no evidence that the Justices were sworn in at this time. It is probable that they had taken the required oaths separately earlier. It is known that Wilson was sworn in by the mayor of Philadelphia on October 5, 1789. The Justices wore robes but discarded the English judicial wigs. The early robes were probably parti-colored, black and red.

The second term, in August, 1790, was again in New York City, without cases on the docket, which was also the conditions at the third term, February, 1791. This session was held in the City Hall of Philadelphia, where the court continued to meet until it moved to Washington. Thomas Johnson of Maryland, who was Rutledge's successor, qualified at the August, 1792, term, and at that time cases were first heard on their merits.

JAY, JOHN, 1745-1829
NEW YORK

Continental Congress, 1774-76, 1778-79, 1784,
President, 1779; New York Provincial Convention; Minister to Spain, but not received;
negotiator of peace with Great Britain; Secretary for Foreign Affairs, 1781-89; Chief Justice of the United States, commissioned,
September 26, 1789, resigned, June 29, 1795,
refused reappointment, 1800; Minister to
England, 1794-95; Governor of New York.

RUTLEDGE, JOHN, 1739-1800
SOUTH CAROLINA

South Carolina Legislature; Stamp Act Congress; Continental Congress, 1774-75, 1782-83;
South Carolina Constitutional Convention, and
Governor; Deputy to United States Constitutional Convention; Associate Justice, 1789-
91, but did not attend; Chief Justice of South
Carolina; sworn in as Chief Justice of the
United States, August 12, 1795, but rejected
by the Senate, December 15.

ELLSWORTH, OLIVER, 1745-1807
CONNECTICUT

Connecticut Legislature; Continental Congress,
1778-83; Governor's Council and State judge;
Deputy to United States Constitutional Con-
vention, but not a Signer; United States Sena-
tor, 1789-96; sworn in as Chief Justice of the
United States, March 8, 1796; mission to
France, 1799-1800; resigned Chief Justiceship,
October, 1800.

MARSHALL, JOHN, 1755-1835
VIRGINIA

Officer in the Revolution; Virginia Legislature;
Virginia Ratification Convention; XYZ Mis-
sion to France, 1797; Congressman, 1799-1800;
Secretary of State, 1800-01; sworn in as Chief
Justice of the United States, February 4,
1801; died in office, July 6, 1835.

TANEY, ROGER BROOKE, 1777-1864
MARYLAND

Maryland Legislature; Attorney General of the United States, 1831-33; recess appointment as Secretary of the Treasury, 1833, but rejected by the Senate; appointed Associate Justice, 1835, but rejected by the Senate; sworn in as Chief Justice of the United States, March 28, 1836; died in office, October 12, 1864.

CHASE, SALMON PORTLAND, 1808-1873
OHIO

United States Senator, 1849-55; Governor of Ohio; Secretary of the Treasury, 1861-64; sworn in as Chief Justice of the United States, December 15, 1864; died in office, May 7, 1873.

WAITE, MORRISON REMICK, 1816-88
OHIO

Ohio Legislature; counsel before Geneva Arbitration Tribunal, 1871-72; President of Ohio Constitutional Convention; sworn in as Chief Justice of the United States, March 4, 1874; died in office, March 23, 1888.

FULLER, MELVILLE WESTON, 1833-1910
ILLINOIS

Active in Democratic politics but held no offices; sworn in as Chief Justice, October 8, 1888; died in office, July 4, 1910.

WHITE, EDWARD DOUGLASS,
1845-1921

LOUISIANA

Confederate soldier; Louisiana Senate; Louisiana Supreme Court; United States Senator,
1891-94; Associate Justice of the Supreme
Court of the United States, 1894-1910; sworn
in as Chief Justice of the United States, December 19, 1910; died in office, May 19, 1921.

TAFT, WILLIAM HOWARD, 1857-1930

OHIO

Superior Court of Ohio; Solicitor General of
the United States, 1890-92; Circuit Judge,
1892-1900; President of Philippine Commission and Governor, 1900-04; Secretary of
War, 1904-08; President of the United States,
1909-13; sworn in as Chief Justice of the
United States, July 11, 1921; resigned,
February 3, 1930.

HUGHES, CHARLES EVANS, 1862—

NEW YORK

Governor of New York; Associate Justice of
the Supreme Court of the United States,
1910-16; Republican candidate for President,
1916; Secretary of State, 1921-25; member
of Permanent Court of Arbitration at The
Hague; sworn in as Chief Justice of the
United States, February 24, 1930.

QUESTIONS AND ANSWERS
PERTAINING TO THE
CONSTITUTION

Q. In what language was Magna Charta written, and to whom was it addressed?

A. It was written in Latin and was addressed "To the archbishops, bishops, abbots, earls, barons, justices, foresters, sheriffs, reeves, ministers, and to all bailiffs, and faithful subjects."

Q. What part of the world was first called America?

A. The name "America" was first applied to Central Brazil, in honor of Amerigo Vespucci, who claimed its discovery. It was first applied to the whole known western world by Mercator, the geographer, in 1538.

Q. When did the phrase, "The United States of America," originate?

A. The first known use of the formal term "United States of America" was in the Declaration of Independence. Thomas Paine, in February, 1776, had written of "Free and independent States of America." The terms "United Colonies," "United Colonies of America," "United Colonies of North America," and also "States," were used in 1775 and 1776.

Q. How were deputies to the Constitutional Convention chosen?

A. They were appointed by the legislatures of the different States.

Q. Were there any restrictions as to the number of deputies a State might send?

A. No.

Q. Which State did not send deputies to the Constitutional Convention?

A. Rhode Island and Providence Plantations.

Q. Were the other twelve States represented throughout the Constitutional Convention?

A. No. Two of the deputies from New York left on July 10, 1787, and after that Hamilton, the third deputy, when he was in attendance did not attempt to cast the vote of his State. The New Hampshire deputies did not arrive until July 23, 1787; so that there never was a vote of more than eleven States.

Q. Where and when did the deputies to the Constitutional Convention assemble?

A. In Philadelphia, in the State House where the Declaration of Independence was signed. The meeting was called for May 14, 1787, but a quorum was not present until May 25.

Q. About how large was the population of Philadelphia?

A. The census of 1790 gave it 28,000; including its suburbs, about 42,000.

Q. What was the average age of the deputies to the Constitutional Convention?

A. About 44.

[162]

Q. Who were the oldest and youngest members of the Constitutional Convention?

A. Benjamin Franklin, of Pennsylvania, then 81; and Jonathan Dayton, of New Jersey, 26.

Q. How many lawyers were members of the Constitutional Convention?

A. There were probably 34, out of 55, who had at least made a study of the law.

Q. From what classes of society were the members of the Constitutional Convention drawn?

A. In addition to the lawyers, there were soldiers, planters, educators, ministers, physicians, financiers, and merchants.

Q. How many members of the Constitutional Convention had been members of the Continental Congress?

A. Forty, and two others were later members.

Q. Were there any members of the Constitutional Convention who never attended any of its meetings?

A. There were nineteen who were never present. Some of these declined, others merely neglected the duty.

Q. Were the members of the Constitutional Convention called "delegates" or "deputies," and is there any distinction between the terms?

A. Some of the States called their representatives "delegates"; some, "deputies"; and some, "commissioners," the terms being often mixed. In the Convention itself they were always referred to as "deputies." Washington, for example, signed his name as "deputy from Virginia." The point is simply that whatever they called themselves, they were representatives of their States. The general practice of historians is to describe them as "delegates."

Q. Who was called the "Sage of the Constitutional Convention"?

A. Benjamin Franklin, of Pennsylvania.

Q. Who was called the "Father of the Constitution"?

A. James Madison, of Virginia, because in point of erudition and actual contributions to the formation of the Constitution he was preeminent.

Q. Was Thomas Jefferson a member of the Constitutional Convention?

A. No. Jefferson was American Minister to France at the time of the Constitutional Convention.

Q. What did Thomas Jefferson have to do with framing the Constitution?

A. Although absent from the Constitutional Convention and during the period of ratification, Jefferson rendered no inconsiderable service to the cause of Constitutional Government, for it was partly through his insistence that the Bill of Rights, consisting of the first ten amendments, was adopted.

Q. Who presided over the Constitutional Convention?

A. George Washington, chosen unanimously.

Q. How long did it take to frame the Constitution?

A. It was drafted in fewer than one hundred working days.

Q. How much was paid for the journal kept by Madison during the Constitutional Convention?

A. President Jackson secured from Congress in 1837 an appropriation of $30,000 with which to buy Madison's journal and other papers left by him.

Q. Was there harmony in the Convention?

A. Serious conflicts arose at the outset, especially between those representing the small and large States.

Q. Who presented the Virginia Plan?

A. Edmund Randolph.

Q. What was the Connecticut Compromise?

A. This was the first great compromise of the Constitutional Convention, whereby it was agreed that in the Senate each State should have two members, and that in the House the number of Representatives was to be based upon population. Thus the rights of the small States were safeguarded, and the majority of the population was to be fairly represented.

Q. Who actually wrote the Constitution?

A. In none of the relatively meager records of the Constitutional Convention is the literary authorship of any part of the Constitution definitely established. The deputies debated proposed plans until, on July 24, 1787, substantial agreement having been reached, a Committee of Detail was appointed, consisting of John Rutledge, of South Carolina; Edmund Randolph, of Virginia; Nathaniel Gorham, of Massachusetts; Oliver Ellsworth, of Connecticut; and James Wilson, of Pennsylvania, who on August 6 reported a draft which included a Preamble and twenty-three articles, embodying fifty-seven sections. Debate continued until September 8, when a new Committee of Style was named to revise the draft. This committee included William Samuel Johnson, of Connecticut; Alexander Hamilton, of New York; Governor Morris, of Pennsylvania; James Madison, of Virginia; and Rufus King, of Massachusetts, and they reported the draft in approximately its final shape on September 12. The actual literary form is believed to be largely that of Morris, and the chief testimony for this is in the letters and papers of Madison, and Morris's claim. However, the document in reality was built slowly and laboriously, with not a piece of material included until it has been shaped and approved. The preamble was written by the Committee of Style.

Q. Who was the penman who, after the text of the Constitution had been agreed on, engrossed it prior to the signing?

A. Jacob Shallus who, at the time, was assistant clerk of the Pennsylvania State Assembly, and whose office was in the same building in which the Convention was held.

Q. Does his name appear on the document or in any of the papers pertaining to its preparation?

A. No. In the financial memoranda there is an entry of $30 for "clerks employed to transcribe & engross."

Q. When and how was the identity of the engrosser determined?

A. In 1937, on the occasion of the 150th anniversary of the Constitution. His identity was determined after a long and careful search of collateral public documents, and is here disclosed for the first time.

Q. Where did Shallus do the engrossing?

A. There is no record of this, but probably in Independence Hall.

Q. Did he realize the importance of the work he had done?

A. Probably not; when he died, in 1796, the Constitution had not yet come to be the firmly established set of governmental principles it since has become.

Q. Did some of the deputies to the Constitutional Convention refuse to sign the Constitution?

A. Only thirty-nine signed. Fourteen deputies had departed for their homes, and three--Randolph and Mason, of Virginia, and Gerry, of Massachusetts--refused to sign. One of the signatures is that of an absent deputy, John Dickinson, of Delaware, added at his request by George Read, who also was from Delaware.

Q. How can it be said that the signing of the Constitution was unanimous, when the deputies of only twelve States signed and some delegates refused to sign?

A. The signatures attest the "Unanimous Consent of the States present." The voting was by States, and the vote of each State that of a majority of its deputies. Hamilton signed this attestation for New York, though as he was the only deputy of the State present he had not been able to cast the vote of his State for the consent, only eleven States voting on the final question. There is an even greater discrepancy about the Signers of the Declaration of Independence. Some seven or eight members present on July 4 never signed; seven Signers, including Richard Henry Lee, of Virginia, who proposed the resolution of independence, were not present on the day; and eight other Signers were not members of Congress until after July 4.

Q. Did George Washington sign the Declaration of Independence?

A. No. He had been appointed Commander-in-Chief of the Continental Army more than a year before and was at the time with the army in New York City.

Q. What are the exact measurements of the originals of the Declaration of Independence and of the Constitution of the United States?

A. The Declaration of Independence: 29 7/8 in. by 24 7/16 in.; The Constitution: four sheets, approximately 28 3/4 in. by 23 5/8 in. each.

Q. How many words are there in the texts in the present volume, and how long does it take to read them?

A. The Constitution has 4,543 words, including the signatures but not the certificate on the interlineations; and takes about half an hour to read. The Declaration of Independence has 1,458 words, with the signatures, but is slower reading, as it takes about ten minutes. The Farewell Address has 7,641 words and requires forty-five minutes to read.

Q. What party names were given to those who favored ratification and to those who opposed it?

A. Those who favored ratification were called Federalists; those who opposed, Anti-federalists.

Q. In ratifying the Constitution, did the people vote directly?

A. No. Ratification was by special State conventions (Art. VII).

Q. The vote of how many States was necessary to ratify the Constitution?

A. Nine (Art. VII).

Q. In what order did the States ratify the Constitution?

A. In the following order: Delaware, Pennsylvania, New Jersey, Georgia, Connecticut, Massachusetts, Maryland, South Carolina, New Hampshire, Virginia, and New York. After Washington had been inaugurated, North Carolina and Rhode Island ratified.

Q. After the Constitution was submitted for ratification, where did the greatest contests occur?

A. In Massachusetts, Virginia, and New York.

Q. In each instance what was the vote?

A. New York ratified the Constitution by a majority of three votes 30 to 27; Massachusetts by 187 to 168; and Virginia by 89 to 79.

Q. In the course of ratification, how many amendments were offered by the State conventions?

A. Seventy-eight; exclusive of Rhode Island's twenty-one, and those demanded by the first convention in North Carolina. There were many others offered which were considered necessary as items of a Bill of Rights. Professor Ames gives 124 as the whole number, inclusive of those of Rhode Island and North Carolina and the Bills of Rights. Various of these covered the same topics.

Q. When did the United States government go into operation under the Constitution?

A. The Constitution became binding upon nine States by the ratification of the ninth State, New Hampshire, June 21, 1788. Notice of this ratification was received by Congress on July 2, 1788. On September 13, 1788, Congress adopted a resolution declaring that electors should be appointed in the ratifying States on the first Wednesday in January, 1789; that the electors vote for President on the first Wednesday in February, 1789; and that "the first Wednesday in March next [March 4, 1789] be the time and the present seat of Congress the place for commencing proceedings under the said constitution." The Convention had also suggested "that after such Publication the Electors should be appointed, and the Senators and Representatives elected." The Constitution left with the States the control over the election of congressmen, and Congress said nothing about this in its resolution; but the States proceeded to provide for it as well as for the appointment of electors. On March 3, 1789, the old Confederation went out of existence and on March 4 the new government of the United States began legally to function, according to a decision of the Supreme Court of the United States (wings v. Speed, 5 Wheat. 420); however, it had no practical existence until April 6, when first the presence of quorums in both Houses permitted organization of Congress. On April 30, 1789, George Washington was inaugurated as President of the United States, so on that date the executive branch of the government under the Constitution became operative. But it was not until February 2, 1790, that the Supreme Court, as head of the third branch of the government, organized and, held its first session;

so that is the date when our government under the Constitution became fully operative.

Q. Did Washington receive the unanimous vote of the electors in his first election as President?

A. Yes, of all who voted. Four, two in Virginia and two in Maryland, did not vote; and the eight votes to which New York was entitled were not cast because the legislature could come to no agreement upon how the electors should be appointed. There should have been 81 votes; he received 69.

Q. How did the first inauguration proceed?

A. The Senate Journal narrates it as follows: "The House of Representatives, preceded by their Speaker, came into the Senate Chamber, and took the seats assigned them; and the joint Committee, preceded by their Chairman, agreeably to order, introduced the President of the United States to the Senate Chamber, where he was received by the Vice President, who conducted him to the Chair; when the Vice President informed him, that 'The Senate and House of Representatives were ready to attend him to take the oath required by the Constitution, and that it would be administered by the Chancellor of the State of New-York'--To which the President replied, he was ready to proceed:--and being attended to the gallery in front of the Senate Chamber, by the Vice President and Senators, the Speaker and Representatives, and the other public characters present, the oath was administered.--After which the Chancellor proclaimed, 'Long live George Washington, President of the United States.' The President having returned to his seat, after a short pause, arose and addressed the Senate and House of Representatives. The President, the Vice President, the Senate and House of Represent-atives, then proceeded to St. Paul's Chapel, where divine service was performed by the Chaplain of Congress, after which the President was conducted to his house, by the Committee appointed for that purpose."

Q. Was Adams sworn in as Vice President before Washington took the oath of office as President?

A. No. Neither the Vice President nor any Senators took the oath of office until June 3. The first act of Congress, June 1, provided for the oath. In the House the Speaker and members present on April 8 had taken an oath provided for by a resolve on April 6 of that House, and the act of June 1 recognized that oath as sufficient for those who had taken it.

Q. What cities have been capitals of the United States government?

A. The Continental Congress sat at Philadelphia, 1774-76, 1777, 1778-83; Baltimore, 1776-77; Lancaster, 1777; York, 1777-78; Princeton, 1783; Annapolis, 1783-84; Trenton, 1784; and New York, 1785-89. The first capital under the Constitution of the United States was in New York, but in 1790 it was moved to Philadelphia. Here it was continued until 1800, when the permanent capital, Washington, in the new District of Columbia, was occupied.

Q. How was the manner of address of the President of the United States decided?

A. Both Houses of Congress appointed committees to consider the proper title to give the President, but they could not agree. The Senate wished it to be "His Highness the President of the United States of America and Protector of their Liberties." The House considered this as too monarchical...

and on May 5 addressed its reply to the inaugural speech merely to "The President of the United States." The Senate on May 14 agreed to this simple form.

Q. What is meant by the term "constitution"?

A. A constitution embodies the fundamental principles of a government. Our constitution, adopted by the sovereign power, is amendable by that power only. To the constitution all laws, executive actions, and, judicial decisions must conform, as it is the creator of the powers exercised by the departments of government.

Q. Why has our Constitution been classed as "rigid"?

A. The term "rigid" is used in opposition to "flexible" because the provisions are in a written document which cannot be legally changed with the same ease and in the same manner as ordinary laws. The British Constitution, which is unwritten, can, on the other hand, be changed overnight by act of Parliament.

Q. What was W. E. Gladstone's famous remark about the Constitution?

A. It was as follows: "As the British Constitution is the most subtle organism which has proceeded from the womb and long gestation of progressive history, so the American Constitution is, so far as I can see, the most wonderful work ever struck off at a given time by the brain and purpose of man."

Q. What is the source of the philosophy found in the Constitution?

A. The book which had the greatest influence upon the members of the Constitutional Convention was Montesquieu's Spirit of Laws, which first appeared in 1748. The great French philosopher had, however, in turn borrowed much of his doctrine from the Englishman John Locke, with whose writings various members of the Convention were also familiar.

Q. Are there original ideas of government in the Constitution?

A. Yes; but its main origins lie in centuries of experience in government, the lessons of which were brought over from England and further developed through the practices of over a century and a half in the colonies and early State governments, and in the struggles of the Continental Congress. Its roots are deep in the past; and its endurance and the obedience and respect it has won are mainly the result of the slow growth of its principles from before the days of Magna Charta.

Q. What state papers should be considered in connecting the Constitution of the United States with Magna Charta?

A. The Great Charter was confirmed several times by later medieval monarchs, and there were various statutes, such as those of Westminster, which also helped to develop the germs of popular government. The Petition of Right, 1628, against the abuse of the royal prerogative, the Habeas Corpus Act, 1679, and the Bill of Rights, 1689, to establish the claims of the Petition, are the great English documents of more modern times on popular freedom. Meanwhile, the colonial charters became the foundation of the Americans' claim to the "rights of Englishmen," and were the predecessors of the State Constitutions, which owed their origin to the American Revolution. The Declaration of Independence established the principles which the Constitution made practical. Plans for colonial union were proposed from time to time, the most important of them being the Albany Plan of 1754, of which Benjamin Franklin was the author. The united efforts to establish independence gave birth to the Articles of Confederation, which though inadequate, were a real step toward the "more perfect Union" of the Constitution.

Q. In what respect had the Confederation failed?

A. It had three great weaknesses. It had no means of revenue independent of that received through its requisitions on the States, which were nothing more than requests, which the States could and did disregard; and it had no control over foreign or interstate commerce. Behind these lacks was its inability to compel the States to honor the national obligations. It could make treaties but had no means to compel obedience to them; or to provide for the payment of the foreign debt. It had responsibility but no power as a national government; no means of coercing the States to obedience even to the very inadequate grant given to the "League of Friendship" by the Articles of Confederation. But its greatest weakness was that it had no direct origin in, or action on, the people themselves; but, unlike both the Declaration of Independence and the later Constitution, knew only the States and was known only to them, calling them sovereign.

Q. How extensively has the Constitution been copied?

A. All later Constitutions show its influence; it has been copied extensively throughout the world.

Q. The United States government is frequently described as one of limited powers. Is this true?

A. Yes. The United States government possesses only such powers as are specifically granted to it by the Constitution.

Q. Then how does it happen that the government constantly exercises powers not mentioned by the Constitution?

A. Those powers simply flow from general provisions. To take a simple example, the Constitution gives to the United States the right to coin money. It would certainly follow, therefore, that the government had the right to make the design for the coinage. This is what the Supreme Court calls "reasonable construction" of the Constitution (Art. I, sec. 8, cl. 18).

Q. Where, in the Constitution, is there mention of education?

A. There is none; education is a matter reserved for the States.

Q. Who was called the "Expounder of the Constitution"?

A. Daniel Webster, of Massachusetts, because of his forceful and eloquent orations interpreting the document.

Q. Must a member of the House of Representatives be a resident of the district which he represents?

A. The Constitution provides only that no person shall be a representative "who shall not, when elected, be an Inhabitant of that State in which he shall be chosen"; but makes no requirement as to residence within the district (Art. I, sec. 2, cl. 2).

Q. Have the English a greater representation in their House of Commons than Americans in their House of Representatives?

A. In Great Britain (England, Scotland, and Wales) there is a member in the House of Commons for approximately every 70,000 of population, while in the United States membership in the lower House is based upon every 279,712 of population (Art. I, sec. 2, cl. 3).

Q. What was the ratio of representation in Congress 100 years ago and what is it now?

A. In 1837 there was apportioned one representative for every 47,700 inhabitants, the total number being 242. In 1937 there was one representative for every 279,712, the total number being 435 (Art I, sec. 2, cl. 3).

Q. Is it possible to impeach a justice of the Supreme Court?

A. It is possible to impeach a Justice of the Supreme Court or any other official. The Constitution makes provision for impeachment by the House and trial of the accused by the Senate sitting as a court of "all civil Officers," which includes the Justices (Art. I, sec. 2, cl. 5; sec. 3, cl. 6, 7; Art. II, sec. 4).

Q. Are Senators, Representatives, and justices of the Supreme Court civil officials of the United. States?

A. Justices are, but the others are probably not. The Constitution in several places seems to make a clear distinction between legislators and officials, though this has been contested. Members of Congress are not subject to impeachment, but are liable to expulsion by the vote of the House of which they are members (Art. I, sec. 5, cl. 2).

Q. What would be the proceeding in case of the impeachment of a Cabinet officer?

A. An impeachment proceeding may be set in motion in the House of Representatives by charges made on the floor on the responsibility of a member or territorial delegate; by charges preferred by a memorial, which is usually referred to a committee for examination; by charges transmitted by the legislature of a State or from a grand jury; or the facts developed and reported by an investigating committee of the House. After the impeachment has been voted by the House, the case is heard by the Senate sitting as a court. When the President of the United States is impeached and tried, the proceedings are the same except that the Senate is then presided over by the Chief Justice of the United States (Art. I, sec. 2, cl. 5; sec. 3, cl. 6, 7; Art. II, sec. 4).

Q. What is meant when it is said that Senators are paired?

A. Sometimes a Senator belonging to one party agrees with a Senator belonging to the other party that neither will vote if the other is absent, the theory being that they would always vote on opposite sides of the question. This is called a pair. Sometimes pairs are secured on a particular vote only. For example, if a Senator is in favor of a certain piece of legislation and is ill or unavoidably detained, his friends arrange for some one on the opposite side not to vote. This insures for each a record as to his views. While many are opposed to general pairs, as the first is called, all are glad to arrange a pair for a specific measure if a Senator is unavoidably prevented from being present (Art. I, sec. 5, cl. 2).

Q. What is the mace of the House of Representatives and what purpose does it serve?

A. The mace consists of thirteen ebony rods, about three feet long, representing the thirteen original States. It is bound together with silver in imitation of the thongs which bound the fasces of ancient Rome. The shaft is surmounted by a globe of solid silver about five inches in diameter upon which rests a massive silver eagle. The mace is the symbol of the paramount authority of the House within its own sphere. In times of riot or disorder upon the floor the Speaker may direct the Sergeant-at-Arms, the executive officer of the House, to bear the mace up and down the aisles as a reminder that the dignity and decorum of the House must not be overthrown. Defiance to such warning is the ultimate disrespect to the House and may lead to expulsion. When the House is sitting as a body the mace rests upright on a pedestal at the right of the Speaker's dais; when the House is sitting in committee of the whole, the mace stands upon the floor at the foot of its pedestal. Thus, when the House wishes to "rise" from committee of the whole and resume business as a legislative body, lifting the mace to its pedestal automatically effects the transition. The origin of the idea of the mace is based upon a similar emblem in the British House of Commons (Art. I, sec. 5, cl. 2).

Q. Who administers the oath of office to the Speaker of the House of Representatives?

A. It is usually administered by the oldest member in point of service (Art. I, sec. 5, cl. 2).

Q. What is meant by the "Father" of the House of Representatives?

A. It is a colloquial title informally bestowed upon the oldest member in point of service (Art. I, sec. 5, cl. 2). It was borrowed originally from the House of Commons.

Q. Why is a member of the House of Representatives referred to on the floor as "the gentleman from New York," for example, instead of by name?

A. It is a custom in all large deliberative bodies to avoid the use of the personal name in debate or procedure. The original purpose of this was to avoid any possible breach of decorum and to separate the political from the personal character of each member (Art. I, sec. 6, cl. 1).

Q. Do members of Congress get extra compensation for their work on committees?

A. No. (Art. I, sec. 6, cl. 1).

Q. Could members of the President's Cabinet be permitted to sit in Congress without amending the Constitution?

A. No. A national officeholder cannot at the same time be a member of either House of Congress (Art. 1, sec. 6, cl. 2).

Q. Must all revenue and appropriation bills originate in the House of Representatives?

A. The Constitution provides that all bills for raising revenue shall originate in the House of Representatives. It is customary for appropriation bills to originate there also (Art. I, sec. 7, cl. 1).

Q. What is meant by the word veto, in the President's powers?

A. The word is from the Latin and means "I forbid." The President is authorized by the Constitution to refuse his assent to a bill presented by Congress if for any reason he disapproves of it. Congress may, however, pass the act over his veto but it must be by a two-thirds majority in both houses. If Congress adjourns before the end of the 10 days, the President can prevent the enactment of the bill by merely not signing it. This is called a pocket veto. (Art. I, sec. 7, cl. 2).

Q. If, after a bill has passed both houses of Congress and gone to the President, Congress desires to recall it, can this be done?

A. A bill which has reached the President may be recalled only by concurrent resolution. The form used is as follows: Resolved, by the House of Representatives (the Senate concurring), That the President be requested to return to the House of Representatives the bill . . . (title). After the concurrent resolution passes both houses it is formally transmitted to the President. The latter might, however, have already signed it, in which case it would have become a law and would have to be repealed in regular fashion (Art. I, sec. 7, cl. 2).

Q. What is the difference between a joint and a concurrent resolution of Congress?

A. A joint resolution has the same force as an act, and must be signed by the President or passed over his veto. A concurrent resolution is not a law, but only a measure on which the two Houses unite for a purpose concerned with their organization and procedure, or expressions of facts, principles, opinions, and purposes, "matters peculiarly within the province of Congress alone," and not embracing "legislative provisions proper" (Art. 1, sec. 7, cl. 3).

Q. Which is the longest term of office in the government, aside from judges?

A. The Comptroller General of the United States and the Assistant Comptroller General have the longest tenure. They hold office for fifteen years (Art. I, sec. 8), cl. 18; sec. 9, cl. 7; Art. II, sec. 2, cl. 2).

Q. What is the term of office of Treasurer of the United States?

A. The Treasurer is appointed by the President of the United States, and no length of term of office is specified (Art. I, sec. 8, cl. 18; sec. 9, cl. 7; Art. II, sec. 2, cl. 2).

Q. When were the various government departments established?

A. Four of the departments are older than the Government under the Constitution. These are Department of Foreign Affairs, Treasury, War, and Post Office. They were re-established by the First Congress under the Constitution, which changed the name of the Department of Foreign Affairs to Department of State. The office of Attorney General was established in 1789, and in 1870 the Department of Justice was established. The Department of the Navy was established in 1798; Department of Interior, 1849; Department of Agriculture, 1889; Department of Commerce and Labor, 1903; Department of Labor, 1913 (Art. I, sec. 8, cl. 18; Art. II, sec. 2, cl. 1).

Q. Does the Postmaster General come before the Secretary of the Navy in order of precedence? A. Yes. The order of creation is: Secretary of State, Secretary of the Treasury, Secretary of War, Attorney General, Postmaster General, Secretary of the Navy, Secretary of the Interior, Secretary of Agriculture, Secretary of Commerce, and Secretary of Labor, and that order gives the precedence; but the Postmaster General was not a member of the Cabinet until Jackson's Administration, many years after the Secretary of the Navy (Art. I, sec. 8, cl. 18; Art. II, sec. 2, cl. 1).

Q. Does the Constitution provide for the formation of a Cabinet?

A. No. The Constitution vests the executive power in the President. Executive departments were created by successive acts of Congress under authority conferred by the Constitution in Art. I, sec. 8, cl. 18. The Depts. of State, Treasury, and War were created by the first session of the First Congress. The Secretaries of these, together with the Attorney General, formed the first President's Cabinet. The Cabinet, it should be distinctly understood, is merely an advisory body whose members hold office only during the pleasure of the President. It has no constitutional function as a Cabinet, and the word does not appear in an act of Congress until February 26,1907 (Art.I, sec.8, cl. 18; Art. II, sec. 1, cl. 1, sec. 2, cl 1).

Q. How many methods of electing the President of the United States were considered by the Constitutional Convention?

A. Five. These were by the Congress; by the people; by State legislatures; by State executives; and by electors. Various methods of appointing the electors were proposed: by popular vote, by lottery from members of Congress, by State legislatures, and by State executives; and the matter was finally compromised by leaving the method to each State legislature. The meeting of the electors in one body was also proposed; and at first the final choice, in case election by electors failed, was given to the Senate, but later, after choice by Congress had been defeated, it was transferred to the House, voting by States.

Q. In the event of the death, resignation, removal, or disability of both President and Vice President, who would become President?

A. In accordance with the Presidential Succession Act of 1886, the succession would devolve upon the Secretary of State, or, if he were not avail-able, upon the Secretary of the Treasury, and so on, according to the order of the creation of their respective departments, provided always that the Cabinet officer fulfilled the qualifications for President as set forth in the Constitution. Thus, for example, if the Secretary of State were born in Canada, the succession would devolve upon the next in rank, the Secretary of the Treasury (Art. II, sec. 1, cl. 6).

Q. If a Cabinet member were to become President while Congress was not in session, would he call a session at once?

A. Yes. In accordance with the act of Congress providing for the succession in such an event, if Congress were not in session, or would not meet within twenty days, such a President would call san extra session (Art. II, sec. 1, cl. 6).

Q. Who appoints the Chief Justice of the United States and for how long a term?

A. The Chief Justice of the United States and the Associate Justices are appointed for life (during good behavior) by the President of the United States, "by and with the Advice and Consent of the Senate," (Art. II, sec. 2, cl. 2; Art. III, sec. 1).

Q. By what authority may the President of the United States call an extra session of Congress?

A. The Constitution provides for this. Art. II, sec. 3, says: ". . . he may, on extraordinary Occasions, convene both Houses, or either of them,"

Q. Can the Secretary of State take action with respect to recognizing a government without the consent of Congress?

A. The Secretary of State, on behalf of the President, may accord recognition without recourse to Congress (Art. II, sec. 3).

Q. Under the new government how was the national judiciary organized?

A. The First Congress passed many notable acts which endured many years as laws. One of the most worthy of these was that organizing the national judiciary, September 24, 1789. The bill was drawn up with extraordinary ability by Senator Oliver Ellsworth, of Connecticut, who had been a deputy to the Constitutional Convention, and who was to become Chief Justice of the United States. The Constitution prescribes a Supreme Court, but left its make-up and provision for other courts to Congress. The Supreme Court was organized with a Chief Justice and five Associates; a district court was provided for each State; and the Supreme Court Justices sat with the district judges in circuit courts. The jurisdiction of the three grades of the judiciary was fixed, and officers--clerks, marshals, and district attorneys--authorized. The Attorney General, also provided for in the act, was for many years little more than the President's legal adviser. Under this law President Washington appointed John Jay, of New York, Chief Justice, and the judiciary was organized on February 2, 1790.

Q. What are the correct style and titles of the Supreme Court of the United States and its members?

A. The correct title for the Supreme Court is "The Supreme Court of the United States"; for the members, one speaks of a Justice, or Associate Justice, of the Supreme Court of the United States, but always of the head of the court as "The Chief Justice of the United States" (Art. III, sec. I).

Q. What has been the number of Justices of the Supreme Court of the United States?

A. The Chief Justice is mentioned in the Constitution but the number of Justices is not specified. The act of September 24, 1789, provided for a Chief Justice and five Associates; that of February 24, 1807, made the Associates six; that of March 3, 1837, eight; and that of March 3, 1863, nine. But on July 23, 1866, a law directed that no appointments be made of Associate Justices until the number of them should be only six. This was to prevent President Johnson from making appointments; but the act of April 10, 1869, restored the number to eight. There were only six at the time that President Grant made the first restorative appointments.

Q. It is frequently asserted that the Supreme Court nullifies an act of Congress. Is this correct?

A. No. The Court has repeatedly declared that it claims no such power. All it does--all it can do--is to examine a law when a suit is brought before it. If the law in question is in accordance with the Constitution, in the opinion of the Supreme Court, the law stands. If the law goes beyond powers granted by the Constitution, then it is no law, and the Supreme Court merely states that fact (Art. III, sec. 2, cl. 1; Art. VI, cl. 2).

Q. In which decision did the Supreme Court first formally assert its authority contrary to an act of Congress?

A. In the famous case of Marbury v. Madison (1803). This was not the first case in which the authority of an act of Congress was questioned in a case before the court. In Hylton v. United States, 1796, the court upheld the constitutionality of a national tax on carriages as an excise that did not have to be apportioned. Also Justices in the circuit court had, as early as 1792, refused to act as commissioners under an act of Congress, considering the law unconstitutional.

Q. What is treason against the United States?

A. Treason against the United States consists in levying war against them, or in adhering to their enemies, giving the latter aid and comfort. No person can be convicted of treason except upon the testimony of two witnesses to the same overt act or on confession in open court (Art. III, sec. 3, cl. 1).

Q. What right has a Territorial Delegate in Congress?

A. A Territorial Delegate sits in the House of Representatives from each organized territory. Delegates may be appointed to committees and have the right to speak on any subject, but not to vote (Art. IV, sec. 3, cl. 2).

Q. Is a constitutional amendment submitted to the President?

A. No. A resolution proposing an amendment to the Constitution, after having passed both houses of Congress by a two-thirds vote, does not go to the President for his signature. It is sent to the States to be ratified either by their legislatures or by conventions, as Congress shall determine (Art. V). The Supreme Court as early as 1798 declared the approval was not requisite (Hollingsworth v. Virginia, 3 Dallas 378).

Q. What constitutes the supreme law of the land?

A. Art. VI, cl. 2 of the Constitution says: "This Constitution, and the Laws of the United States which shall be made in Pursuance thereof; and all Treaties made, or which shall be made, under the Authority of the United States, shalt be the supreme Law of the Land; and the Judges in every State shall be bound thereby, any Thing in the Constitution or Laws of any State to the Contrary notwithstanding."

Q. When referring to various States in the Union, is the term "sovereign States" correct?

A. No. A sovereign is that person or State which recognizes no superior. The States of the Union have a superior--the Constitution of the United States, which is "the supreme Law of the Land . . . any Thing in the Constitution or Laws of any State to the Contrary notwithstanding" (Art. VI, cl. 2).

Q. Is there a clause in the Constitution prohibiting members of certain religious denominations from becoming President of the United States?

A. No. Art. VI, cl. 3 of the Constitution provides that "no religious Test shall ever be required as a Qualification to any Office of public Trust under the United States."

Q. Should the amendments be called articles?

A. The amendments proposed by the first Congress were sent out as "Articles in addition to, and Amendment of the Constitution of the United States of America," and the term "article" is used in self-application in all the amendments since the Twelfth, except the Seventeenth, which uses the term "amendment." This would seem to give official sanction to calling the amendments "articles," but as it causes some confusion, they are better placed by the use of "amendment" only, with the proper number.

Q. How many amendments to the Constitution have been proposed to Congress?

A. About 3,200. Professor Ames lists some 1,500 separate proposals during the first century of the operation of the Constitution, not including the 124 suggested in the State ratification conventions. Since 1889 and down through 1935 there have been about 1,700. Many of these cover the same subject and the same proposal has been repeatedly offered, since all such matters must be renewed with each Congress. The desires for change cover all phases of the Constitution and reflect in their emphasis the prominent economic, social, and political questions of the period concerned. Besides the twenty-one amendments which have been adopted, five others have failed to receive the necessary State ratification. Two of them were presented with the first ten amendments, and related to apportionment and compensation in Congress. In 1810 one forbidding a citizen to accept titles of nobility passed Congress; in 1861 one forbidding interference with slavery in the States; and in 1924 one prohibiting child labor. This last is considered as still pending, since it has not the time limit added to later proposals. Besides these, various other proposed amendments have passed one or the other House.

Q. Has there been any movement for a convention to propose amendments to the Constitution?

A. Article V says that "on the Application of the Legislatures of two thirds of the 'several States, shall call a Convention for proposing Amendments." While the Constitution was under consideration by the ratification conventions, there was much demand for a second convention, and the legislatures of New York and Virginia made formal application to the First Congress for one. In 1832 Georgia and in 1833 Alabama renewed the request. Between 1893 and 1935 there have been proposals from 33 State legislatures, some for a general consideration of amendments and others with reference to particular matters. Some legislatures have voted for a convention several times. It is claimed that since more than two-thirds of the States have asked for a convention, it is the duty of Congress to summon one, since the Constitution says nothing about the time within which such two-thirds application must be made. The Supreme Court has, however, said in one of its statements about the ratification of amendments that "we conclude that the fair inference or implication from Article V is that the ratification must be within some reasonable time after the proposal." This reasoning would apply to proposals for a convention.

Q. In the first session of the First Congress how many proposed amendments were considered?

A. All of the amendments proposed by the State conventions were considered, but only approximately 90 separate amendments were formally introduced. Professor Ames lists 312 through the First Congress, which includes the 124 proposed by the States and all reports and amendments to those proposed, in Congress.

Q. Who proposed the creation of the first executive departments and the first amendments to the Constitution?

A. James Madison, of Virginia, proposed the resolutions for the formation of the first executive depts. and a series of twelve amendments to the Constitution of which ten were finally ratified by the States.

Q. What constitutes the Bill of Rights?

A. The first ten amendments to the Constitution.

Q. It is said that when the first amendments to the Constitution were submitted, there were twelve, of which ten were adopted. What were the other two about?

A. The two amendments of the twelve submitted as the Bill of Rights which were rejected were the one which related to the apportionment of Representatives in Congress and the one fixing the compensation of members of Congress. (Note: The rejected second amendment was ratified on May 7,1992 as the 27th amendment.)

Q. Do the first ten amendments bind the States?

A. No. They restrict the powers of the national government. They do not bind the States; but various of their restrictions have been applied to the States by the Fourteenth Amendment.

Q. Does not the Constitution give us our rights and liberties?

A. No, it does not, it only guarantees them. The people had all their rights and liberties before they made the Constitution. The Constitution was formed, among other purposes, to make the people's liberties secure-- secure not only as against foreign attack but against oppression by their own government. They set specific limits upon their national government and upon the States, and reserved to themselves all powers that they did not grant. The Ninth Amendment declares: "The enumeration in the Constitution, of certain rights, shall not be construed to deny or disparage others retained by the people."

Q. What protection is given to a person accused of crime under the jurisdiction of the United States?

A. The Fifth Amendment declares that no person, except one serving in the land or naval forces or the militia in time of war or public danger, can be held to answer for a capital or other infamous crime unless on a presentment or indictment of a grand jury. No person can be twice put in jeopardy of life or limb for the same offense. No one in a criminal case can be compelled to be a witness against himself, or be deprived of life, liberty, or property without due process of law. Private property cannot be taken for public use without just compensation. By the Eighth Amendment excessive bail and fines and cruel and unusual punishments are prohibited. The original Constitution forbids ex post facto laws and bills of attainder, limits the punishment for treason, protects the right to a writ of habeas corpus, and secures trial by jury.

Q. Is the right to speedy trial guaranteed?

A. Yes. The Sixth Amendment expressly states that in all criminal prosecutions the accused shall enjoy the right to a speedy and public trial by an impartial jury within the district of the crime, and to be informed of the nature and cause of the accusation. He is entitled to be confronted with the witnesses against him, to be allowed to compel the attendance of witnesses in his favor, and to have the assistance of counsel for his defense.

Q. Is the right of trial by jury in civil cases also assured?

A. Yes. Amendment Seven preserves the right of trial by jury in suits of common law involving the value of more than twenty dollars.

Q. What has been the longest period during which no amendment has been added to the Constitution?

A. Sixty-one years, from 1804 to 1865. This period elapsed between the Twelfth and Thirteenth Amendments.

Q. Since the organization of the present Republican Party have more amendments been added to the Constitution during the Republican or Democratic administrations?

A. Five amendments have been added during Republican administrations; two during Democratic administrations; and two were sent to the States during Republican administrations and ratified during Democratic administrations.

Q. How long did it take the States to ratify the income tax amendment?

A. The Sixteenth Amendment was proposed to the States on July 12, 1909, deposited with the Secretary of State on July 21, ratified by the thirty-sixth state on February 3, 1913, and, declared ratified on February 25, 1913.

Q. It has been stated that the Prohibition Amendment was the first instance of incorporating a statute in the Constitution. Is this so?

A. No. Those portions of the Constitution which specifically dealt with slavery and the slave trade (Art. I, sec. 9, cl. 1; Art. IV, sec. 2, cl. 3) were both of this character. They were made obsolete by time limit in one case and the Civil War in the other.

Q. How many amendments to the Constitution have been repealed?

A. Only one -- the Eighteenth (Prohibition).

Q. How is an amendment repealed?

A. By adding another amendment.

Q. If the Eighteenth Amendment is repealed, why is it necessary to call the new one repealing it the Twenty-first?

A. The Eighteenth Amendment will indeed remain in the Constitution, but a notation will be added to the effect that it is repealed by the Twenty-first.

Q. What is the Twentieth Amendment and when was it adopted?

A. This is the so-called "Lame Duck" Amendment, which changes the time for the beginning of the terms of the President, Vice President, and the members of Congress. The term of the President and Vice President begins on January 20, and that of members of Congress on January 3. It was adopted upon the ratification by the thirty-sixth State, January 23, 1933, and certified in effect on February 6.

Q. Why was a constitutional amendment necessary to change the date of the beginning of the terms of President, Vice President, and members of Congress?

A. The Constitution fixes the terms of President and, Vice President at four years, of Senators at six years, and of Representatives at two years. Any change of date would affect the terms of the incumbents. It was therefore necessary to amend the Constitution to make the change.

Q. If the President-elect dies, who becomes President at the beginning of the term for which he was elected?

A. The Twentieth Amendment provides that in this case the Vice President-elect shall become President.

Q. Does the Twentieth Amendment do away with the Electoral College?

A. It does not.

Q. It takes how many States to block an amendment?

A. Thirteen, without respect to population or importance; but while approval is considered final, rejection is not while within the time limit, if one is prescribed by the amendment.

The Heart and Soul of the Constitution
Address by
Sol, BLOOM, Director General of the
United States Constitution Sesquicentennial Commission

In discussing the Constitution of the United States I wish here to consider it from a new angle. We all agree that as a legal document it establishes a successful system of government. Its precision and brevity are admirable. Millions of words have been devoted to its governmental principles. Great jurists have interpreted the meaning of the Constitution in almost all its parts. As a frame of government it has stood the test of time, war, and depression. It is based on truth, and, like truth, it laughs at the assaults of time.

But what I should like to discuss at this time is the heart and soul of the Constitution—its qualities that spring from the human heart, and not merely from the human intellect.

Unless the Constitution satisfies the aspirations of the heart, unless it feeds the human soul, unless it stirs our emotions, it cannot be regarded as a complete expression of the American spirit.

Why was the Constitution formed? Who were its framers? What was the emergency before them? What did they aim to accomplish?

In a nutshell, the Constitution was formed for the purpose of perpetuating American liberty by uniting the States in a firm Union. All other aims were subordinate to the safeguarding of the liberty that had been won by the Revolution. It was evident after the Revolution that American liberty would be lost unless the States banded themselves together to preserve it.

If you and I believe that life comes from God, and that the Creator endows man with the right of liberty when He breathes life into him, we must agree that the framers of the Constitution were obeying the will of God when they sought a way to perpetuate liberty.

Life and the right to enjoy liberty come from God. The guaranty of the right to enjoy liberty, the power to maintain liberty, must come from the human heart and soul. The Constitution is this guaranty. It enables the American people to exercise their power to maintain their liberty against foreign attack or internal dissension.

[179]

The signers of the Declaration of Independence pledged their lives to liberty. Their hearts directed their hands when they sent forth this declaration of war for freedom.

The framers of the Constitution were no less in earnest. They saw the light of liberty dying in America as the States quarreled and threatened to disband. It was a new Declaration of Independence which the Constitution-makers prepared for the approval of the people—a declaration that their hard-won liberty should not perish, but should be made perpetual by joining the hearts and souls of the people of all the States in an indestructible Union.

These framers of the Constitution were chosen by their States to meet together. They were soldiers, planters, lawyers, physicians, merchants, and judges. Some of them were rich and others were poor. One of them, a luminous star in the human firmament, had been a penniless printer. Another, Roger Sherman, who, with Robert Morris, had the honor of signing the Declaration of Independence, the Articles of Confederation and the Constitution, had been a poor shoemaker who studied at night to become a lawyer. The university which fitted George Washington to preside over this body of men was the stern school of war.

Being human, these delegates had human failings. They were devoted to State and local interests. Those from large States were bent upon exercising the strength of large States. Those from small States shrank from a Union that might make them the pawns of greater States. The commercial North and the agricultural South had clashing interests. All the States had been disappointed by the failure of such central government as was exercised under the Articles of Confederation. They were suspicious of any proposal for a national government. They feared it would swallow the States and the liberties of the people, or be just another failure like the Confederation.

After many jarring sessions, in which misunderstandings, jealousies, and selfish sectional interest bore down their efforts to agree, the delegates were almost in despair. Their hearts cried out for union, but their minds seemed to be overwhelmed. At this crisis, the venerable Benjamin Franklin suggested that they call upon Providence to give them guidance, that their appeal to the Almighty Father might soften their temper, and, drawing strength by relying upon Divine aid, they might go forward together in common sympathy.

What their hearts desired their minds discovered. They found a way to make American liberty forever secure.

We have all read the Constitution. We all know, at least in a general way, how it fulfills the people's will by uniting the States. But have we analyzed the Constitution, to search out its heart and soul? I maintain that, next to the Bible, "that holy book by which men live and die," the most precious expression of the human soul is the Constitution. In the Bible man finds solace, refreshment, and instruction in the most secret and sacred relation of the soul—its relation to God.

In the Constitution we find solace and security in the next most important thing in life—our liberty. Every word in the Constitution serves to safeguard us in our life, liberty, and pursuit of happiness. Every American, as he studies the marvelous framework of the Constitution, can say with truth and pride: "This was made for me. It is my fortress. When danger threatens my life or liberty I can take safe refuge in the Constitution. Into that fortress neither President nor Congress nor armies nor mobs can enter and take away my life or liberty."

You may ask me, where in the Constitution is there any language that throbs with a human heartbeat? Where is the soul of the Constitution? My answer is, in every .paragraph. All its parts are mighty links that bind the people in an unbreakable chain of Union—a chain so beautifully wrought that it reminds us of the mystical golden chain which the poet saw binding earth to God's footstool.

Let us consider the preamble to the Constitution. We do not know from whose brain it came, but we know that it sounds the heartbeat of the framers. It is the majestic voice of the people, giving expression to their soul's desire.

"We the People of the United*States, in order to form a more perfect Union." For what purpose? To make our liberties secure. For how long? So long as humanity wanders through the wilderness of time. For whom? For every man, woman, and child under the American flag.

"Establish Justice." What is justice but a guardian of liberty? My rights and immunities made secure against tyranny. Your right safeguarded against my wrong-doing. Your widow and your child protected when you are gone. Can there be a higher aspiration of the soul than to establish justice?

Justice is an attribute of the Almighty Himself; for He said, "I, the Lord thy God, am a just God."

"Insure domestic Tranquility." The people longed for harmony. The framers of the Constitution saw that a central government would bring the States into common accord on all national questions, while removing other vexatious causes of disagreement. The very fact of equality of States was a guarantee of domestic tranquility. But the Constitution also provided a means whereby the government could protect the people against disturbances of public order and private security. The great charter thereby insured domestic order and peace, both among the States and among the people.

"Provide for the common defence." It was well understood that the separated States were not strong enough to ward off foreign aggression. Divided, they invited invasion and con-quest, even from the second-rate foreign powers. United, they constituted a nation capable of defending itself in every part. The framers therefore clothed the common government with power to make war and peace, to raise armies and navies, to use the State militia for common defense, to build arsenals and navy yards. All that a mighty nation can do to defend its people and territory the United States of America can do; and even in its infancy the United States became a powerful nation through union of the States. The protection provided by the Constitution is the protection which a wise father provides for his family. This nation is like a strong fort defended by armed men. And far out at sea, prepared to meet and destroy any assailant, the United States Navy rides the waves in unwearied and vigilant patrol.

"Promote the general Welfare." This provision has a far wider sweep than latter-day commentators accord to it. They seem to think that the government has limited powers in promoting the general welfare. They speak of relief of unemployment, flood-control, and drought-control as examples of pro-vision for the general welfare. Those objects may come within the scope of the government's general welfare powers, it is true, but those powers extend far beyond that point. The general welfare is promoted by the unification of the States. They are thus enabled to pool their resources and concentrate their energies. An example of promotion of the general welfare is the establishment of the postal system. Another example is provision for uniform coinage and currency. Still another is the consolidation of defense forces of which I have just spoken. Indeed, the promotion of the general welfare by unification of the States is manifest in nearly every paragraph of the Constitution.

And finally, the Preamble declares that the Constitution is established to "secure the Blessings of Liberty to ourselves and our Posterity." Who are we but the posterity of the great souls who wrought for our perpetual liberty? Can you agree that the forefathers of America were selfish and heartless men, when this proof is given that 150 years ago they were thinking of us, their posterity and heirs? Are we of this day equally fore-sighted? Do we give thought to our posterity that will live 150 years from now? If we are ready to pledge our lives, our fortunes, and our sacred honor for our distant posterity, we are worthy of the forefathers who did that much for us.

Summed up, the Preamble declares that our forefathers sought Union, Justice, Tranquility, Safety, Welfare, and Liberty. These are the virtues enjoined upon mankind by their Heavenly Father. He who seeks justice is blest with the benediction of God. It is God's wish that mankind should be free. In securing their liberty, the people obey God's will.

We hear it said that the Constitution is faulty because it does not invoke the name of the Deity. I hold that it does more than lean upon Divine strength. It strives to do God's will on earth, as it is done in heaven. Not a line, not a word in the Constitution is in conflict with the Divine will. On the contrary, every word and every declaration breathes an ardent desire to pattern the American Nation in accordance with God's holy will.

Can an atheist become President of the United States? I maintain that the spirit of the Constitution forbids it. The Constitution prescribes an oath or affirmation which the President must take in order to qualify for his office. This oath or affirmation in its essence is a covenant with the people which the President pledges himself to keep with the help of Almighty God. All officers of the United States and of the States, all judges and defenders of the Union must bind themselves to support the Constitution. Whether given by oath or affirmation, this pledge is essentially an appeal for Divine help in keeping inviolate a sacred obligation

Upon all the coins of the United States appears the inscription, "*In God we trust.*" Every word of the Constitution breathes this trust in God. Read the Preamble again and again. Give wings to your thought, so that you may poise like an eagle over time and the universe, and you will find within those words all the most ardent hopes of the human heart, the holiest aspirations of the human soul. That this nation is established upon the rock of God's favor and protection will be proved, we devoutly believe, by its indestructibility. Time does not wear down nor eat away the eternal truths of the Constitution. War cannot overturn the temple of our liberty so long as American sons are worthy of their forefathers. Instead of fading with age, the glory of the Constitution takes on new splendor with the passing of the centuries. The faith of the forefathers gave them strength to plan for the ages. May we, with equal faith, guard our birth-right and hand it down to our posterity as their most precious heirloom—liberty, "the immediate jewel of the soul."

INDEX

History of the Great Seal

The colored plate on the outside back (top left) shows the obverse of the present Great Seal of the United States, which with slight modification of details is the same as that adopted originally in 1782. The reverse of the seal is never used and has not, indeed, ever been cut. On July 4, 1776, the day of the adoption of the Declaration of Independence, the Continental Congress appointed a committee consisting of Benjamin Franklin, John Adams, and Thomas Jefferson to devise a seal of the new nation. The committee reported a design on August 20, but of that plan nothing was ever used, except the motto. Another committee offered a new sketch in 1780, which included a shield with red and white stripes and the constellation in a cloud. In 1782, William Barton, a private citizen of Philadelphia, submitted designs to an-other committee. Of these the reverse was adopted; but the obverse was considered further by Charles Thomson, the Secretary of the Continental Congress. He made an eagle with expanded wings as the central figure and borrowed other elements from earlier reports. On June 20, 1782, Congress adopted the seal thus devised and the obverse was cut and put in use. The new government under the National Constitution took over the seal, by act of September 15, 1789, and placed it in the custody of the Secretary of State, where it has remained. In 1841 the Secretary, without authority, had a new die of the seal cut, which made changes that were contrary to the design as prescribed by the original law. This die, called the "illegal seal," remained in use until the act of July 7, 1884, authorized a new one in close adherence to the original form. A further seal was cut in 1903. Its use is restricted to papers bearing the signature of the President, different seals being used for other purposes, and also for several minor papers which have the presidential signature. Though the reverse is never used as a seal, both the obverse and reverse appear on the new one dollar bill.

C-9-37-300 – original imprint on this page
[192]

Last Page Of Original Sol Bloom Book

P.S. God Bless Sol Bloom for his Patriotism, and for his devotion to the God who watches over America. May Mr. Bloom, a great Patriot for sure, live in eternity with the angels on high! Thank you for your life's work and 1937! Thank you for your patriotism and for your love of this book. Me too!

193

LETS GO PUBLISH! Books by Brian Kelly:
(sold at www.bookhawkers.com Amazon.com, and Kindle.).

LETS GO PUBLISH! is proud to announce that more AS/400 and Power i books are becoming available to help you inexpensively address your AS/400 and Power i education and training needs: Our general titles precede specific AS/400 and other technology books.

Why Trump?
You Already Know… But, this book will tell you anyway

Saving America The Trump Way!
A book that tells you how President Donald Trump will help Merica dn Americans wind up on top

The US Immigration Fix
It's all in here. You won't want to put it down

Great Moments in Penn State Football Check out the particulars of this great book at bookhawkers.com.

Great Moments in Notre Dame Football Check out the particulars of this great book at bookhawkers.com or www.notredamebooks.com

WineDiets.Com Presents The Wine Diet Learn how to lose weight while having fun. Four specific diets and some great anecdotes fill this book with fun and the opportunity to lose weight in the process.

Wilkes-Barre, PA; Return to Glory Wilkes-Barre City's return to glory begins with dreams and ideas. Along with plans and actions, this equals leadership.

The Lifetime Guest Plan. This is a plan which if deployed today would immediately solve the problem of 60 million illegal aliens in the United States.

Geoffrey Parsons' Epoch... The Land of Fair Play Better than the original. The greatest re-mastering of the greatest book ever written on American Civics. It was built for all Americans as the best govt. design in the history of the world.

The Bill of Rights 4 Dummmies! This is the best book to learn about your rights. Be the first, to have a "Rights Fest" on your block. You will win for sure!

Sol Bloom's Epoch ...Story of the Constitution This work by Sol Bloom was written to commemorate the Sesquicentennial celebration of the Constitution. It has been remastered by Lets Go Publish! – An excellent read!

The Constitution 4 Dummmies! This is the best book to learn about the Constitution. Learn all about the fundamental laws of America.

America for Dummmies!
All Americans should read to learn about this great country.

Just Say No to Chris Christie for President!
Discusses the reasons why Chris Christie is a poor choice for US President

The Federalist Papers by Hamilton, Jay, Madison w/ intro by Brian Kelly
Complete unabridged, easier to read version of the original Federalist Papers

Kill the Republican Party!
Demonstrates why the Republican Party must be abandoned by conservatives

Bring On the American Party!
Demonstrates how conservatives can be free from the party of wimps by starting its own national party called the American Party.

No Amnesty! No Way!
In addition to describing the issue in detail, this book also offers a real solution.

Saving America
This how-to book is about saving our country using strong mercantilist principles. These same principles that helped the country from its founding.

RRR:
A unique plan for economic recovery and job creation

Kill the EPA
The EPA seems to hate mankind and love nature. They are also making it tough for asthmatics to breathe and for those with malaria to live. It's time they go.

Obama's Seven Deadly Sins.
In the Obama Presidency, there are many concerns about the long-term prospects and sustainability of the country. We examine each of the President's seven deadliest sins in detail, offering warnings and a number of solutions. Be careful. Book may nudge you to move to Canada or Europe.

Taxation Without Representation Second Edition
At the time of the Boston Tea Party, there was no representation. Now, there is no representation again but there are "representatives."

Healthcare Accountability
Who should pay for your healthcare? Whose healthcare should you pay for? Is it a lifetime free ride on others or should those once in need of help have to pay it back when their lives improve?

Jobs! Jobs! Jobs!
Where have all the American Jobs gone and how can we get them back?

Other IBM I Technical Books

The All Everything Operating System:
Story about IBM's finest operating system; its facilities; how it came to be.

The All-Everything Machine
Story about IBM's finest computer server.

Chip Wars
The story of ongoing wars between Intel and AMD and upcoming wars between Intel and IBM. Book may cause you to buy / sell somebody's stock.

Can the AS/400 Survive IBM?
Exciting book about the AS/400 in a System i5 World.

The IBM i Pocket SQL Guide.
Complete Pocket Guide to SQL as implemented on System i5. A must have for SQL developers new to System i5. It is very compact yet very comprehensive and it is example driven. Written in a part tutorial and part reference style, Tons of SQL coding samples, from the simple to the sublime.

The IBM i Pocket Query Guide.
If you have been spending money for years educating your Query users, and you find you are still spending, or you've given up, this book is right for you. This one QuikCourse covers all Query options.

The IBM I Pocket RPG & RPG IV Guide.
Comprehensive RPG & RPGIV Textbook -- Over 900 pages. This is the one RPG book to have if you are not having more than one. All areas of the language covered smartly in a convenient sized book Annotated PowerPoint's available for self-study (extra fee for self-study package)

The IBM I RPG Tutorial and Lab Guide – Recently Revised.
Your guide to a hands-on Lab experience. Contains CD with Lab exercises and PowerPoint's. Great companion to the above textbook or can be used as a standalone for student Labs or tutorial purposes

The IBM i Pocket Developers' Guide.
Comprehensive Pocket Guide to all of the AS/400 and System i5 development tools - DFU, SDA, etc. You'll also get a big bonus with chapters on Architecture, Work Management, and Subfile Coding.

The IBM i Pocket Database Guide.
Complete Pocket Guide to System i5 integrated relational database (DB2/400) – physical and logical files and DB operations - Union, Projection, Join, etc. Written in a part tutorial and part reference style. Tons of DDS coding samples.

Getting Started with The WebSphere Development Studio Client for System i5 (WDSc).
Focus is on client server and the Web. Includes CODE/400, VisualAge RPG, CGI, WebFacing, and WebSphere Studio. Case study continues from the Interactive Book.

The System i5 Pocket WebFacing Primer.
This book gets you started immediately with WebFacing. A sample case study is used as the basis for a conversion to WebFacing. Interactive 5250 application is WebFaced in a case study form before your eyes.

Getting Started with WebSphere Express Server for IBM i Step-by-Step Guide for Setting up Express Servers
A comprehensive guide to setting up and using WebSphere Express. It is filled with examples, and structured in a tutorial fashion for easy learning.

The WebFacing Application Design & Development Guide:
Step by Step Guide to designing green screen IBM i apps for the Web. Both a systems design guide and a developers guide. Book helps you understand how to design and develop Web applications using regular RPG or COBOL programs.

The System i5 Express Web Implementer's Guide.
Your one stop guide to ordering, installing, fixing, configuring, and using WebSphere Express, Apache, WebFacing, System i5 Access for Web, and HATS/LE.

Joomla! Technical Books

Best Damn Joomla Tutorial Ever
Learn Joomla! By example.

Best Damn Joomla Intranet Tutorial Ever
This book is the only book that shows you how to use Joomla on a corporate intranet.

Best Damn Joomla Template Tutorial Ever
This book teaches you step-by step how to work with templates in Joomla!

Best Damn Joomla Installation Guide Ever
Teaches you how to install Joomla! On all major platforms besides IBM i.

Best Damn Blueprint for Building Your Own Corporate Intranet.
This excellent timeless book helps you design a corporate intranet for any platform while using Joomla as its basis.
4
IBM i PHP & MySQL Installation & Operations Guide
How to install and operate Joomla! on the IBM i Platform

IBM i PHP & MySQL Programmers Guide
programs for IBM i

www.ingramcontent.com/pod-product-compliance
Lightning Source LLC
Chambersburg PA
CBHW072120270326
41931CB00010B/1613